Garfield GOES BANANAS

BY JIM DAVIS

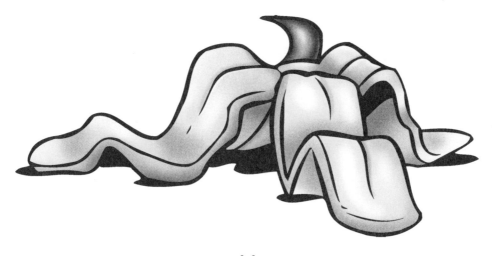

Ballantine Books • **New York**

A Ballantine Books Trade Paperback

Copyright © 2007 by PAWS, Inc.

Published in the United States by Ballantine Books, an imprint of The Random House Publishing Group, a division of Random House, Inc., New York.

BALLANTINE and colophon are registered trademarks of Random House, Inc.

"GARFIELD" and the GARFIELD characters are trademarks of PAWS, Inc.

ISBN 978-0-345-91346-3

Printed in the United States of America

www.ballantinebooks.com

9 8 7 6 5 4

Cats Rule Dogs Drool

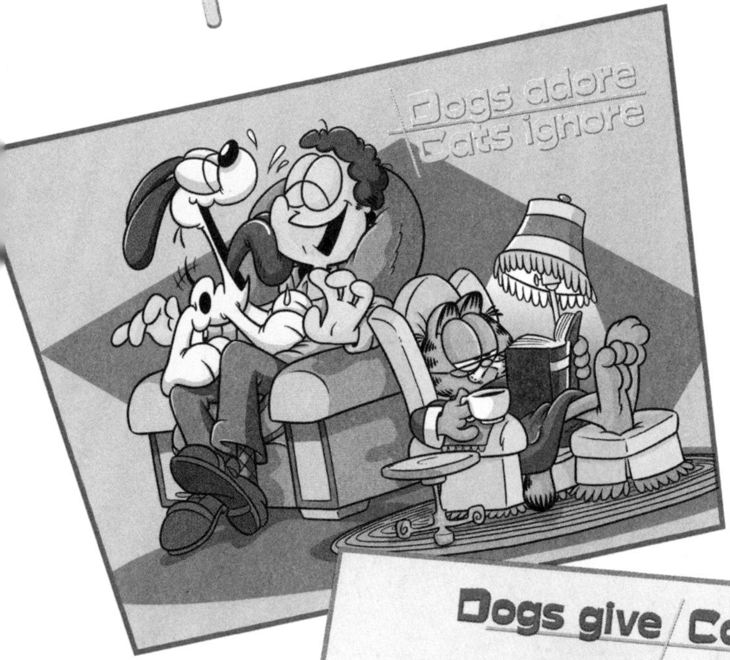
Dogs adore
Cats ignore

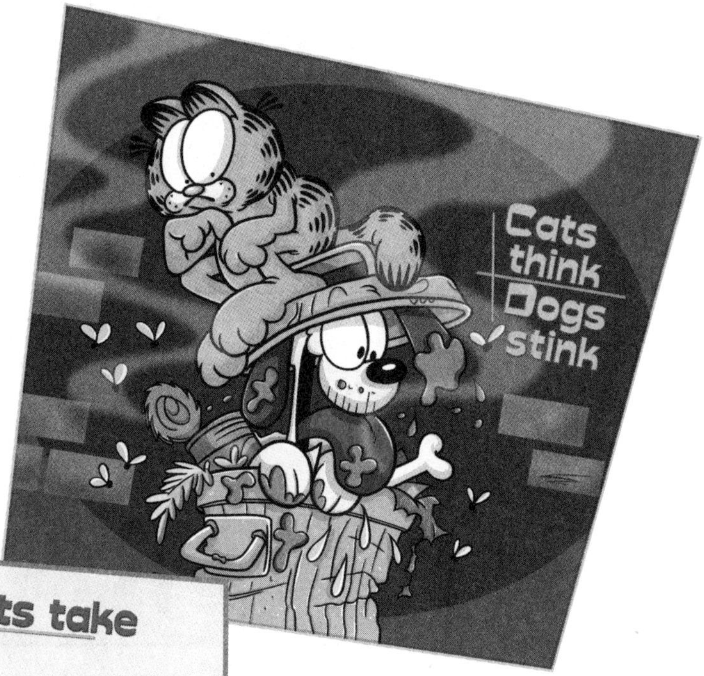
Cats
think
Dogs
stink

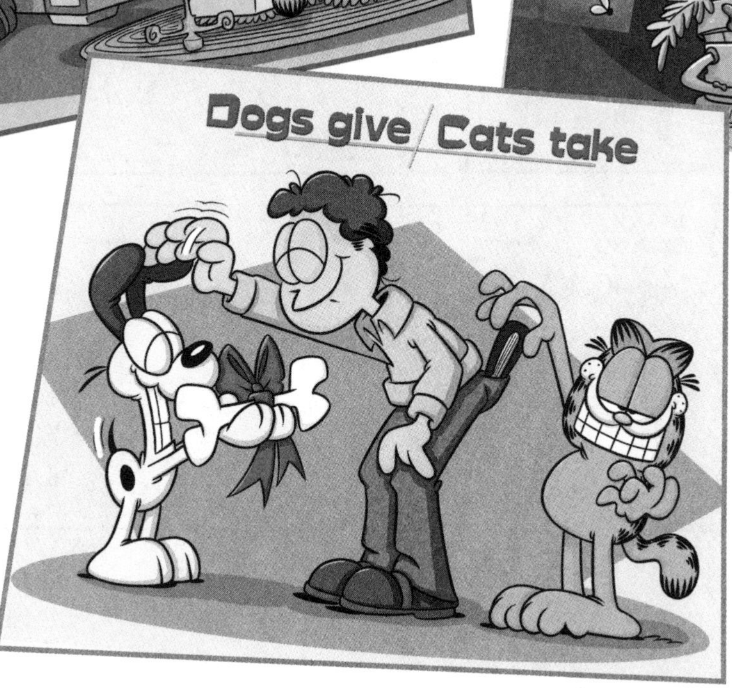
Dogs give / Cats take

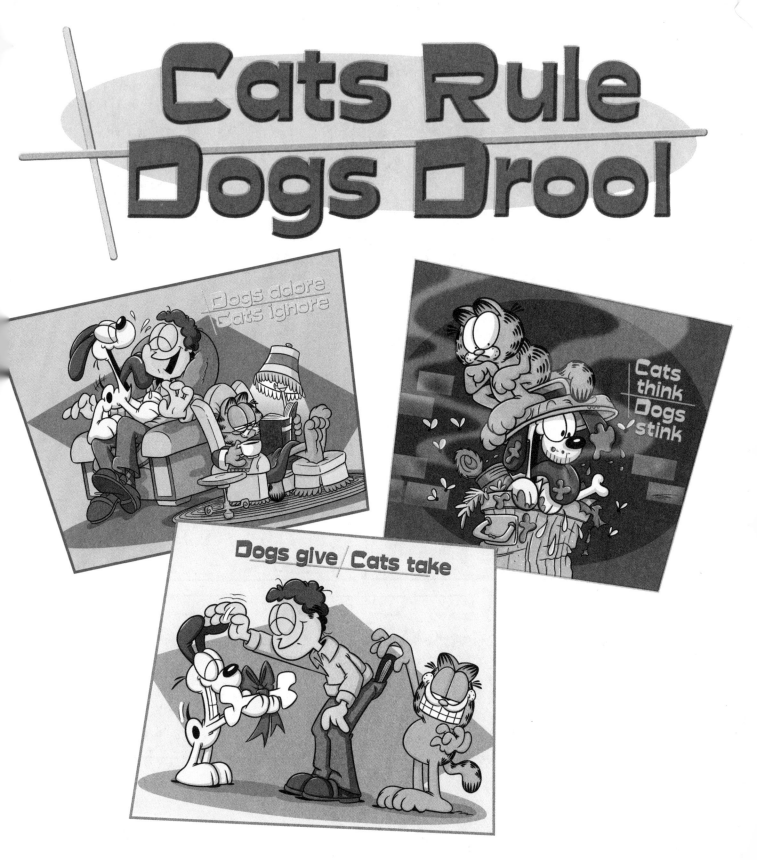

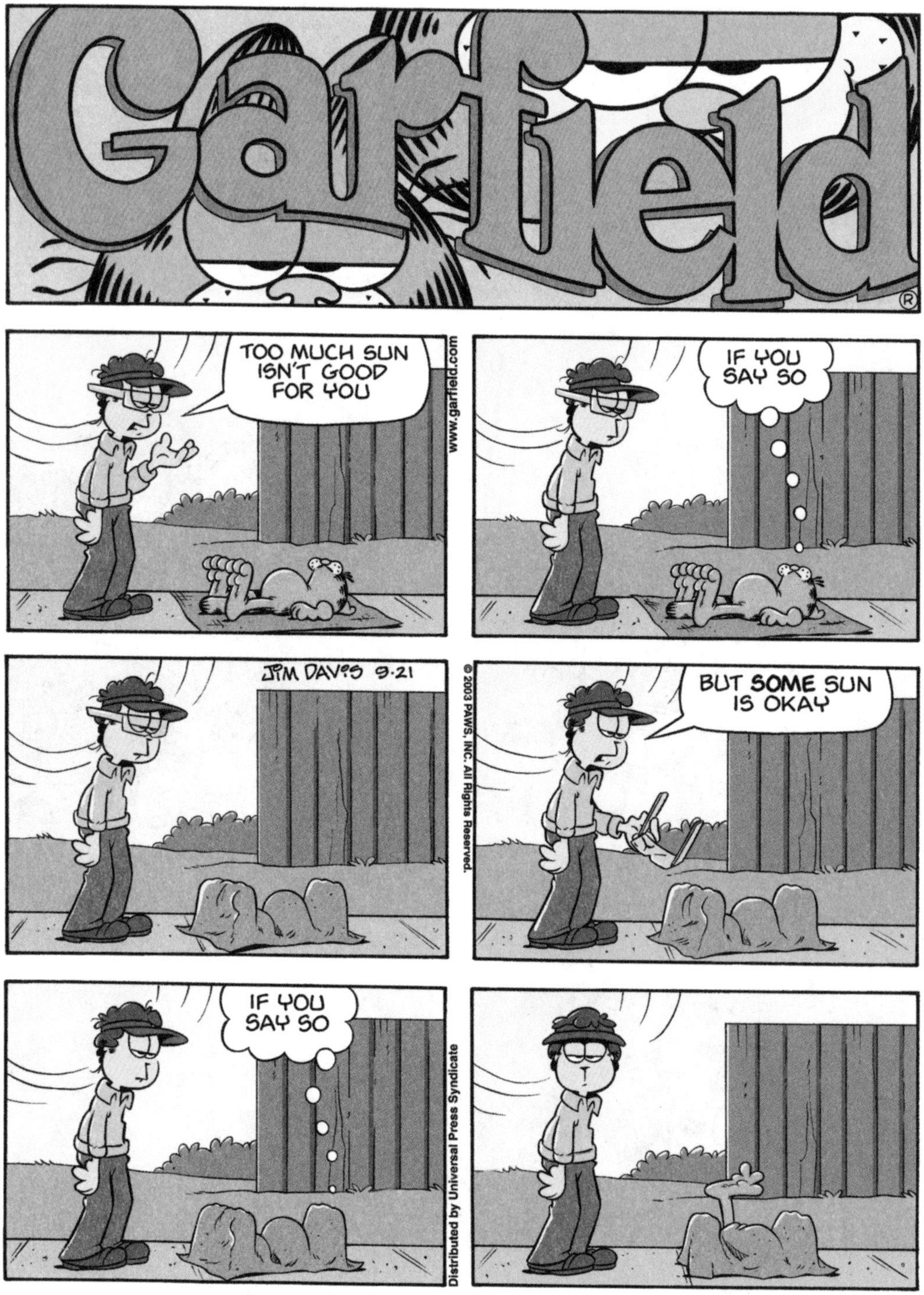
Garfield
TOO MUCH SUN ISN'T GOOD FOR YOU
IF YOU SAY SO
JIM DAVIS 9-21
BUT SOME SUN IS OKAY
IF YOU SAY SO
www.garfield.com
© 2003 PAWS, INC. All Rights Reserved.
Distributed by Universal Press Syndicate

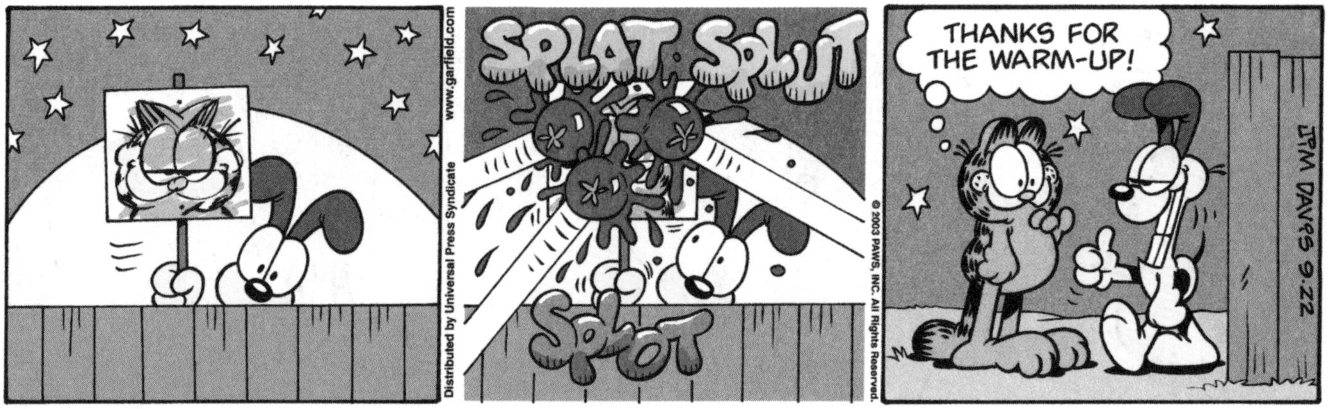
www.garfield.com
Distributed by Universal Press Syndicate
SPLAT SPLAT SPLUT
SPLOT
© 2003 PAWS, INC. All Rights Reserved.
THANKS FOR THE WARM-UP!
JIM DAVIS 9-22

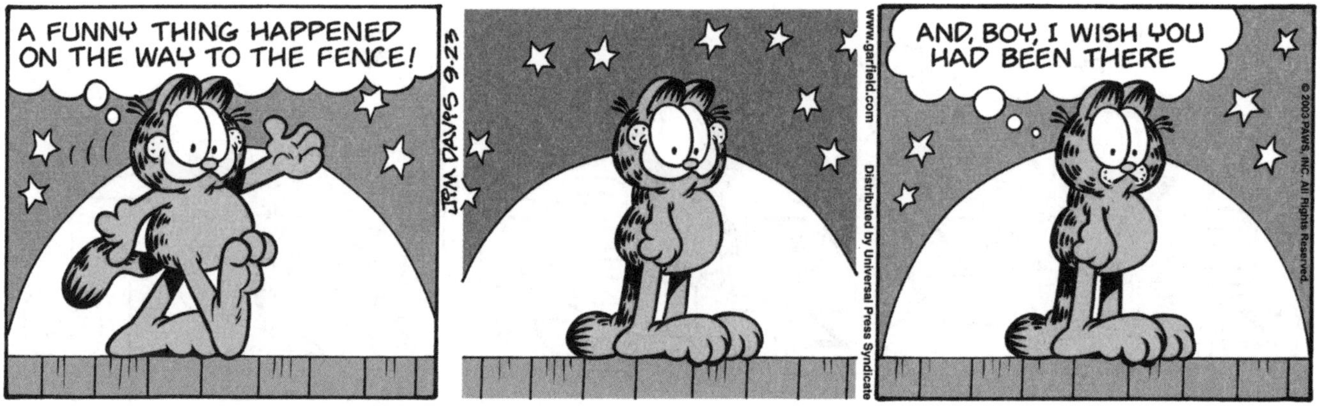
A FUNNY THING HAPPENED ON THE WAY TO THE FENCE!
JIM DAVIS 9-23
www.garfield.com
Distributed by Universal Press Syndicate
AND, BOY, I WISH YOU HAD BEEN THERE
© 2003 PAWS, INC. All Rights Reserved.

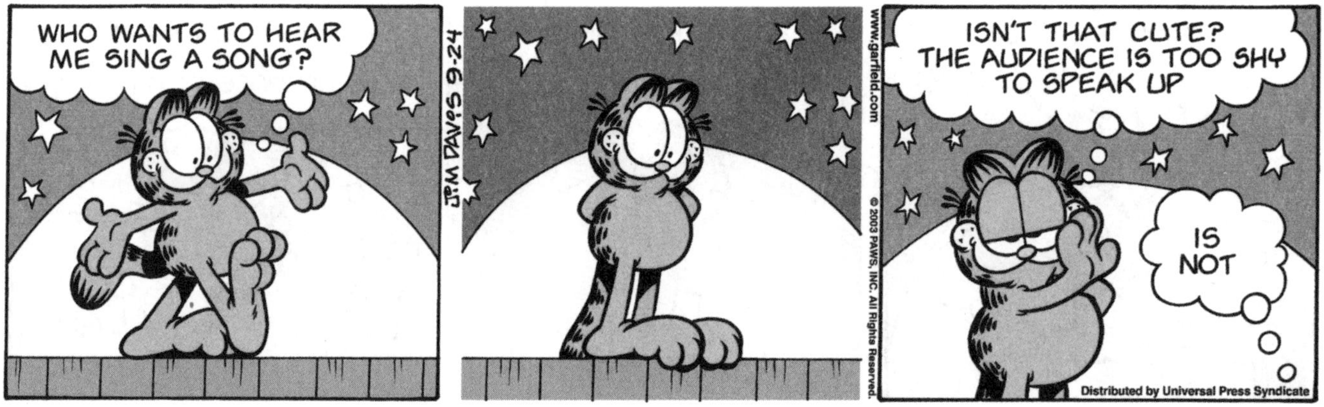
WHO WANTS TO HEAR ME SING A SONG?
JIM DAVIS 9-24
www.garfield.com
© 2003 PAWS, INC. All Rights Reserved.
ISN'T THAT CUTE? THE AUDIENCE IS TOO SHY TO SPEAK UP
IS NOT
Distributed by Universal Press Syndicate

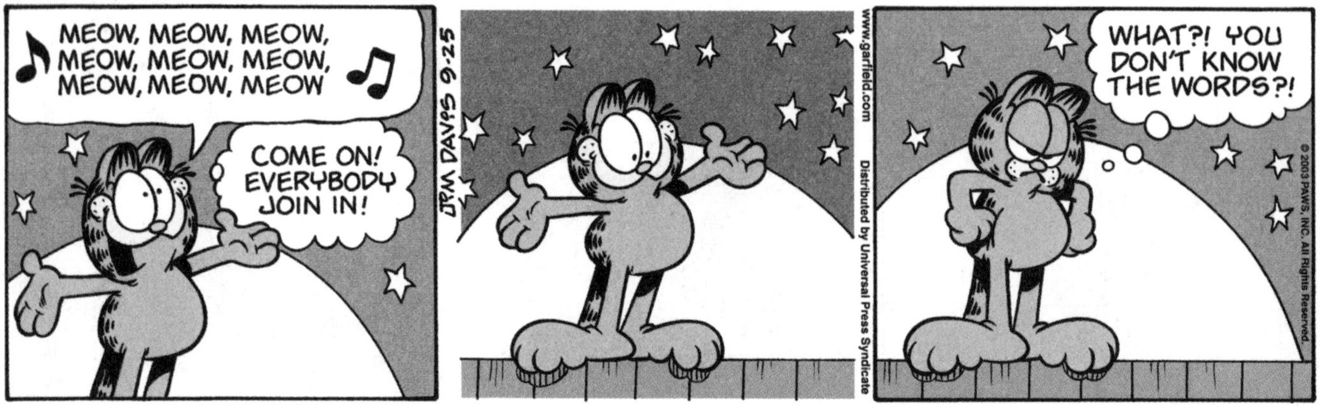
MEOW, MEOW, MEOW, MEOW, MEOW, MEOW, MEOW, MEOW, MEOW
COME ON! EVERYBODY JOIN IN!
JPM DAVIS 9-25
www.garfield.com
Distributed by Universal Press Syndicate
WHAT?! YOU DON'T KNOW THE WORDS?!
© 2003 PAWS, INC. All Rights Reserved.

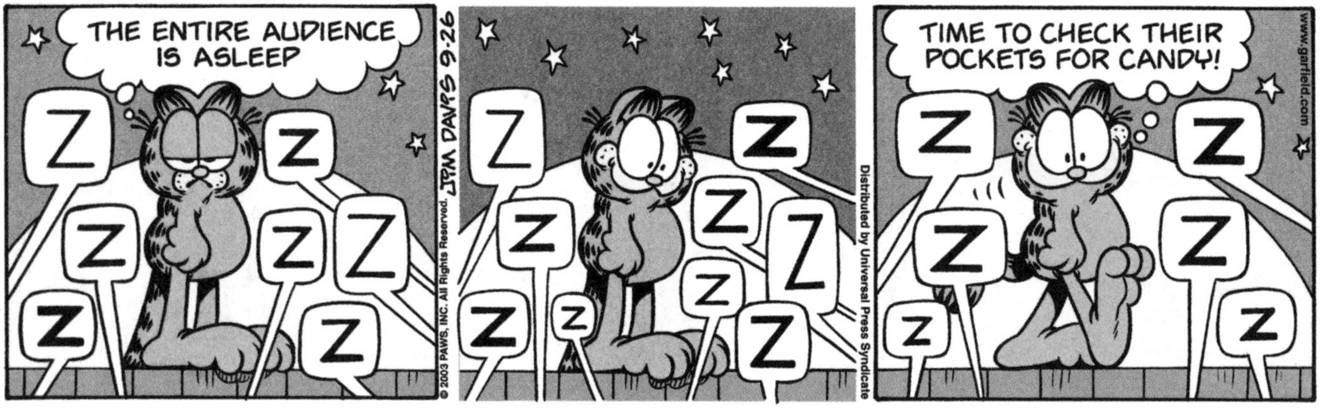
THE ENTIRE AUDIENCE IS ASLEEP
Z Z Z Z Z Z Z
© 2003 PAWS, INC. All Rights Reserved.
JPM DAVIS 9-26
Z Z Z Z Z Z Z Z
Distributed by Universal Press Syndicate
TIME TO CHECK THEIR POCKETS FOR CANDY!
Z Z Z Z Z
www.garfield.com

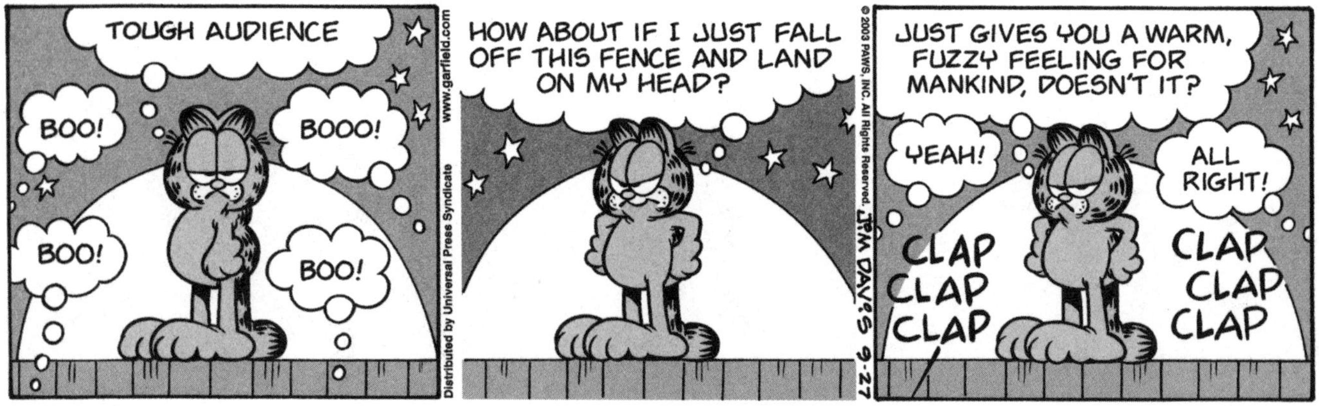
TOUGH AUDIENCE
BOO!
BOOO!
BOO!
BOO!
www.garfield.com
Distributed by Universal Press Syndicate
HOW ABOUT IF I JUST FALL OFF THIS FENCE AND LAND ON MY HEAD?
JPM DAVIS 9-27
© 2003 PAWS, INC. All Rights Reserved.
JUST GIVES YOU A WARM, FUZZY FEELING FOR MANKIND, DOESN'T IT?
YEAH!
ALL RIGHT!
CLAP CLAP CLAP
CLAP CLAP CLAP

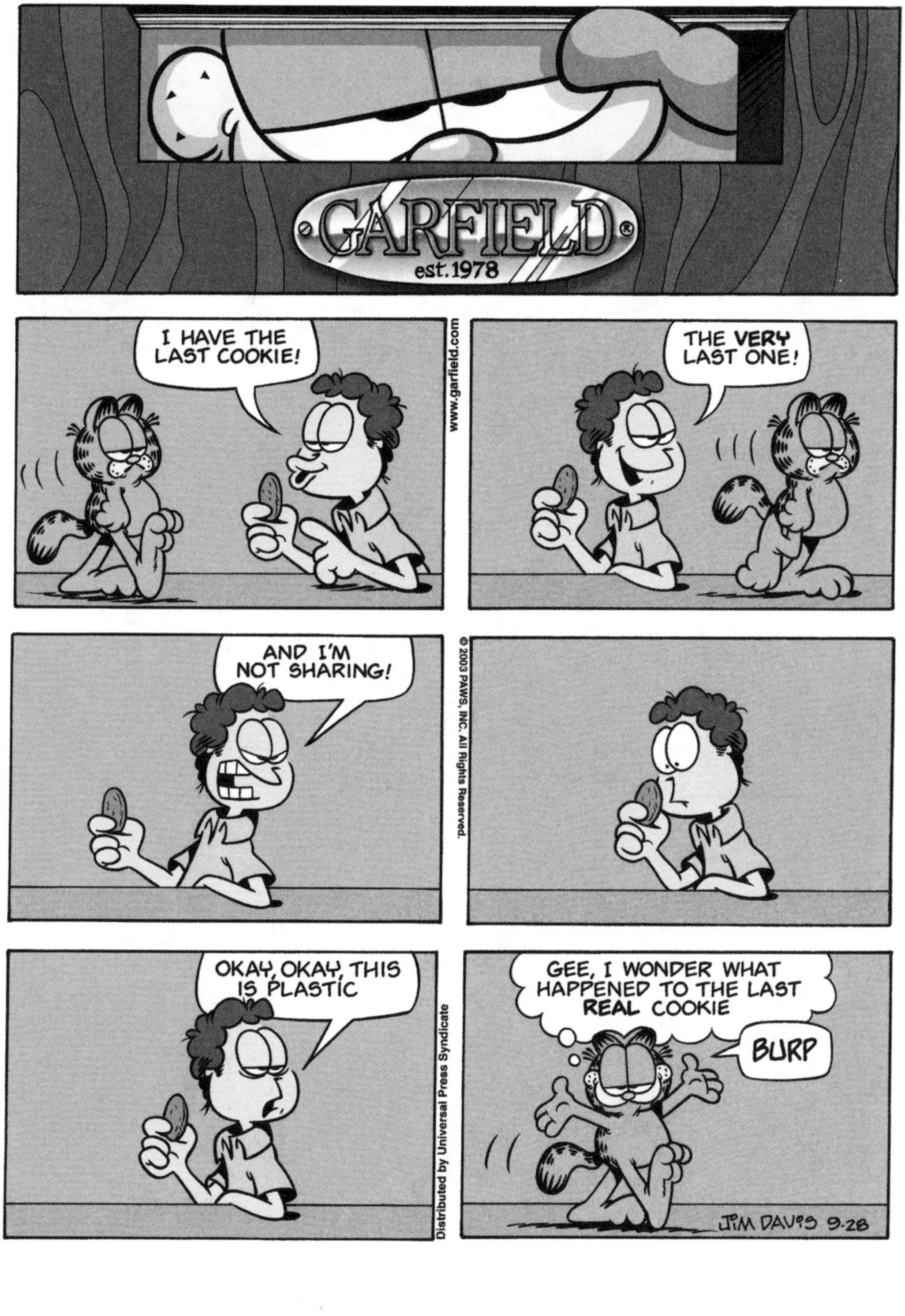
GARFIELD®
est. 1978
I HAVE THE LAST COOKIE!
THE **VERY** LAST ONE!
AND I'M NOT SHARING!
OKAY, OKAY, THIS IS PLASTIC
GEE, I WONDER WHAT HAPPENED TO THE LAST **REAL** COOKIE
BURP
JIM DAVIS 9-28
www.garfield.com
© 2003 PAWS, INC. All Rights Reserved.
Distributed by Universal Press Syndicate

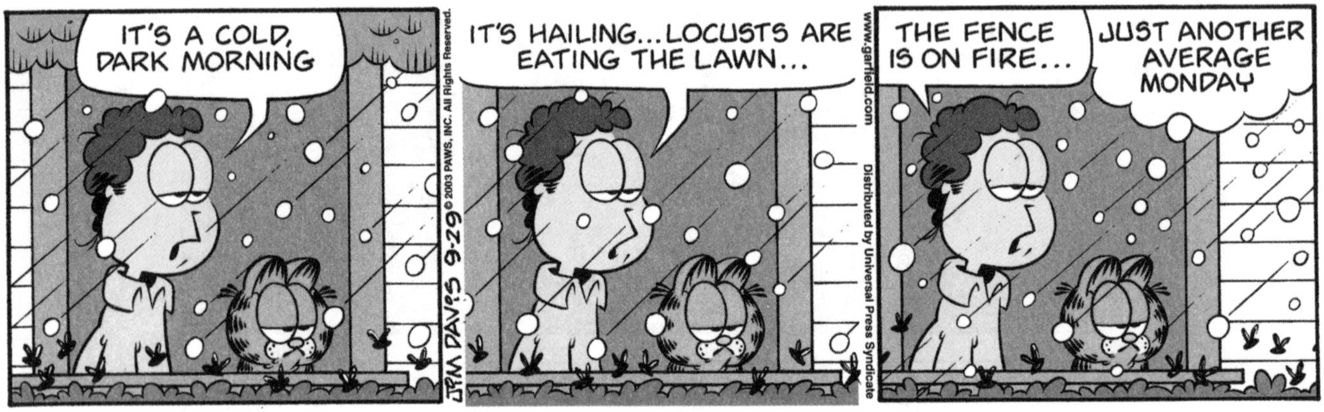
IT'S A COLD, DARK MORNING
JIM DAVIS 9-29
© 2003 PAWS, INC. All Rights Reserved.
IT'S HAILING...LOCUSTS ARE EATING THE LAWN...
www.garfield.com
Distributed by Universal Press Syndicate
THE FENCE IS ON FIRE...
JUST ANOTHER AVERAGE MONDAY

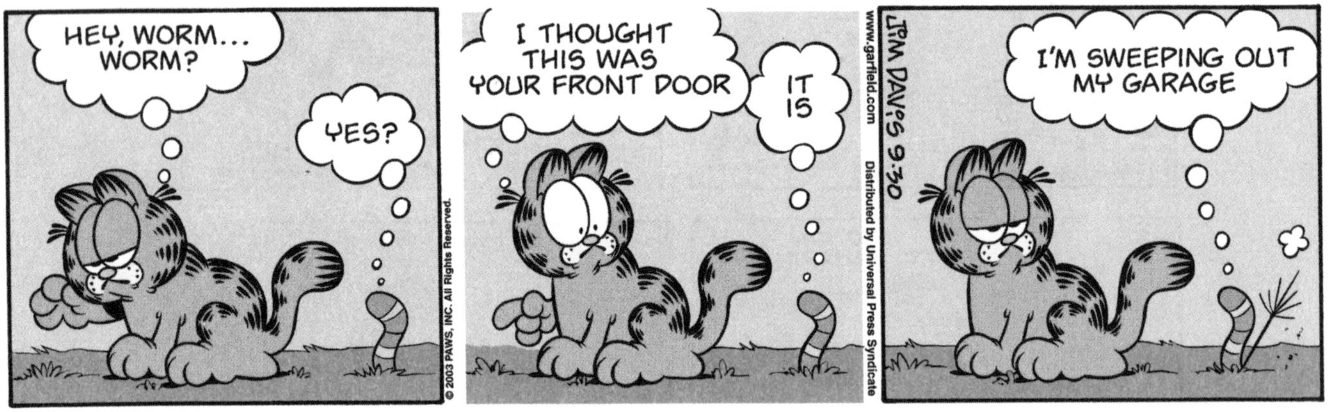
HEY, WORM... WORM?
YES?
© 2003 PAWS, INC. All Rights Reserved.
I THOUGHT THIS WAS YOUR FRONT DOOR
IT IS
JIM DAVIS 9-30
www.garfield.com
Distributed by Universal Press Syndicate
I'M SWEEPING OUT MY GARAGE

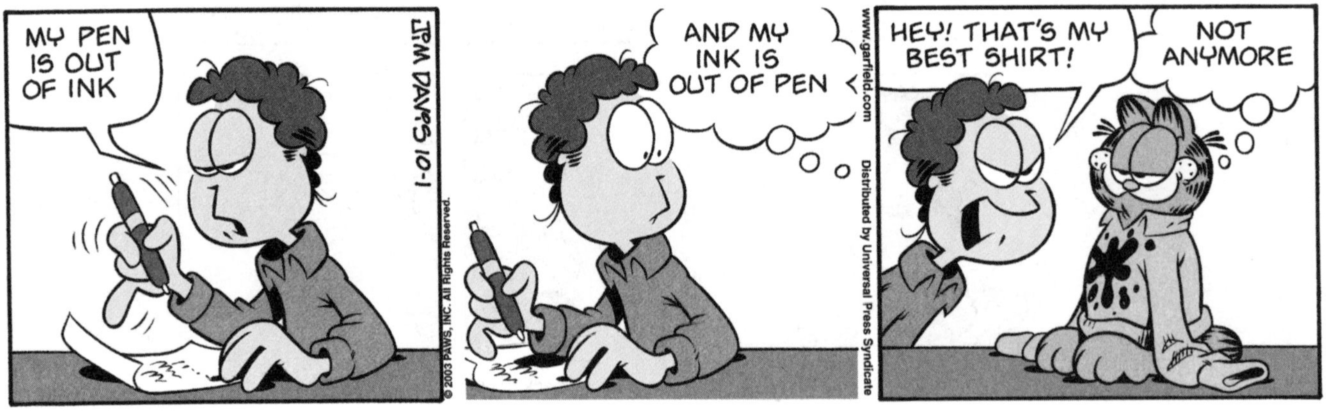
MY PEN IS OUT OF INK
JIM DAVIS 10-1
© 2003 PAWS, INC. All Rights Reserved.
AND MY INK IS OUT OF PEN
www.garfield.com
Distributed by Universal Press Syndicate
HEY! THAT'S MY BEST SHIRT!
NOT ANYMORE

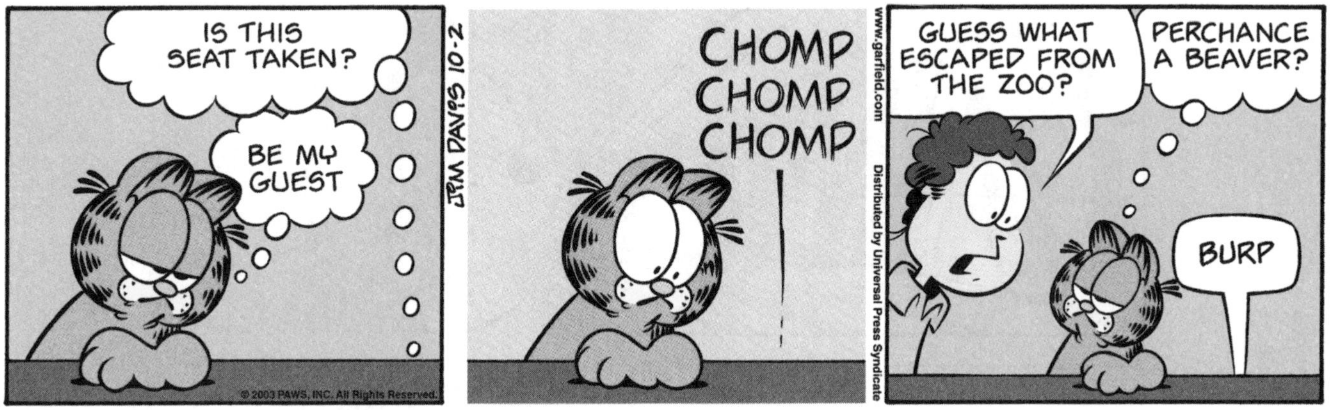
IS THIS SEAT TAKEN?
BE MY GUEST
JPM DAVPS 10-2
© 2003 PAWS, INC. All Rights Reserved.
CHOMP CHOMP CHOMP
www.garfield.com Distributed by Universal Press Syndicate
GUESS WHAT ESCAPED FROM THE ZOO?
PERCHANCE A BEAVER?
BURP

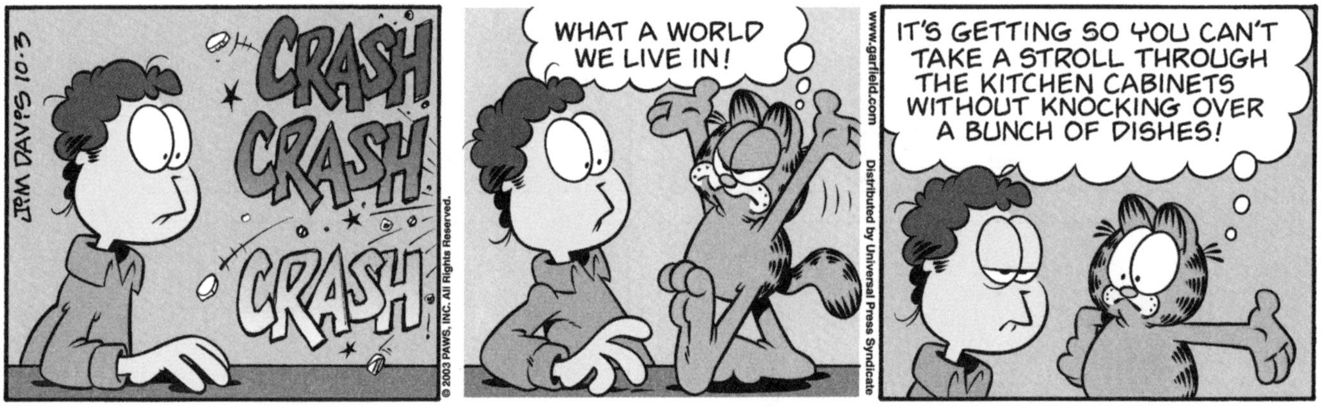
JPM DAVPS 10-3
CRASH CRASH CRASH
© 2003 PAWS, INC. All Rights Reserved.
WHAT A WORLD WE LIVE IN!
www.garfield.com Distributed by Universal Press Syndicate
IT'S GETTING SO YOU CAN'T TAKE A STROLL THROUGH THE KITCHEN CABINETS WITHOUT KNOCKING OVER A BUNCH OF DISHES!

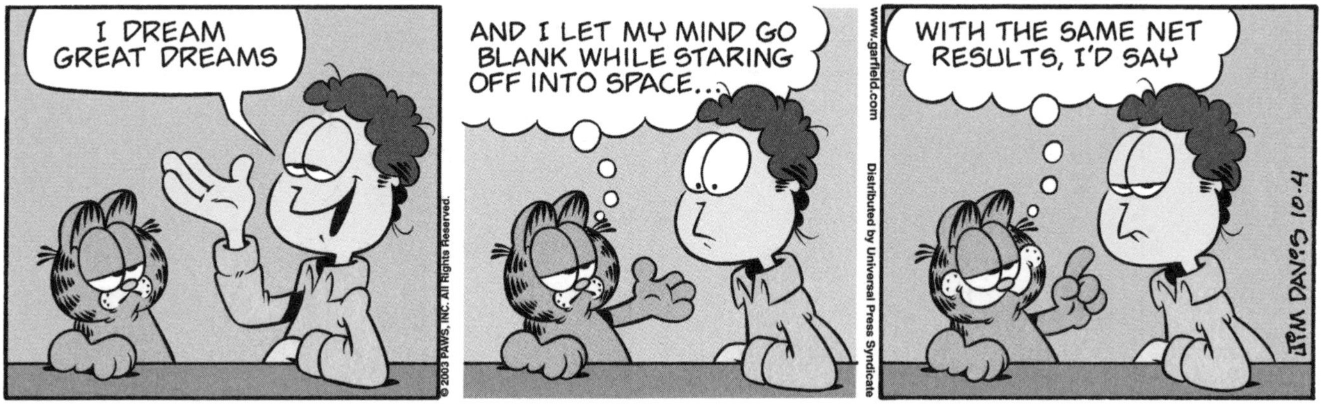
I DREAM GREAT DREAMS
© 2003 PAWS, INC. All Rights Reserved.
AND I LET MY MIND GO BLANK WHILE STARING OFF INTO SPACE...
www.garfield.com Distributed by Universal Press Syndicate
WITH THE SAME NET RESULTS, I'D SAY
JPM DAVPS 10-4

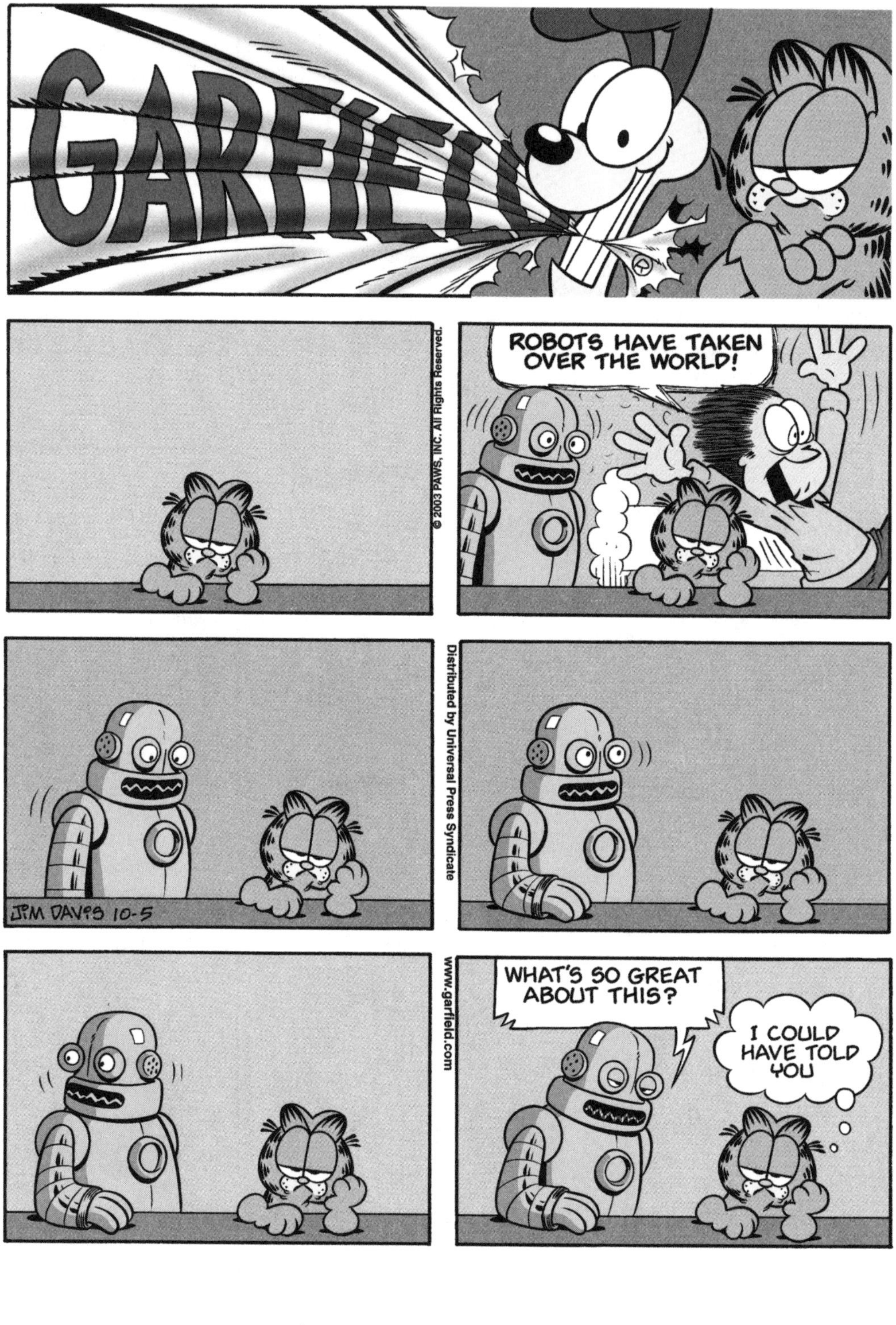
GARFIELD
© 2003 PAWS, INC. All Rights Reserved.
ROBOTS HAVE TAKEN OVER THE WORLD!
Distributed by Universal Press Syndicate
JIM DAVIS 10-5
www.garfield.com
WHAT'S SO GREAT ABOUT THIS?
I COULD HAVE TOLD YOU

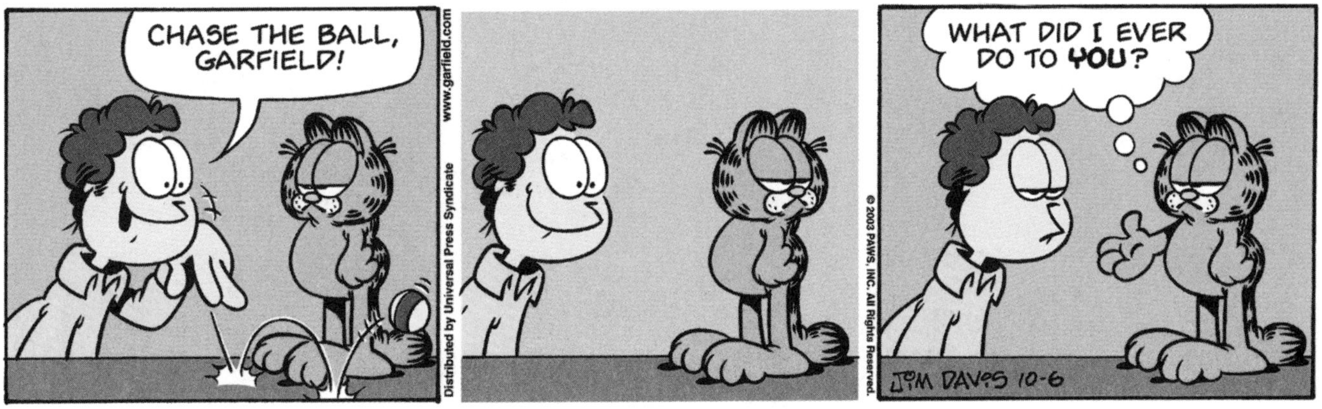
CHASE THE BALL, GARFIELD!
www.garfield.com
Distributed by Universal Press Syndicate
WHAT DID I EVER DO TO YOU?
© 2003 PAWS, INC. All Rights Reserved.
JIM DAVIS 10-6

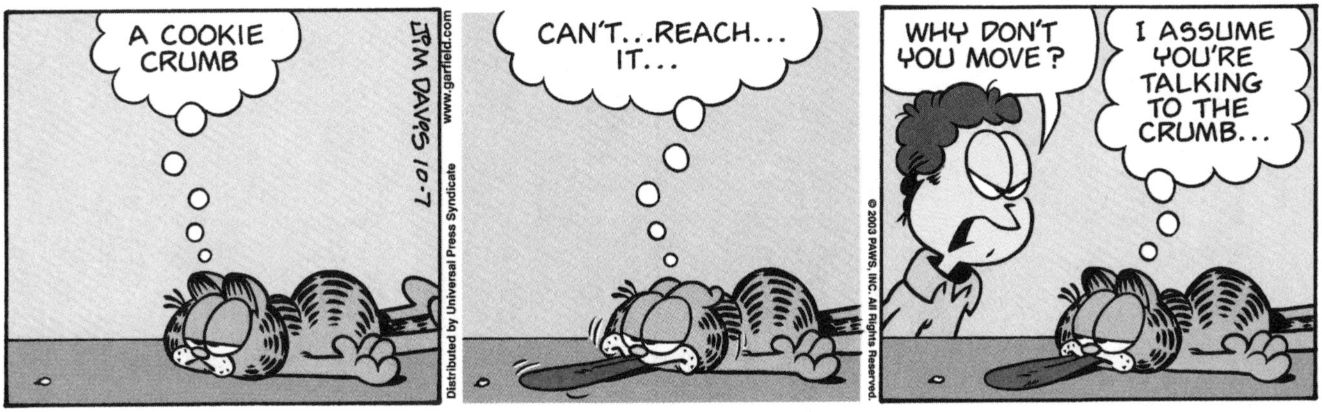
A COOKIE CRUMB
JIM DAVIS 10-7
www.garfield.com
Distributed by Universal Press Syndicate
CAN'T...REACH... IT...
© 2003 PAWS, INC. All Rights Reserved.
WHY DON'T YOU MOVE?
I ASSUME YOU'RE TALKING TO THE CRUMB...

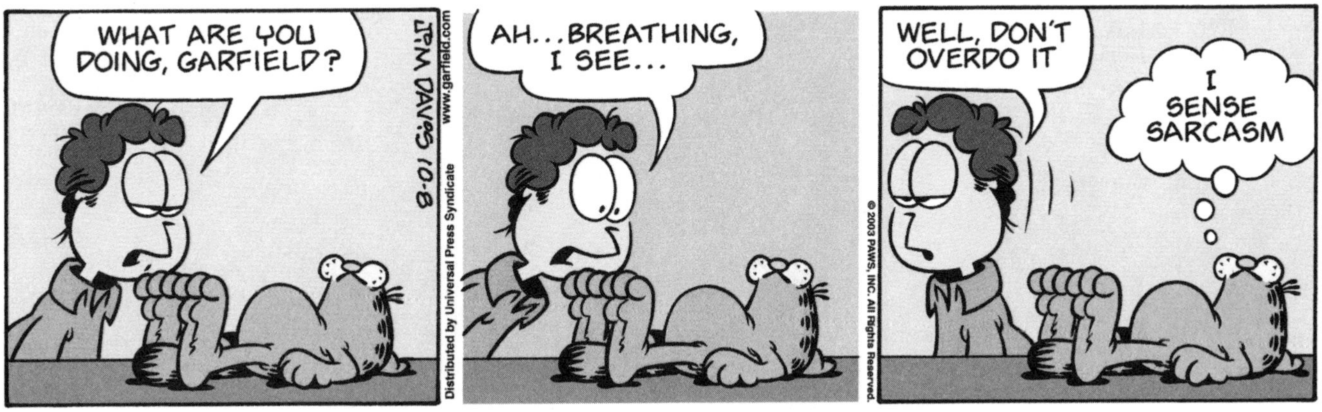
WHAT ARE YOU DOING, GARFIELD?
JIM DAVIS 10-8
www.garfield.com
Distributed by Universal Press Syndicate
AH...BREATHING, I SEE...
© 2003 PAWS, INC. All Rights Reserved.
WELL, DON'T OVERDO IT
I SENSE SARCASM

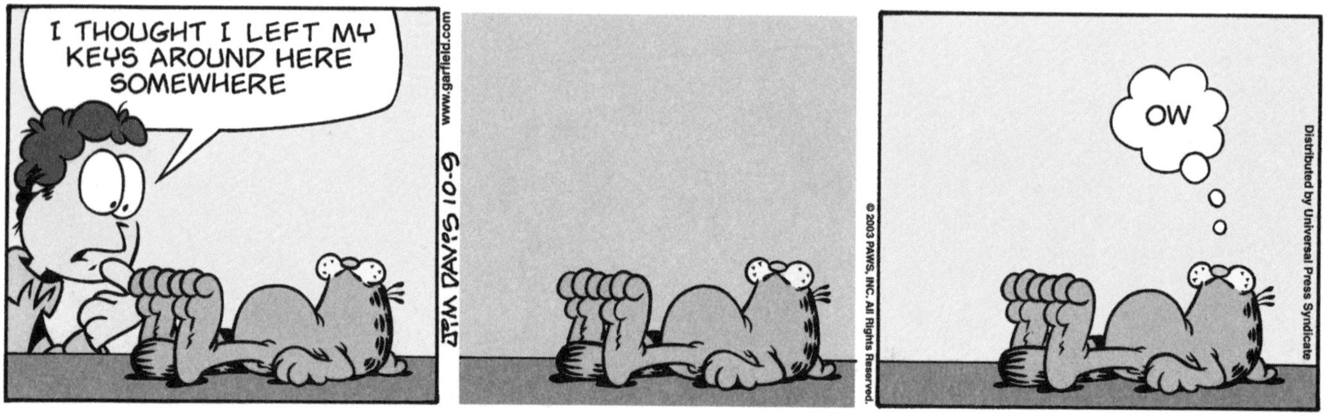
I THOUGHT I LEFT MY KEYS AROUND HERE SOMEWHERE
JPM DAVIS 10-9
www.garfield.com
© 2003 PAWS, INC. All Rights Reserved.
OW
Distributed by Universal Press Syndicate

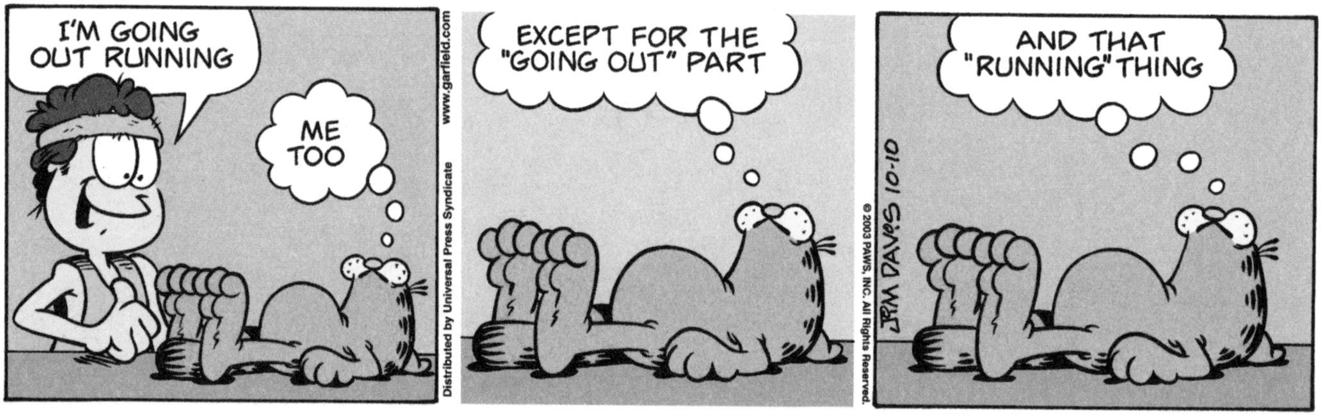
I'M GOING OUT RUNNING
ME TOO
www.garfield.com
Distributed by Universal Press Syndicate
EXCEPT FOR THE "GOING OUT" PART
© 2003 PAWS, INC. All Rights Reserved.
JPM DAVIS 10-10
AND THAT "RUNNING" THING

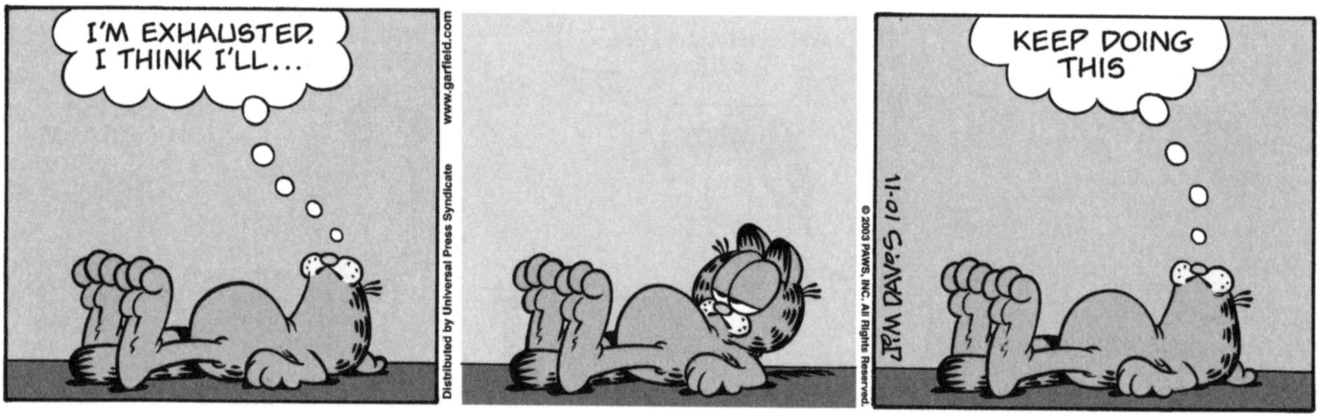
I'M EXHAUSTED. I THINK I'LL...
www.garfield.com
Distributed by Universal Press Syndicate
© 2003 PAWS, INC. All Rights Reserved.
JPM DAVIS 10-11
KEEP DOING THIS

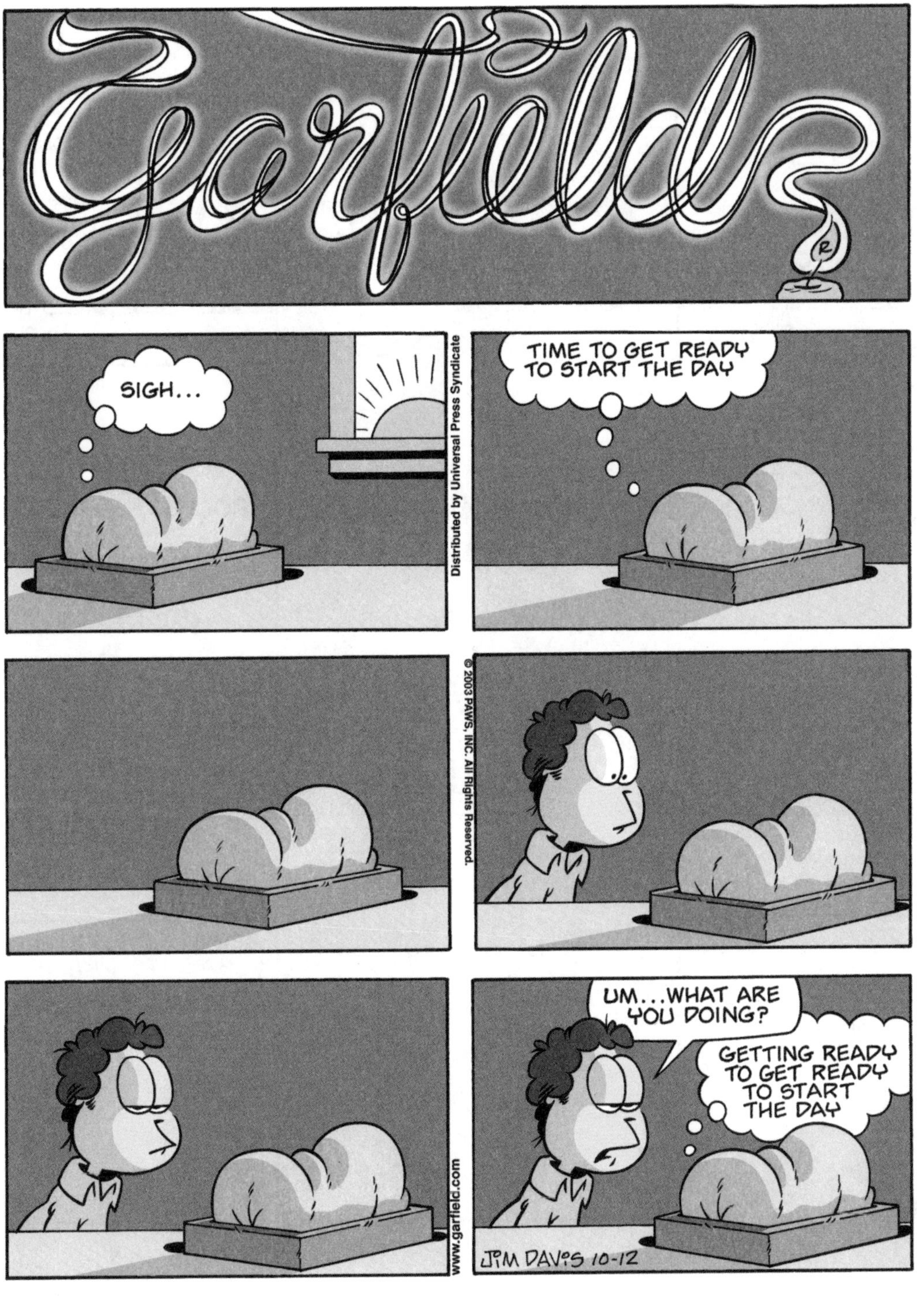
Garfield
SIGH...
TIME TO GET READY TO START THE DAY
UM...WHAT ARE YOU DOING?
GETTING READY TO GET READY TO START THE DAY
JIM DAVIS 10-12
Distributed by Universal Press Syndicate
© 2003 PAWS, INC. All Rights Reserved.
www.garfield.com

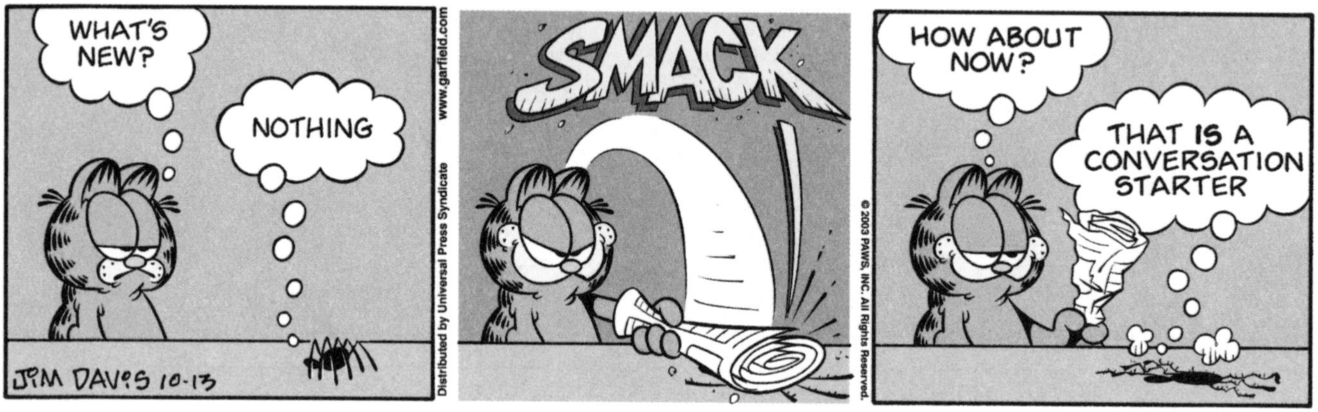
WHAT'S NEW?
NOTHING
JIM DAVIS 10-13
Distributed by Universal Press Syndicate www.garfield.com
SMACK
© 2003 PAWS, INC. All Rights Reserved.
HOW ABOUT NOW?
THAT IS A CONVERSATION STARTER

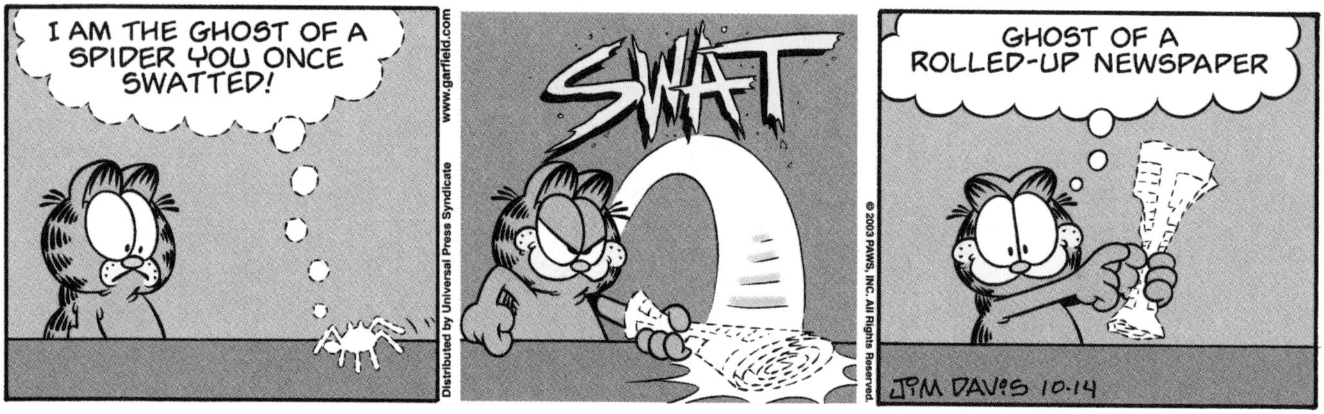
I AM THE GHOST OF A SPIDER YOU ONCE SWATTED!
Distributed by Universal Press Syndicate www.garfield.com
SWAT
© 2003 PAWS, INC. All Rights Reserved.
GHOST OF A ROLLED-UP NEWSPAPER
JIM DAVIS 10-14

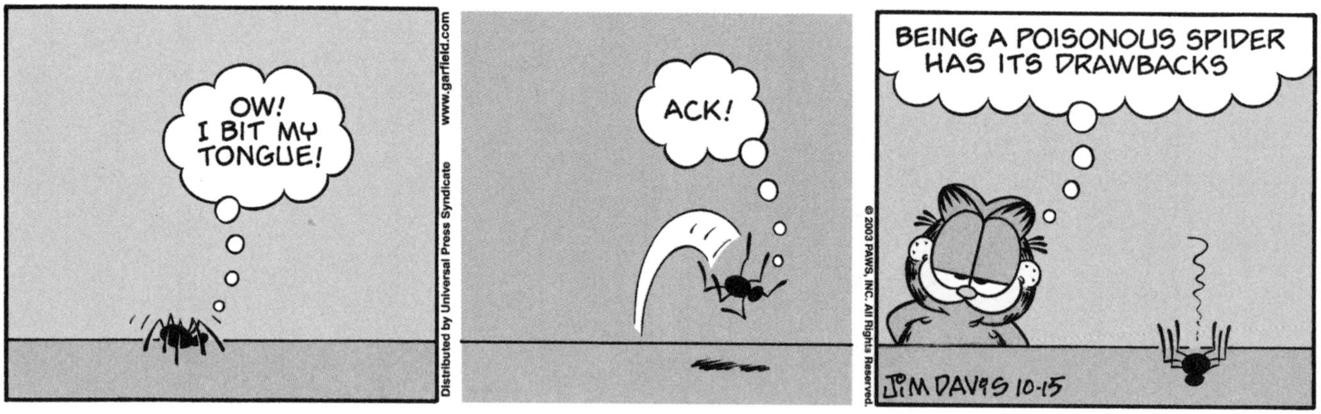
OW! I BIT MY TONGUE!
Distributed by Universal Press Syndicate www.garfield.com
ACK!
© 2003 PAWS, INC. All Rights Reserved.
BEING A POISONOUS SPIDER HAS ITS DRAWBACKS
JIM DAVIS 10-15

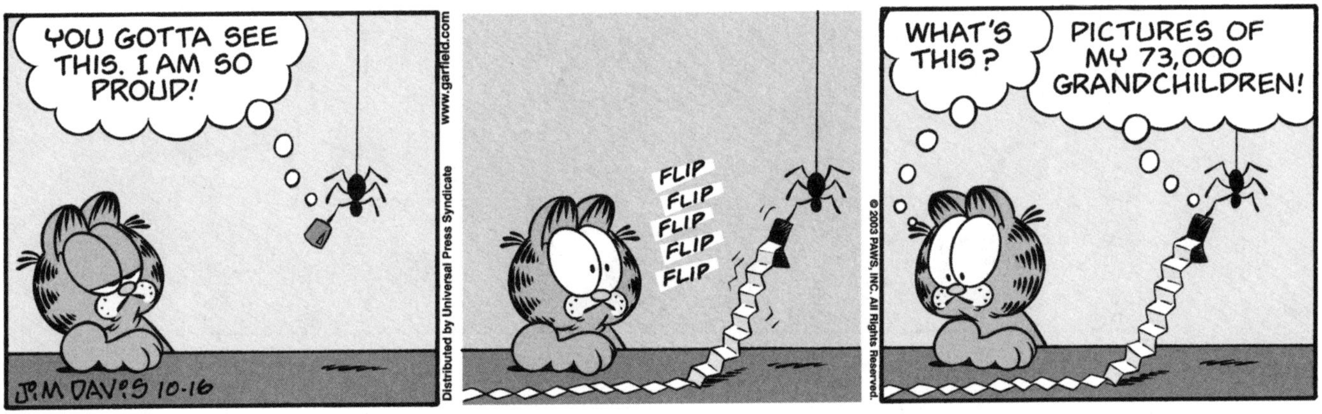
YOU GOTTA SEE THIS. I AM SO PROUD!
JIM DAVIS 10-16
www.garfield.com
Distributed by Universal Press Syndicate
FLIP FLIP FLIP FLIP FLIP
© 2003 PAWS, INC. All Rights Reserved.
WHAT'S THIS?
PICTURES OF MY 73,000 GRANDCHILDREN!

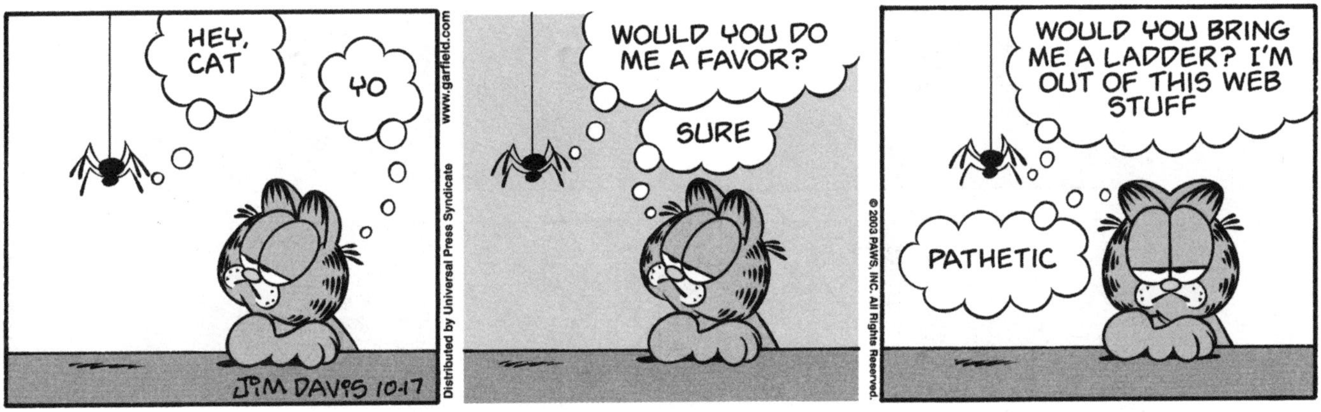
HEY, CAT
YO
JIM DAVIS 10-17
www.garfield.com
Distributed by Universal Press Syndicate
WOULD YOU DO ME A FAVOR?
SURE
© 2003 PAWS, INC. All Rights Reserved.
WOULD YOU BRING ME A LADDER? I'M OUT OF THIS WEB STUFF
PATHETIC

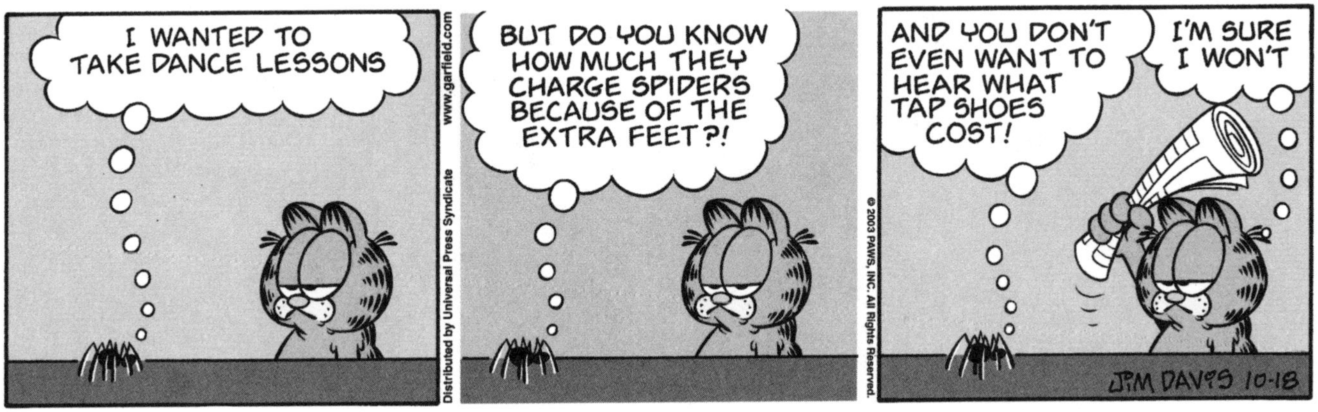
I WANTED TO TAKE DANCE LESSONS
www.garfield.com
Distributed by Universal Press Syndicate
BUT DO YOU KNOW HOW MUCH THEY CHARGE SPIDERS BECAUSE OF THE EXTRA FEET?!
© 2003 PAWS, INC. All Rights Reserved.
AND YOU DON'T EVEN WANT TO HEAR WHAT TAP SHOES COST!
I'M SURE I WON'T
JIM DAVIS 10-18

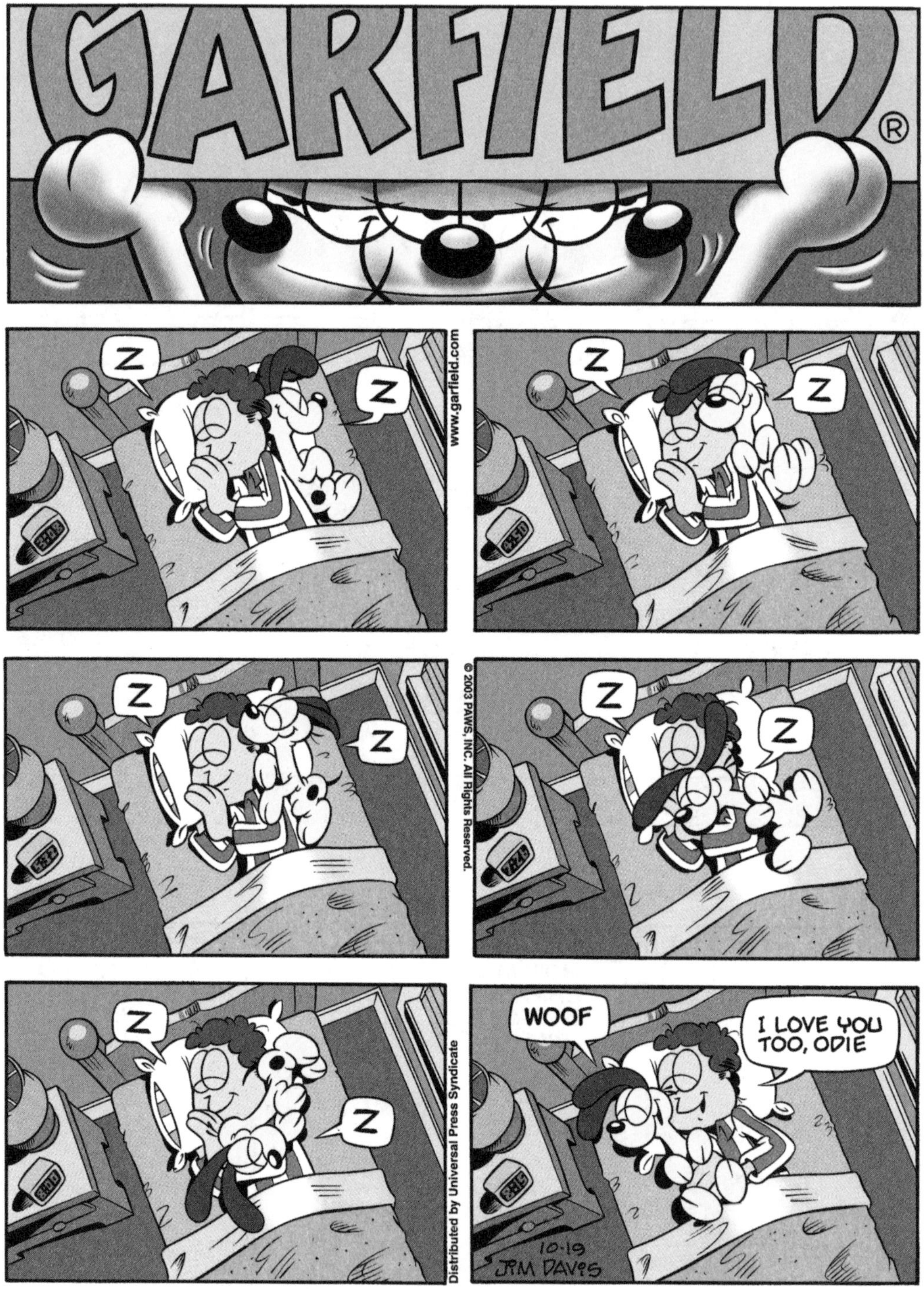
GARFIELD®
Z
Z
www.garfield.com
Z
Z
Z
Z
© 2003 PAWS, INC. All Rights Reserved.
Z
Z
Z
Z
Distributed by Universal Press Syndicate
WOOF
I LOVE YOU TOO, ODIE
10-19
JIM DAVIS

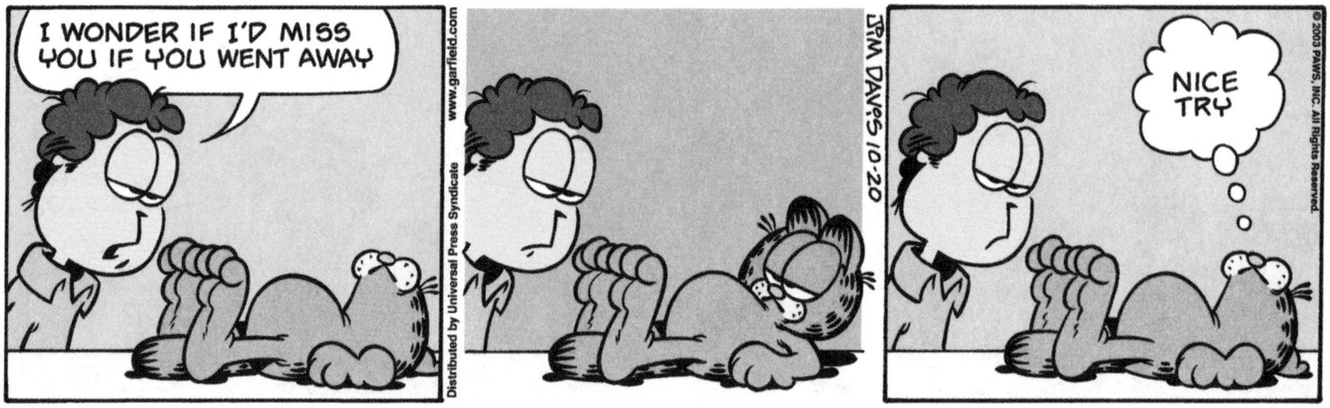
I WONDER IF I'D MISS YOU IF YOU WENT AWAY
NICE TRY
JIM DAVIS 10-20
www.garfield.com
Distributed by Universal Press Syndicate
© 2003 PAWS, INC. All Rights Reserved.

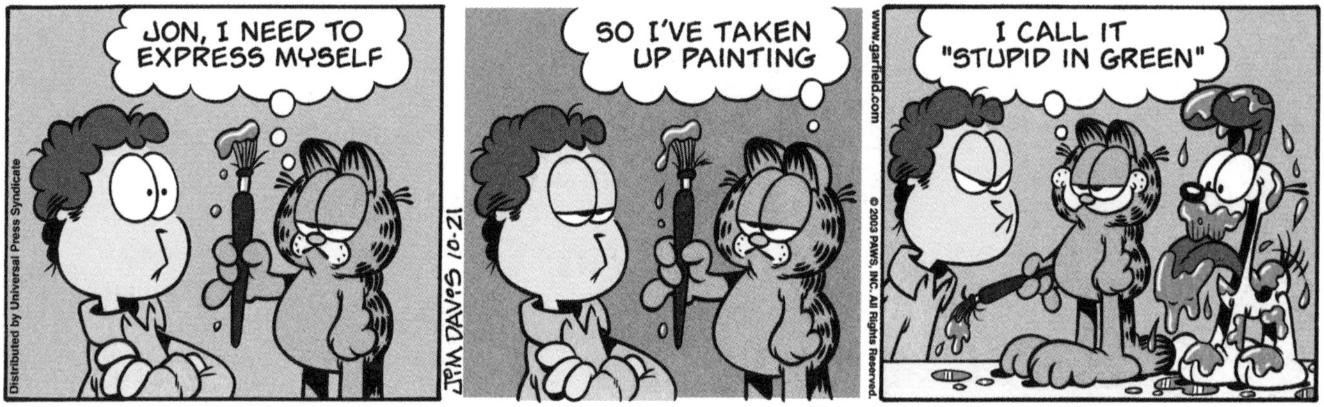
JON, I NEED TO EXPRESS MYSELF
SO I'VE TAKEN UP PAINTING
I CALL IT "STUPID IN GREEN"
JIM DAVIS 10-21
Distributed by Universal Press Syndicate
www.garfield.com
© 2003 PAWS, INC. All Rights Reserved.

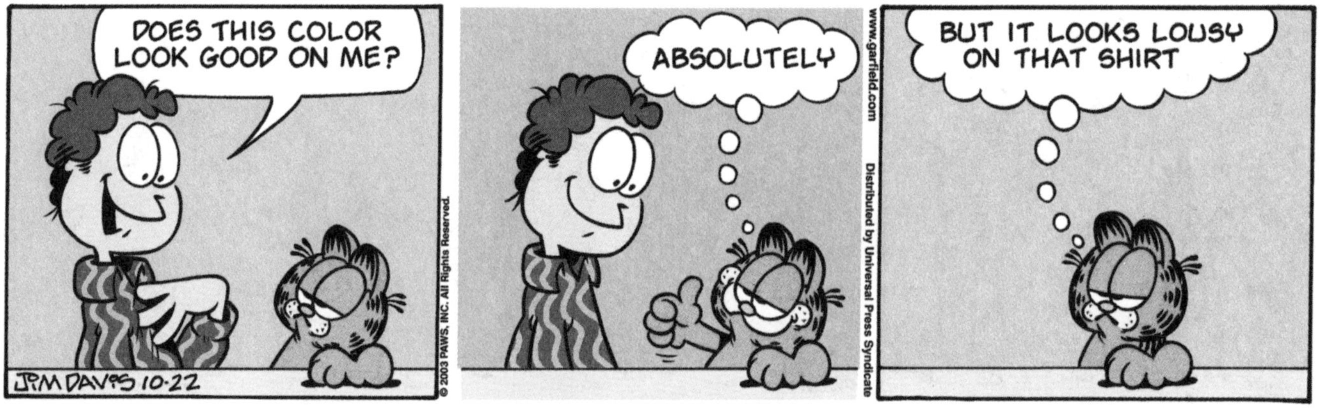
DOES THIS COLOR LOOK GOOD ON ME?
ABSOLUTELY
BUT IT LOOKS LOUSY ON THAT SHIRT
JIM DAVIS 10-22
© 2003 PAWS, INC. All Rights Reserved.
www.garfield.com
Distributed by Universal Press Syndicate

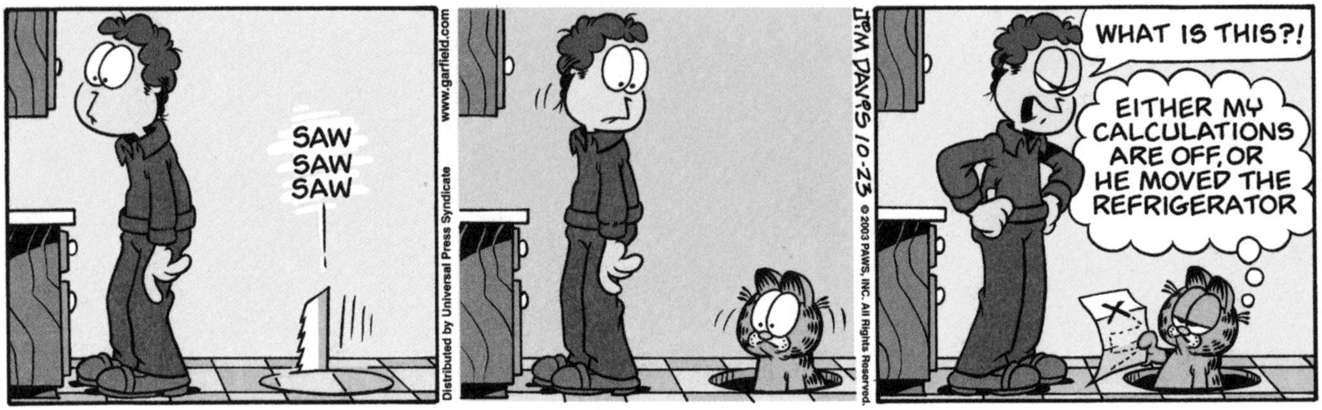
SAW
SAW
SAW
WHAT IS THIS?!
EITHER MY CALCULATIONS ARE OFF, OR HE MOVED THE REFRIGERATOR

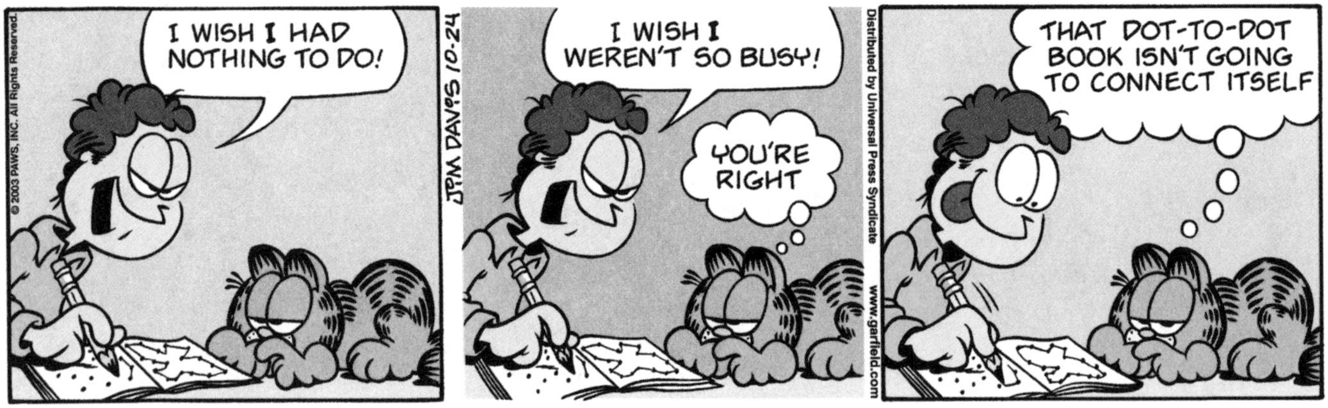
I WISH I HAD NOTHING TO DO!
I WISH I WEREN'T SO BUSY!
YOU'RE RIGHT
THAT DOT-TO-DOT BOOK ISN'T GOING TO CONNECT ITSELF

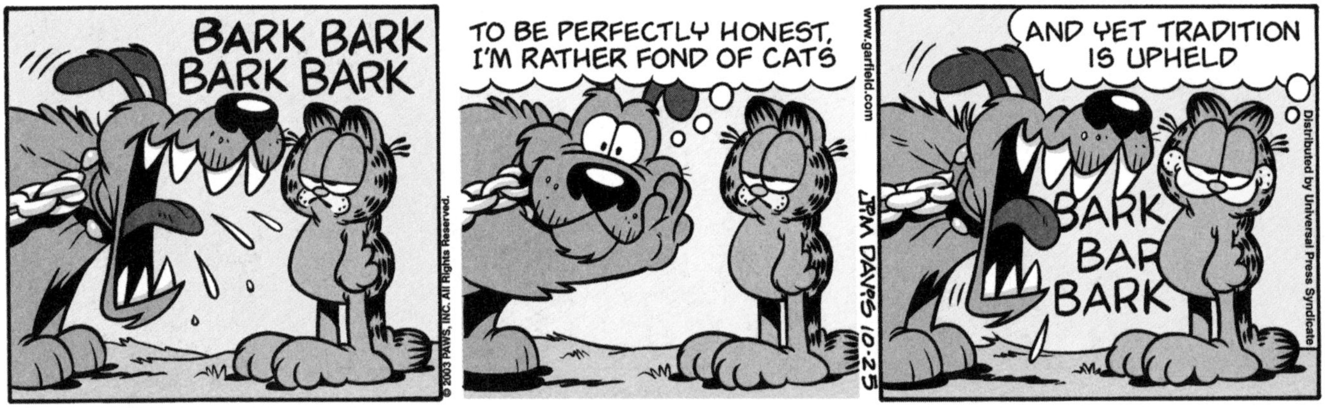
BARK BARK
BARK BARK
TO BE PERFECTLY HONEST, I'M RATHER FOND OF CATS
AND YET TRADITION IS UPHELD
BARK
BAR
BARK

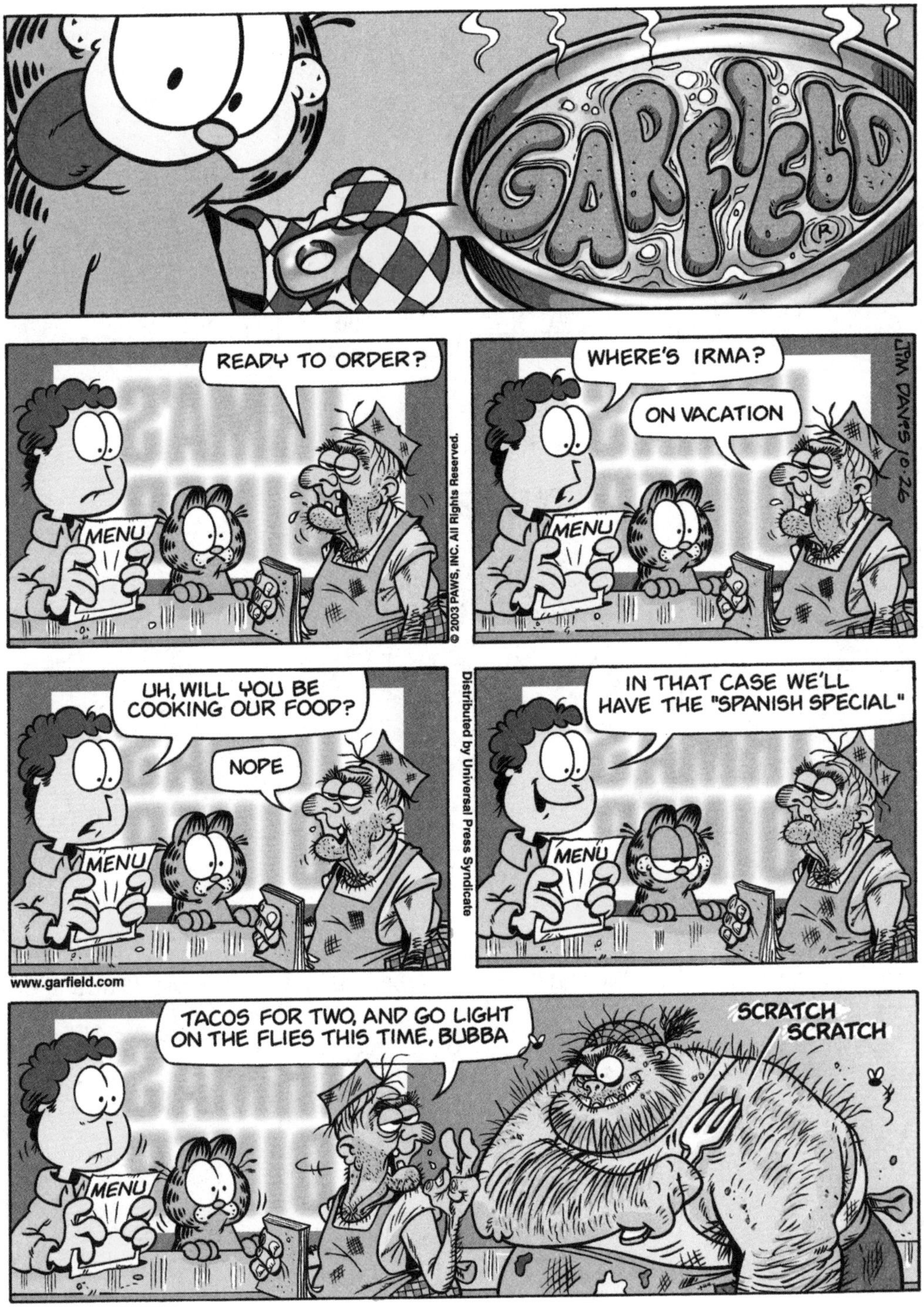
GARFIELD®
READY TO ORDER?
WHERE'S IRMA?
ON VACATION
JIM DAVIS 10-26
UH, WILL YOU BE COOKING OUR FOOD?
NOPE
IN THAT CASE WE'LL HAVE THE "SPANISH SPECIAL"
TACOS FOR TWO, AND GO LIGHT ON THE FLIES THIS TIME, BUBBA
SCRATCH SCRATCH
MENU

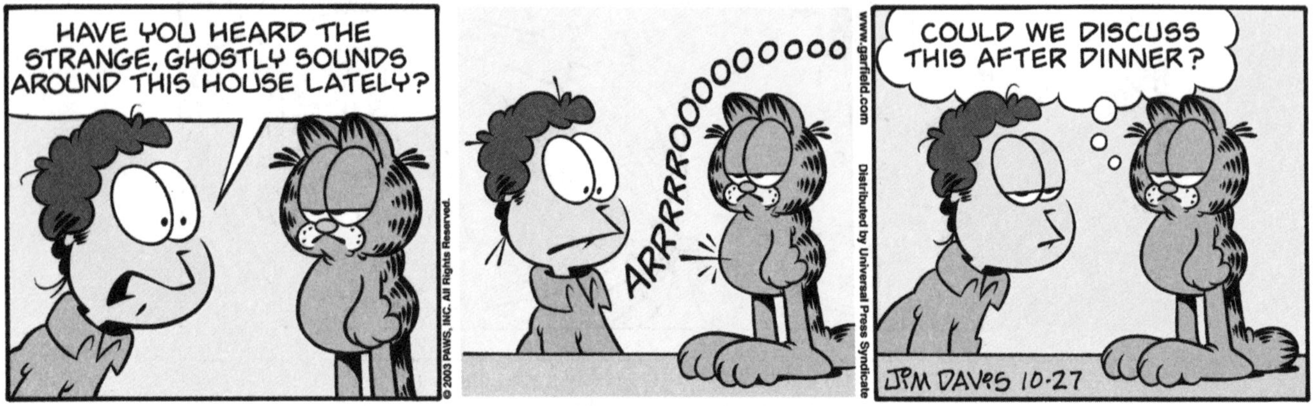
HAVE YOU HEARD THE STRANGE, GHOSTLY SOUNDS AROUND THIS HOUSE LATELY?
© 2003 PAWS, INC. All Rights Reserved.
ARRRRROOOOOOOOOOOO
www.garfield.com Distributed by Universal Press Syndicate
COULD WE DISCUSS THIS AFTER DINNER?
JIM DAVIS 10-27

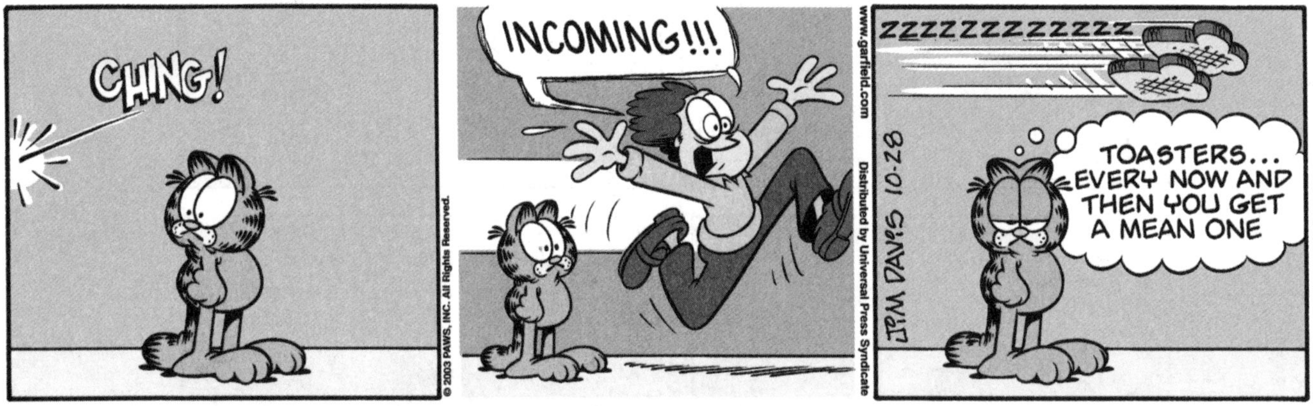
CHING!
© 2003 PAWS, INC. All Rights Reserved.
INCOMING!!!
www.garfield.com Distributed by Universal Press Syndicate
JIM DAVIS 10-28
ZZZZZZZZZZZZ
TOASTERS... EVERY NOW AND THEN YOU GET A MEAN ONE

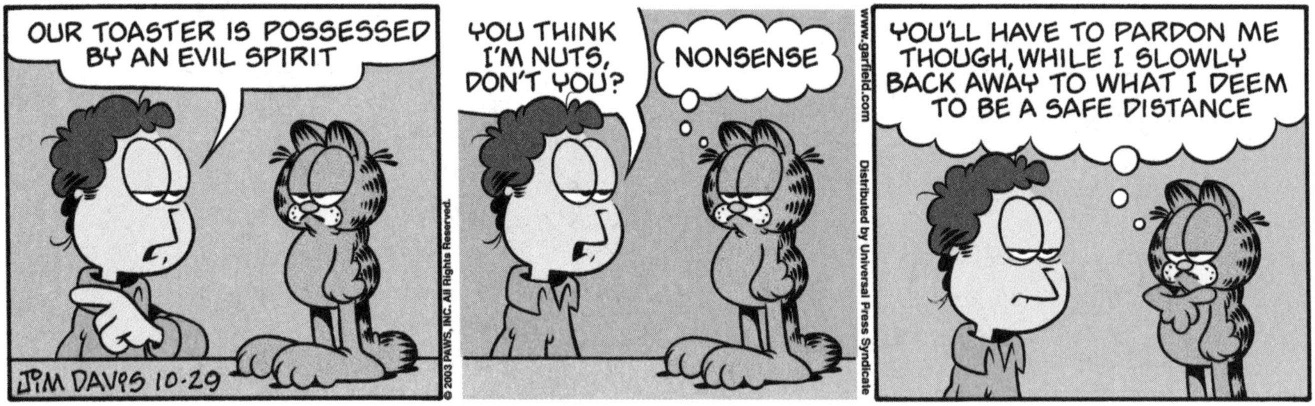
OUR TOASTER IS POSSESSED BY AN EVIL SPIRIT
JIM DAVIS 10-29
© 2003 PAWS, INC. All Rights Reserved.
YOU THINK I'M NUTS, DON'T YOU?
NONSENSE
www.garfield.com Distributed by Universal Press Syndicate
YOU'LL HAVE TO PARDON ME THOUGH, WHILE I SLOWLY BACK AWAY TO WHAT I DEEM TO BE A SAFE DISTANCE

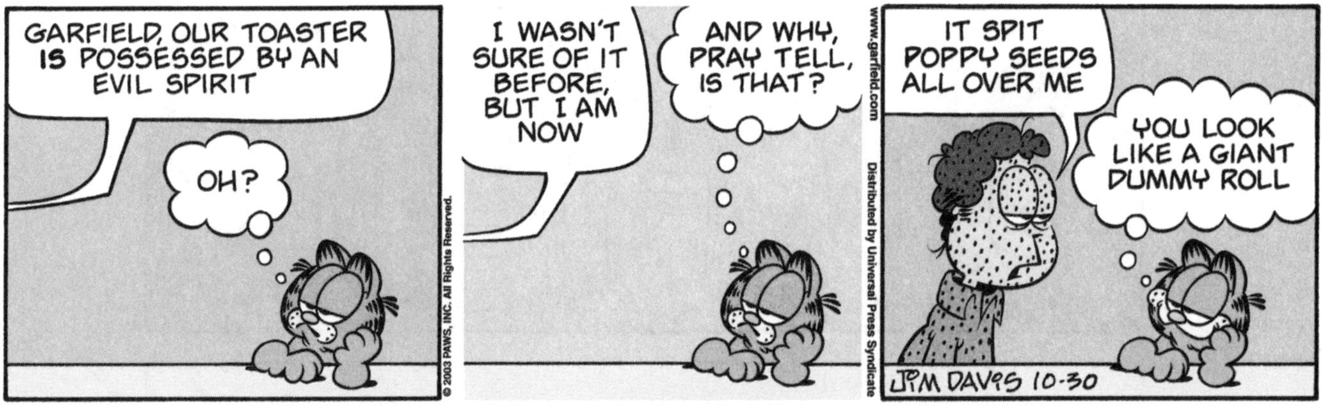
GARFIELD, OUR TOASTER IS POSSESSED BY AN EVIL SPIRIT
OH?
I WASN'T SURE OF IT BEFORE, BUT I AM NOW
AND WHY, PRAY TELL, IS THAT?
IT SPIT POPPY SEEDS ALL OVER ME
YOU LOOK LIKE A GIANT DUMMY ROLL
JIM DAVIS 10-30
© 2003 PAWS, INC. All Rights Reserved.
www.garfield.com Distributed by Universal Press Syndicate

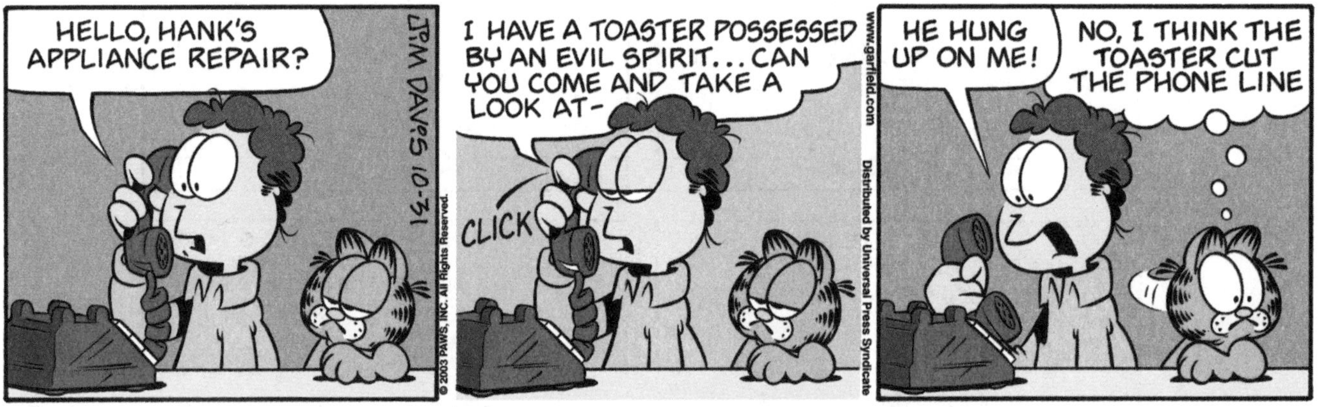
HELLO, HANK'S APPLIANCE REPAIR?
JIM DAVIS 10-31
I HAVE A TOASTER POSSESSED BY AN EVIL SPIRIT... CAN YOU COME AND TAKE A LOOK AT-
CLICK
HE HUNG UP ON ME!
NO, I THINK THE TOASTER CUT THE PHONE LINE
© 2003 PAWS, INC. All Rights Reserved.
www.garfield.com Distributed by Universal Press Syndicate

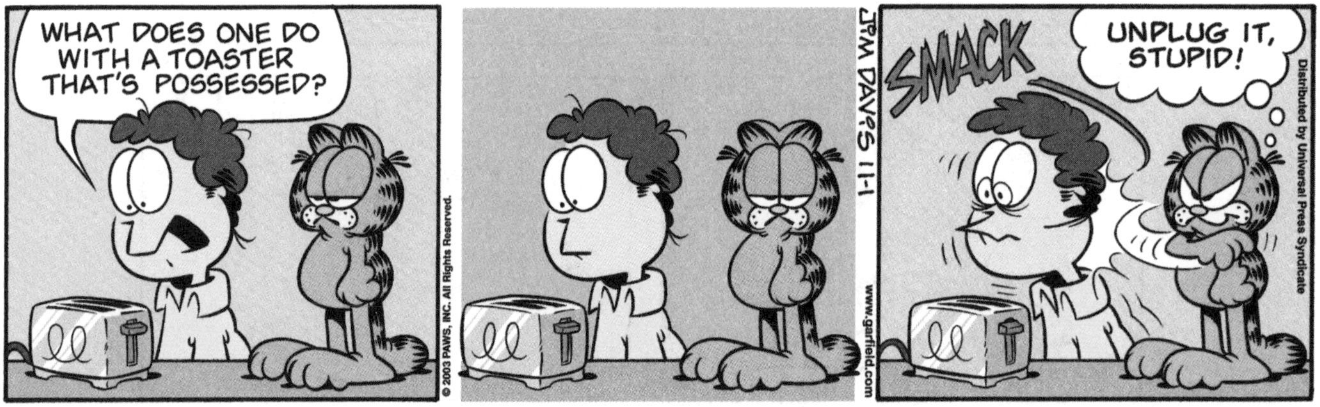
WHAT DOES ONE DO WITH A TOASTER THAT'S POSSESSED?
JIM DAVIS 11-1
SMACK
UNPLUG IT, STUPID!
© 2003 PAWS, INC. All Rights Reserved.
www.garfield.com Distributed by Universal Press Syndicate

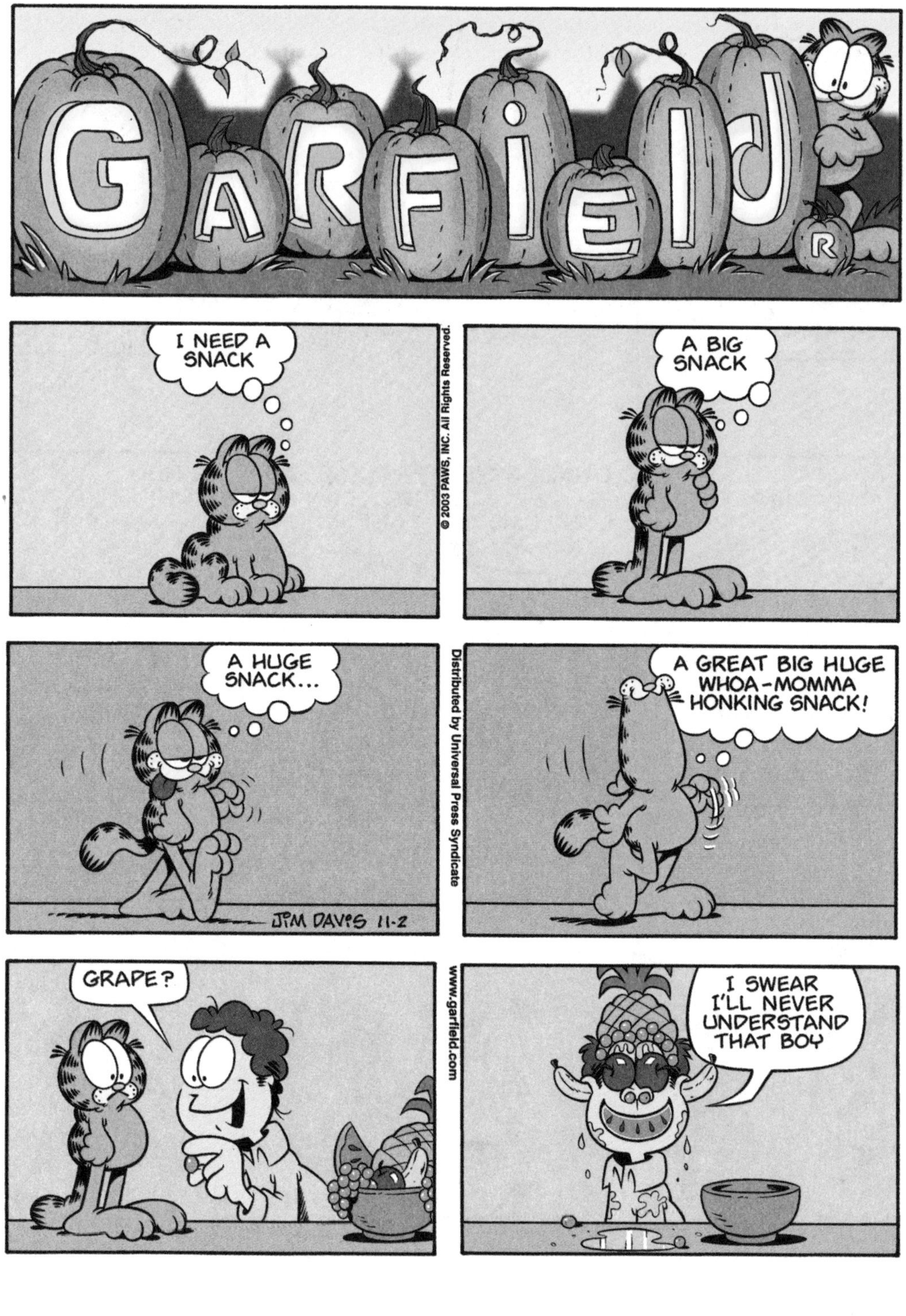
GARFIELD R
I NEED A SNACK
A BIG SNACK
A HUGE SNACK...
A GREAT BIG HUGE WHOA-MOMMA HONKING SNACK!
JIM DAVIS 11-2
GRAPE?
I SWEAR I'LL NEVER UNDERSTAND THAT BOY
© 2003 PAWS, INC. All Rights Reserved.
Distributed by Universal Press Syndicate
www.garfield.com

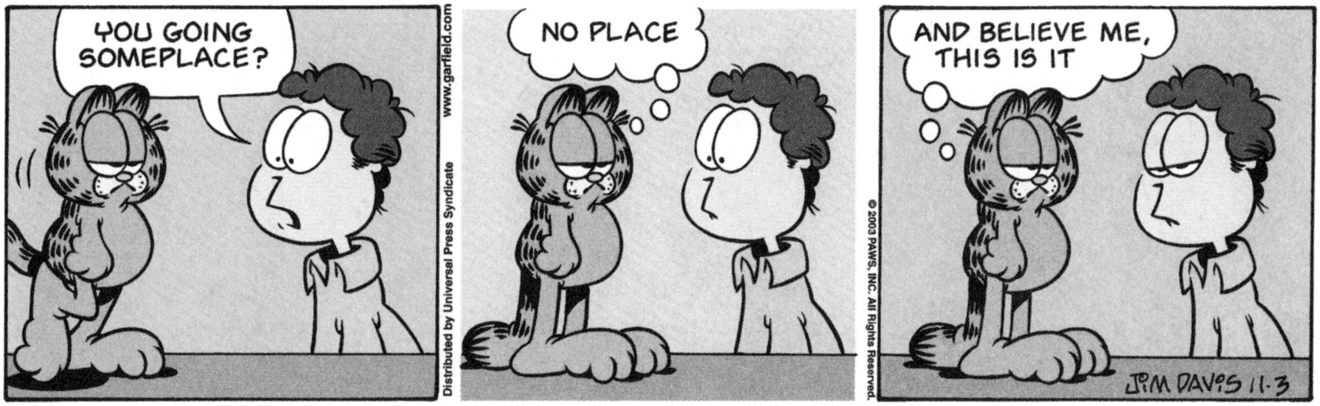
YOU GOING SOMEPLACE?
NO PLACE
AND BELIEVE ME, THIS IS IT
Distributed by Universal Press Syndicate www.garfield.com
© 2003 PAWS, INC. All Rights Reserved.
JIM DAVIS 11-3

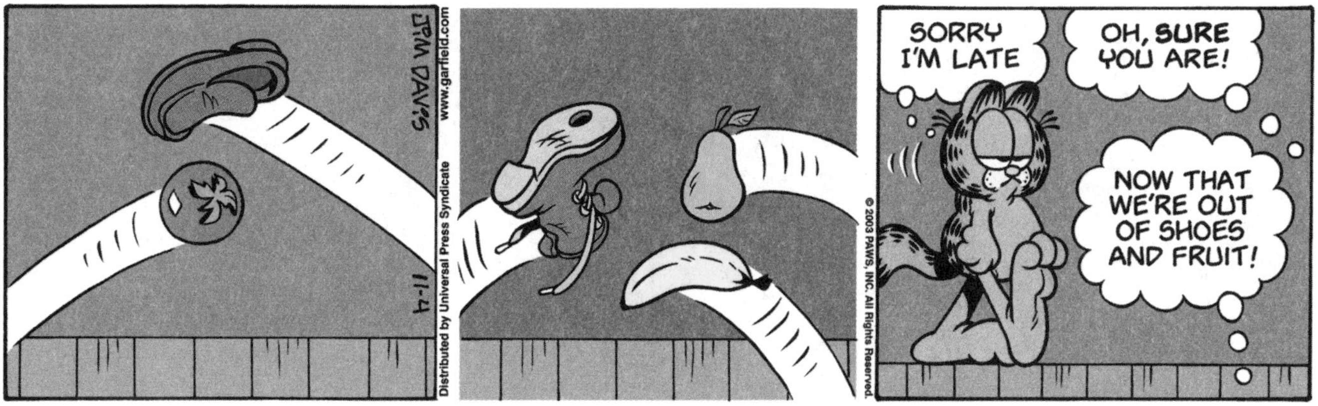
JIM DAVIS 11-4
Distributed by Universal Press Syndicate www.garfield.com
© 2003 PAWS, INC. All Rights Reserved.
SORRY I'M LATE
OH, SURE YOU ARE!
NOW THAT WE'RE OUT OF SHOES AND FRUIT!

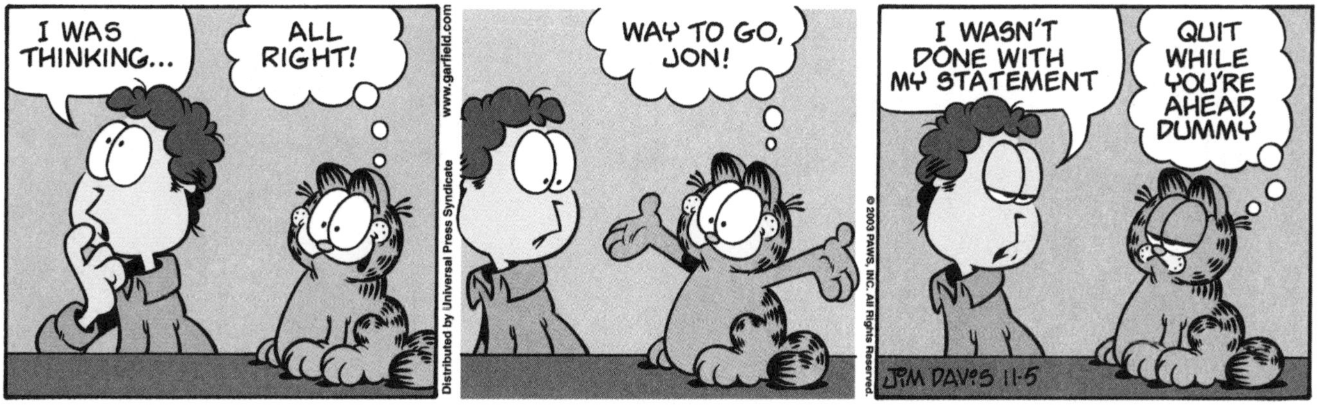
I WAS THINKING...
ALL RIGHT!
Distributed by Universal Press Syndicate www.garfield.com
WAY TO GO, JON!
© 2003 PAWS, INC. All Rights Reserved.
I WASN'T DONE WITH MY STATEMENT
QUIT WHILE YOU'RE AHEAD, DUMMY
JIM DAVIS 11-5

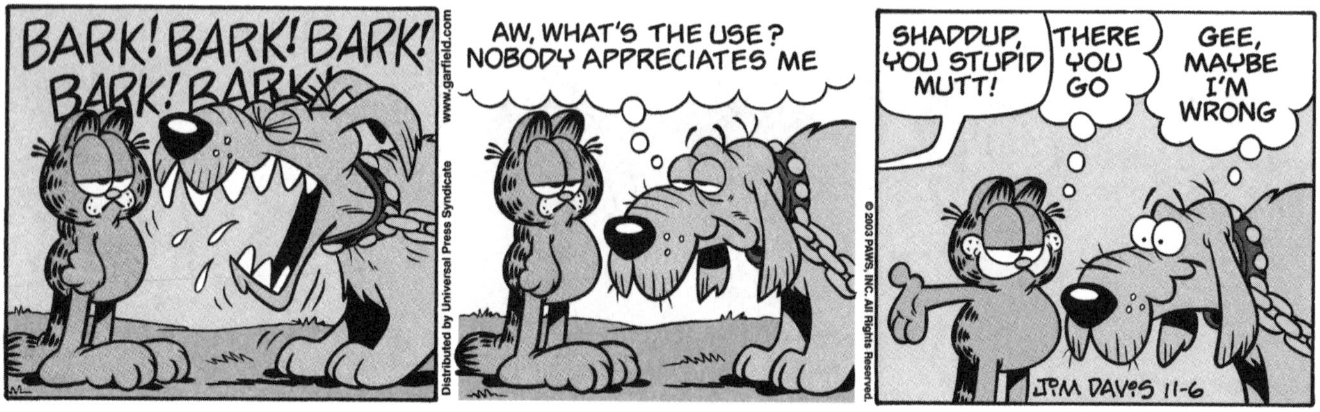
BARK! BARK! BARK! BARK! BARK!
www.garfield.com
Distributed by Universal Press Syndicate
AW, WHAT'S THE USE? NOBODY APPRECIATES ME
© 2003 PAWS, INC. All Rights Reserved.
SHADDUP, YOU STUPID MUTT!
THERE YOU GO
GEE, MAYBE I'M WRONG
JIM DAVIS 11-6

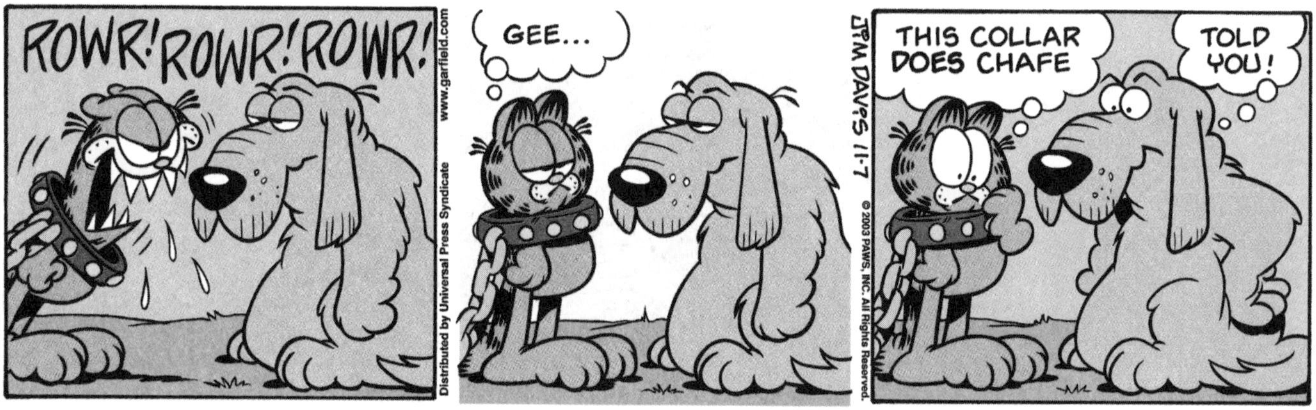
ROWR! ROWR! ROWR!
www.garfield.com
Distributed by Universal Press Syndicate
GEE...
JIM DAVIS 11-7
© 2003 PAWS, INC. All Rights Reserved.
THIS COLLAR DOES CHAFE
TOLD YOU!

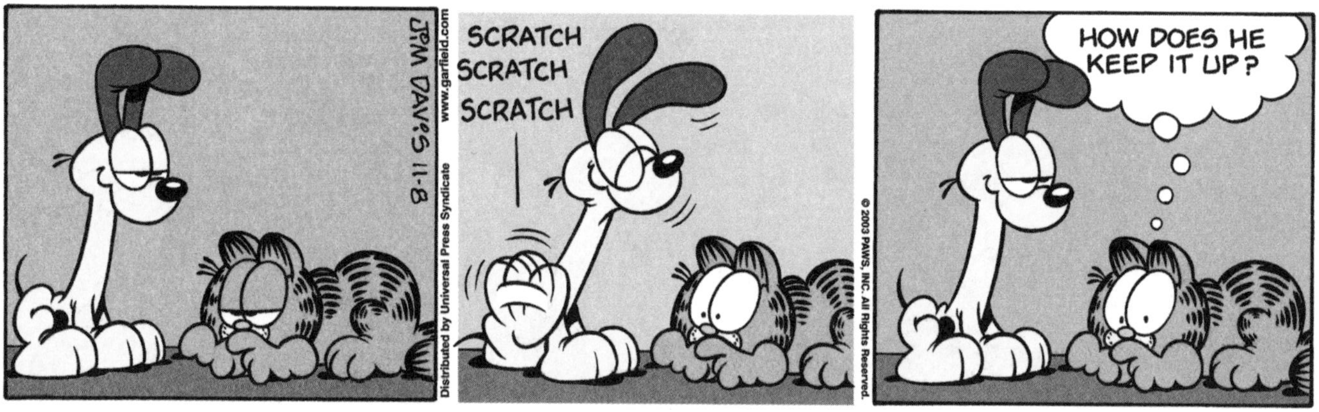
JIM DAVIS 11-8
www.garfield.com
Distributed by Universal Press Syndicate
SCRATCH
SCRATCH
SCRATCH
© 2003 PAWS, INC. All Rights Reserved.
HOW DOES HE KEEP IT UP?

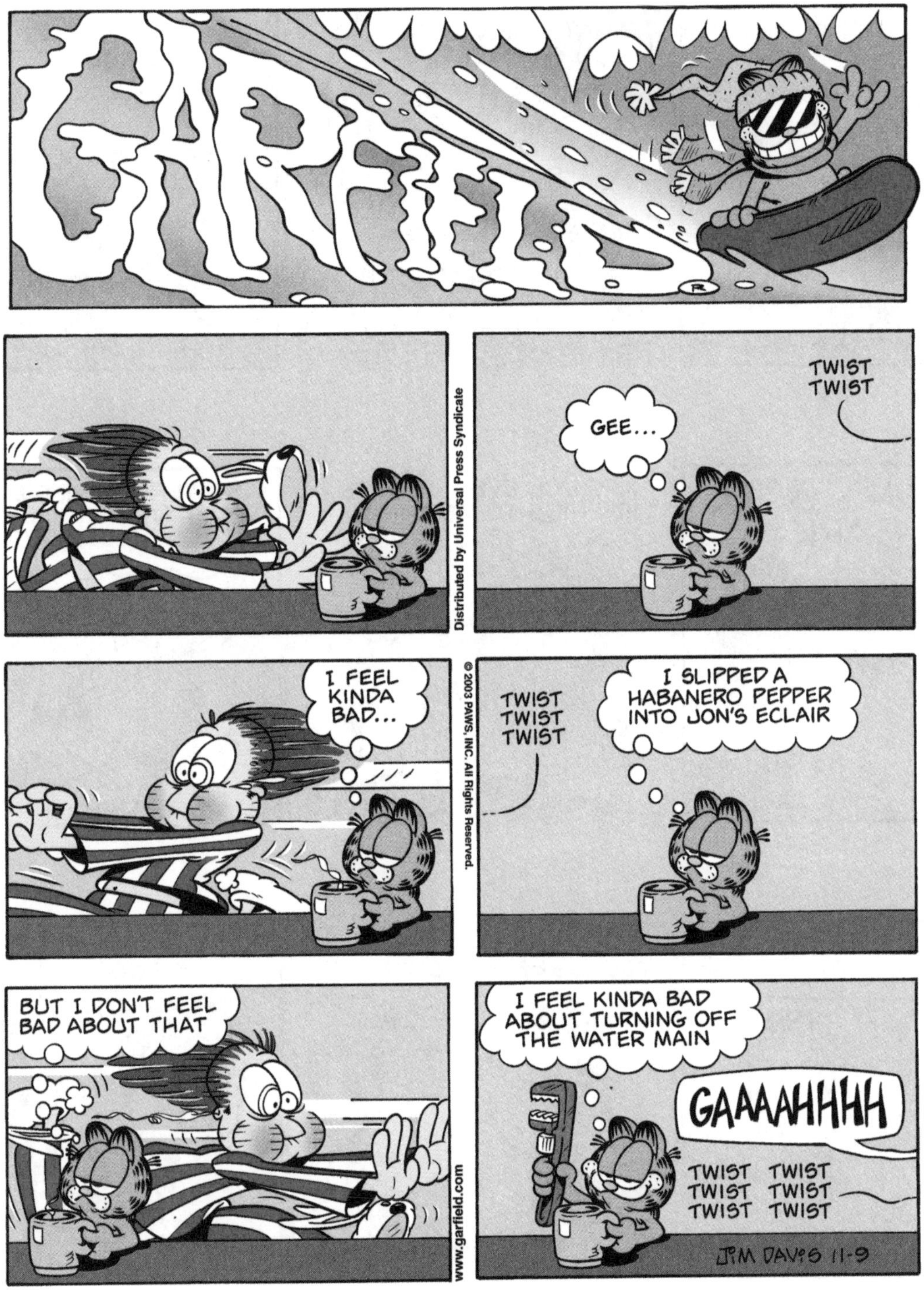
GARFIELD®
GEE...
TWIST TWIST
I FEEL KINDA BAD...
TWIST TWIST TWIST
I SLIPPED A HABANERO PEPPER INTO JON'S ECLAIR
BUT I DON'T FEEL BAD ABOUT THAT
I FEEL KINDA BAD ABOUT TURNING OFF THE WATER MAIN
GAAAAHHHH
TWIST TWIST TWIST TWIST TWIST TWIST
JIM DAVIS 11-9
Distributed by Universal Press Syndicate
© 2003 PAWS, INC. All Rights Reserved.
www.garfield.com

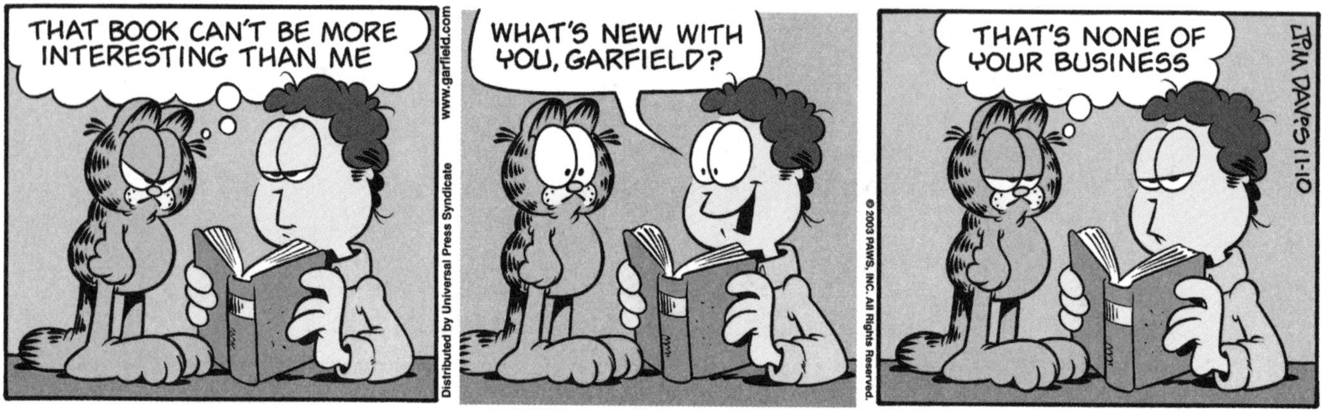
THAT BOOK CAN'T BE MORE INTERESTING THAN ME
www.garfield.com
Distributed by Universal Press Syndicate
WHAT'S NEW WITH YOU, GARFIELD?
© 2003 PAWS, INC. All Rights Reserved.
THAT'S NONE OF YOUR BUSINESS
JIM DAVIS 11-10

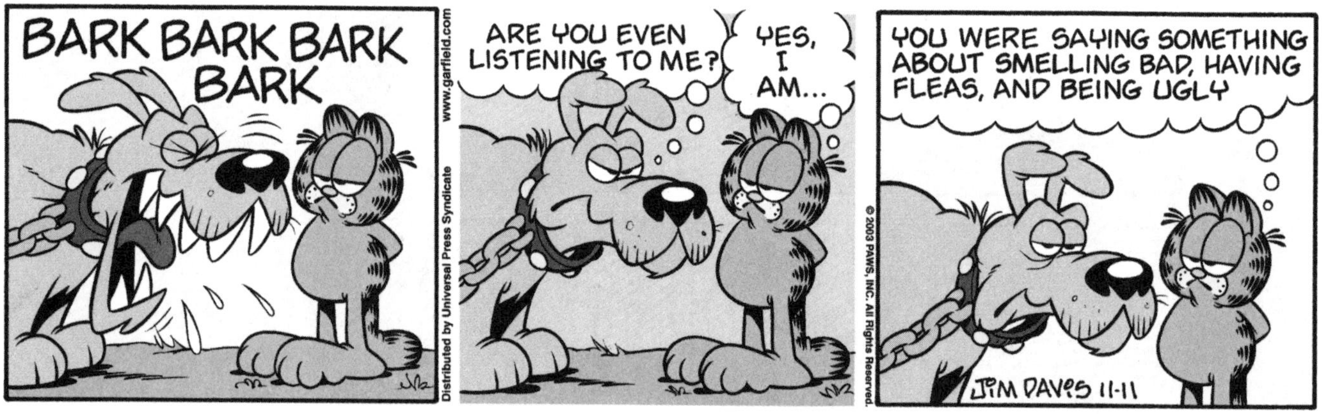
BARK BARK BARK BARK
www.garfield.com
Distributed by Universal Press Syndicate
ARE YOU EVEN LISTENING TO ME?
YES, I AM...
© 2003 PAWS, INC. All Rights Reserved.
YOU WERE SAYING SOMETHING ABOUT SMELLING BAD, HAVING FLEAS, AND BEING UGLY
JIM DAVIS 11-11

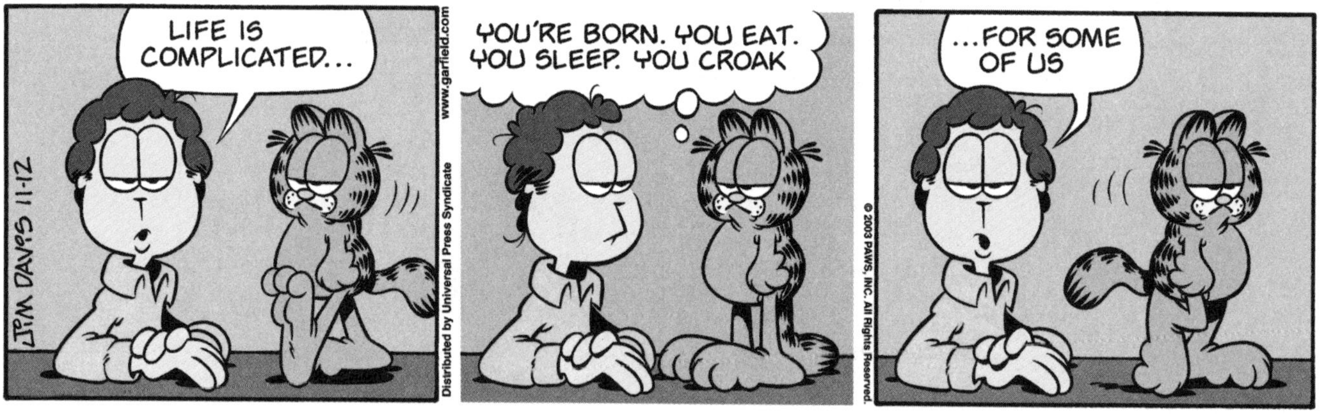
LIFE IS COMPLICATED...
JIM DAVIS 11-12
www.garfield.com
Distributed by Universal Press Syndicate
YOU'RE BORN. YOU EAT. YOU SLEEP. YOU CROAK
© 2003 PAWS, INC. All Rights Reserved.
...FOR SOME OF US

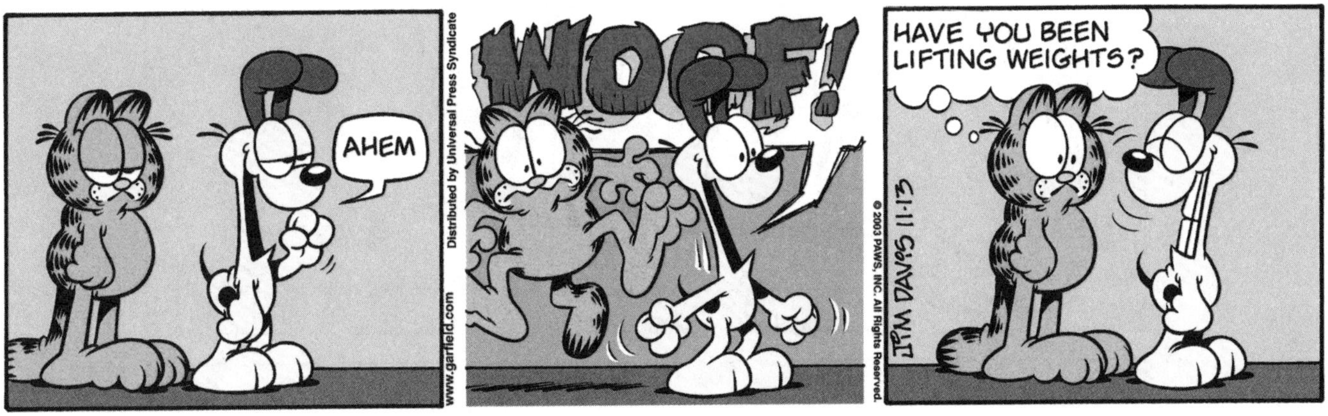
AHEM
www.garfield.com
Distributed by Universal Press Syndicate
WOOF!
© 2003 PAWS, INC. All Rights Reserved.
JIM DAVIS 11-13
HAVE YOU BEEN LIFTING WEIGHTS?

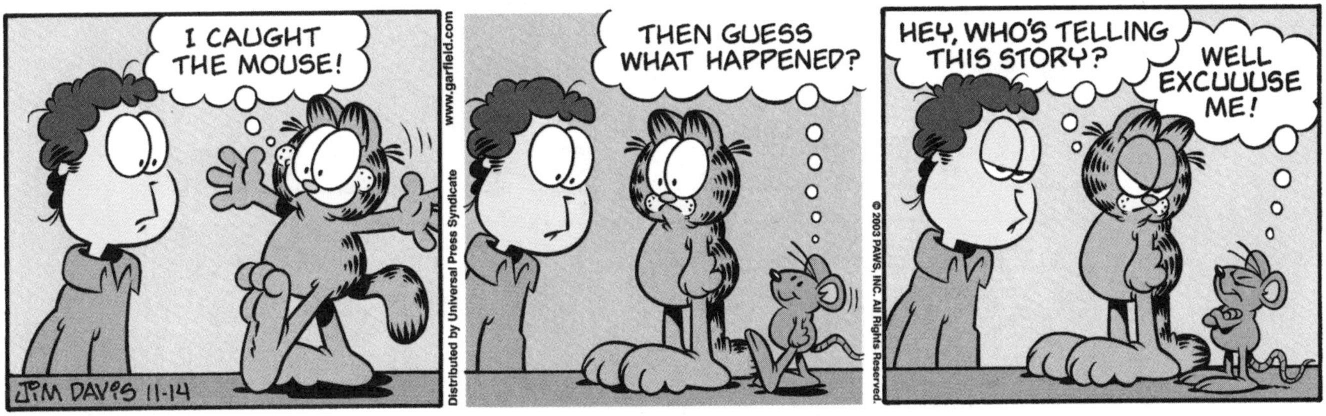
I CAUGHT THE MOUSE!
JIM DAVIS 11-14
Distributed by Universal Press Syndicate
www.garfield.com
THEN GUESS WHAT HAPPENED?
© 2003 PAWS, INC. All Rights Reserved.
HEY, WHO'S TELLING THIS STORY?
WELL EXCUUUSE ME!

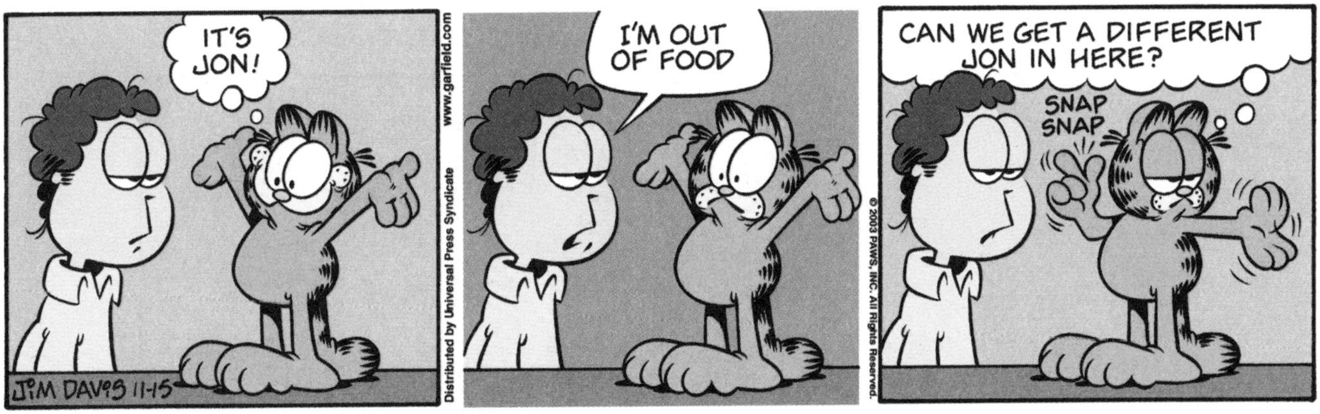
IT'S JON!
JIM DAVIS 11-15
Distributed by Universal Press Syndicate
www.garfield.com
I'M OUT OF FOOD
© 2003 PAWS, INC. All Rights Reserved.
CAN WE GET A DIFFERENT JON IN HERE?
SNAP SNAP

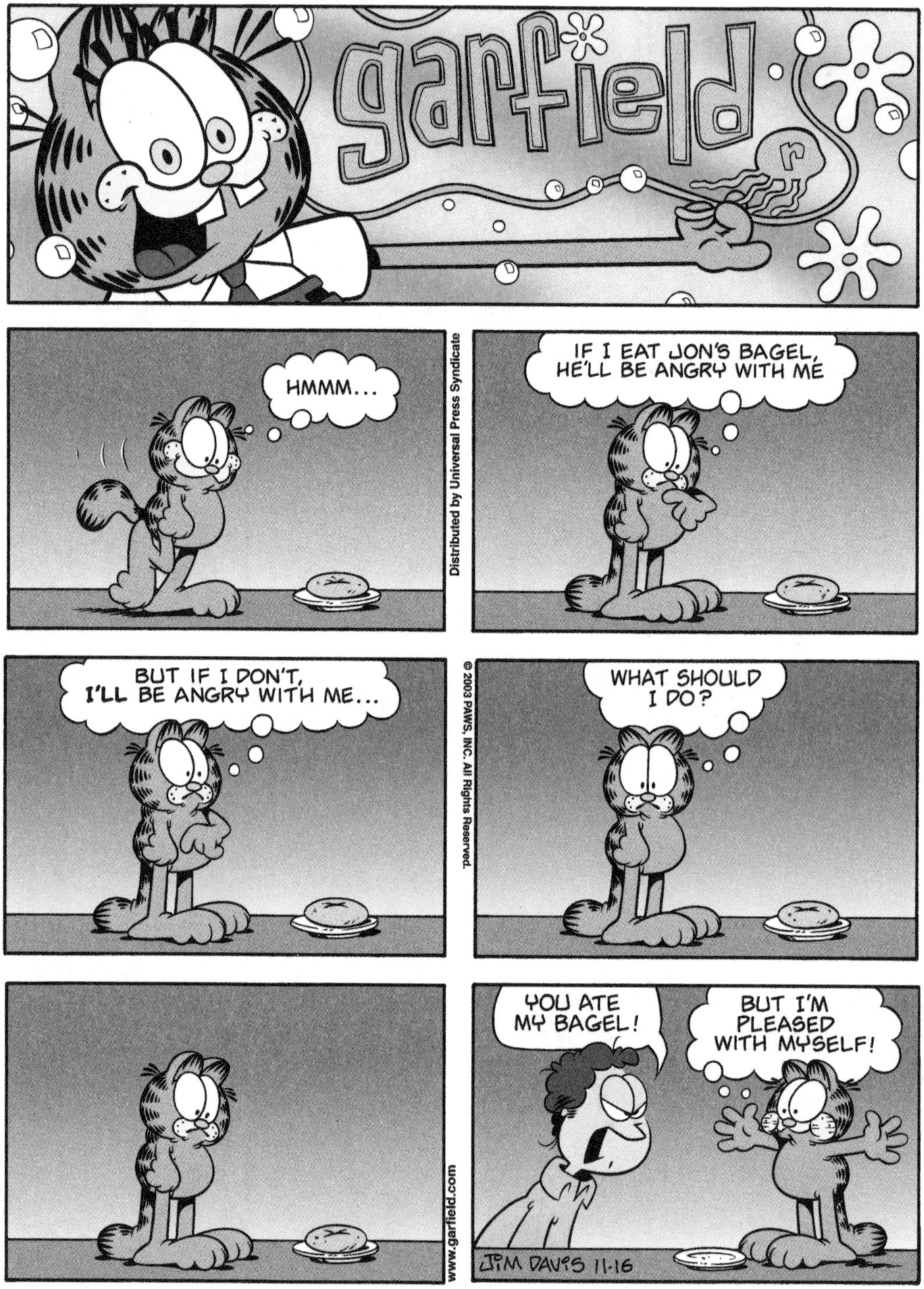
garfield
HMMM...
IF I EAT JON'S BAGEL, HE'LL BE ANGRY WITH ME
BUT IF I DON'T, **I'LL** BE ANGRY WITH ME...
WHAT SHOULD I DO?
YOU ATE MY BAGEL!
BUT I'M PLEASED WITH MYSELF!
JIM DAVIS 11-16
Distributed by Universal Press Syndicate
© 2003 PAWS, INC. All Rights Reserved.
www.garfield.com

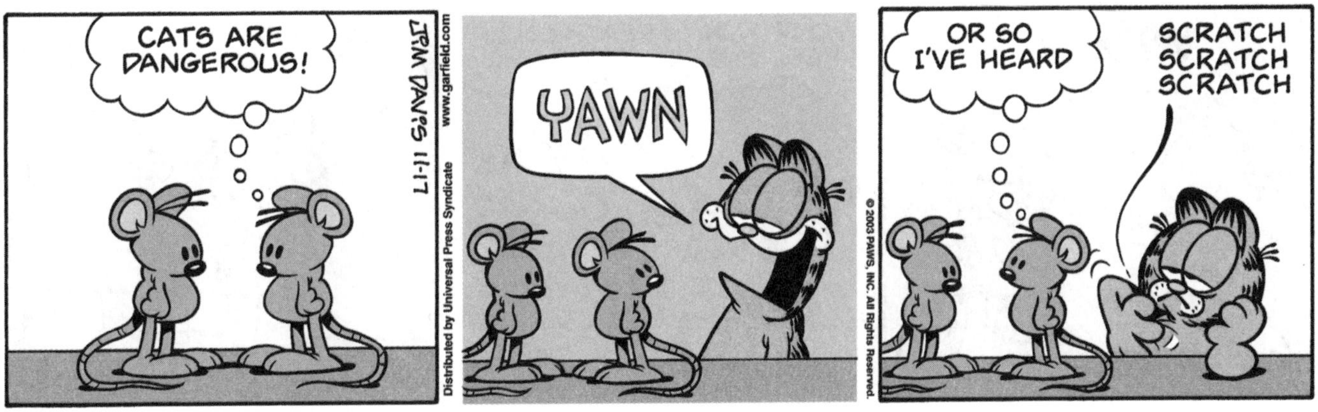
CATS ARE DANGEROUS!
JIM DAVIS 11-17
www.garfield.com
Distributed by Universal Press Syndicate
YAWN
© 2003 PAWS, INC. All Rights Reserved.
OR SO I'VE HEARD
SCRATCH SCRATCH SCRATCH

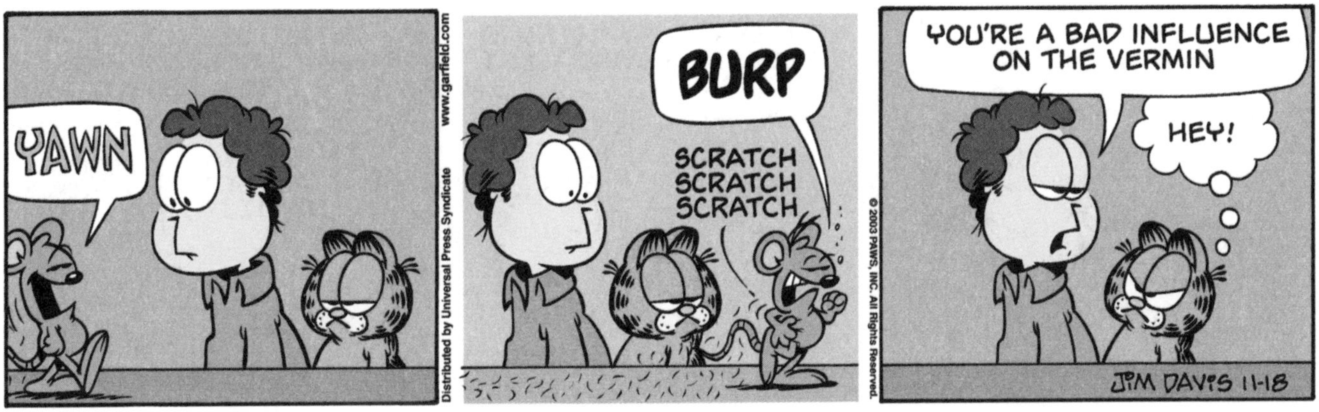
YAWN
www.garfield.com
Distributed by Universal Press Syndicate
BURP
SCRATCH SCRATCH SCRATCH
© 2003 PAWS, INC. All Rights Reserved.
YOU'RE A BAD INFLUENCE ON THE VERMIN
HEY!
JIM DAVIS 11-18

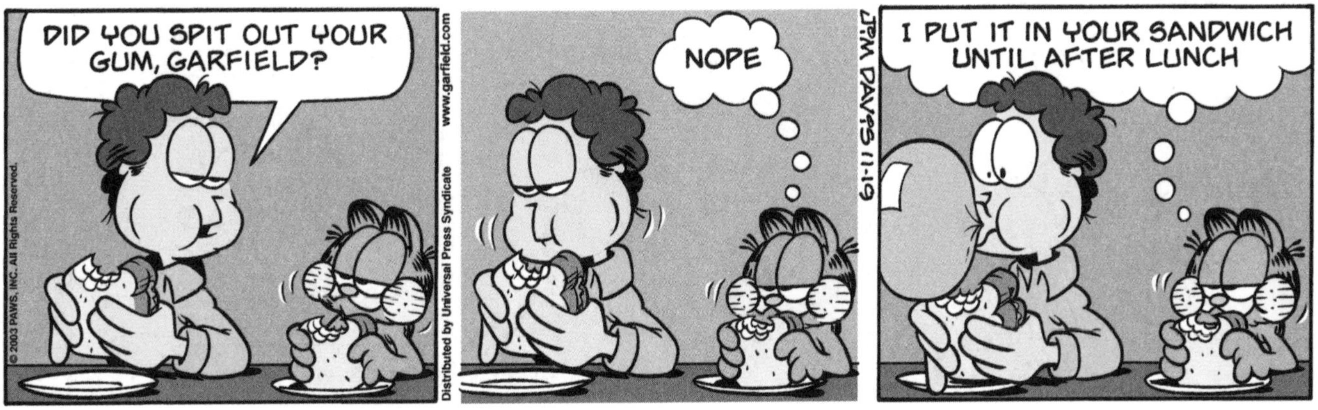
DID YOU SPIT OUT YOUR GUM, GARFIELD?
© 2003 PAWS, INC. All Rights Reserved.
www.garfield.com
Distributed by Universal Press Syndicate
NOPE
JIM DAVIS 11-19
I PUT IT IN YOUR SANDWICH UNTIL AFTER LUNCH

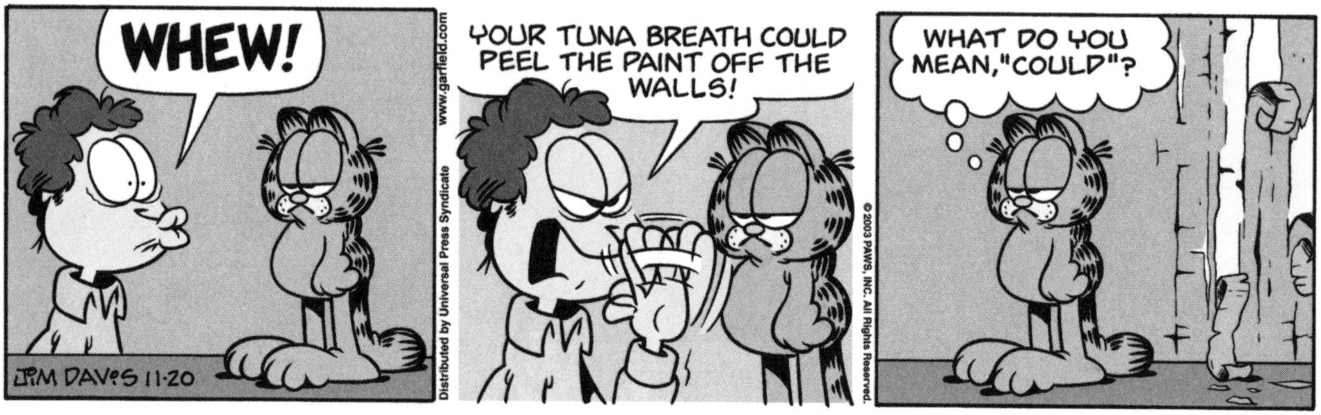
WHEW!
JIM DAVIS 11-20
Distributed by Universal Press Syndicate www.garfield.com
YOUR TUNA BREATH COULD PEEL THE PAINT OFF THE WALLS!
© 2003 PAWS, INC. All Rights Reserved.
WHAT DO YOU MEAN, "COULD"?

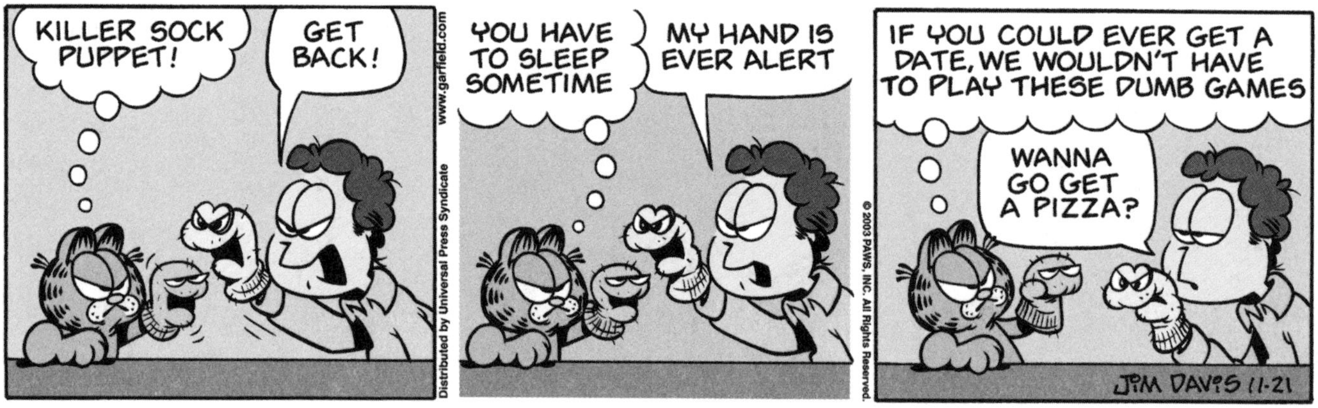
KILLER SOCK PUPPET!
GET BACK!
Distributed by Universal Press Syndicate www.garfield.com
YOU HAVE TO SLEEP SOMETIME
MY HAND IS EVER ALERT
© 2003 PAWS, INC. All Rights Reserved.
IF YOU COULD EVER GET A DATE, WE WOULDN'T HAVE TO PLAY THESE DUMB GAMES
WANNA GO GET A PIZZA?
JIM DAVIS 11-21

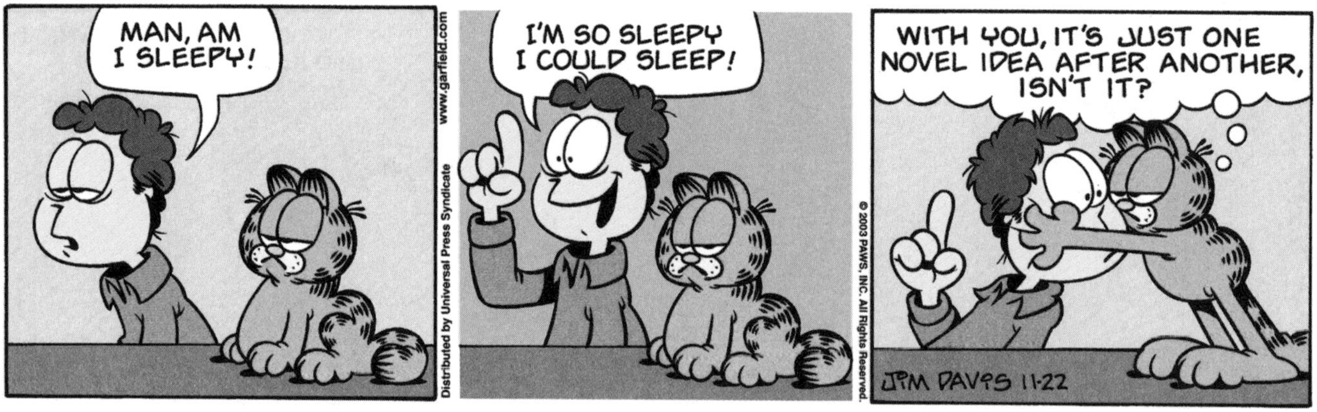
MAN, AM I SLEEPY!
Distributed by Universal Press Syndicate www.garfield.com
I'M SO SLEEPY I COULD SLEEP!
© 2003 PAWS, INC. All Rights Reserved.
WITH YOU, IT'S JUST ONE NOVEL IDEA AFTER ANOTHER, ISN'T IT?
JIM DAVIS 11-22

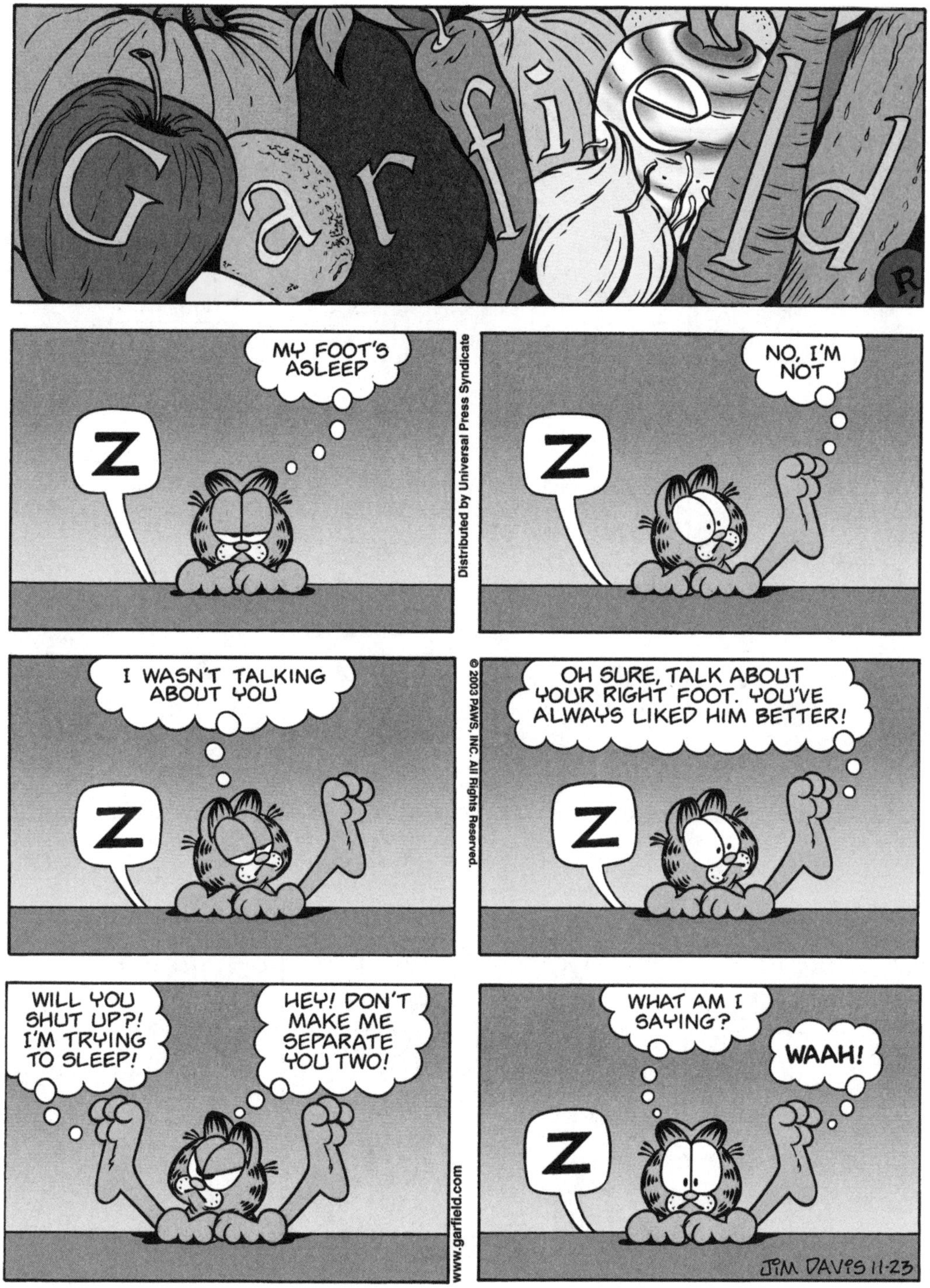
Garfield
MY FOOT'S ASLEEP
Z
Distributed by Universal Press Syndicate
NO, I'M NOT
Z
I WASN'T TALKING ABOUT YOU
Z
© 2003 PAWS, INC. All Rights Reserved.
OH SURE, TALK ABOUT YOUR RIGHT FOOT. YOU'VE ALWAYS LIKED HIM BETTER!
Z
WILL YOU SHUT UP?! I'M TRYING TO SLEEP!
HEY! DON'T MAKE ME SEPARATE YOU TWO!
www.garfield.com
WHAT AM I SAYING?
WAAH!
Z
JIM DAVIS 11-23

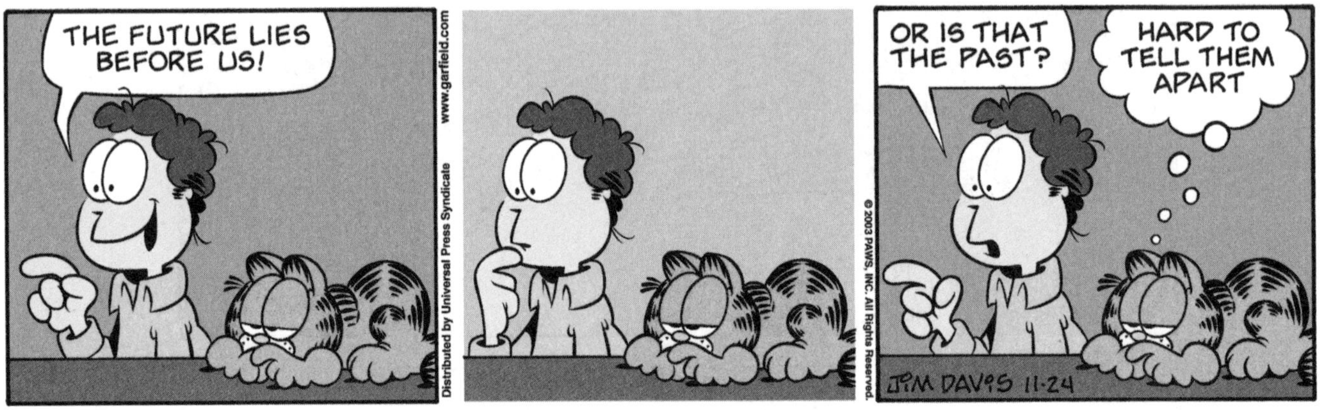
THE FUTURE LIES BEFORE US!
OR IS THAT THE PAST?
HARD TO TELL THEM APART
JIM DAVIS 11-24
www.garfield.com
Distributed by Universal Press Syndicate
© 2003 PAWS, INC. All Rights Reserved.

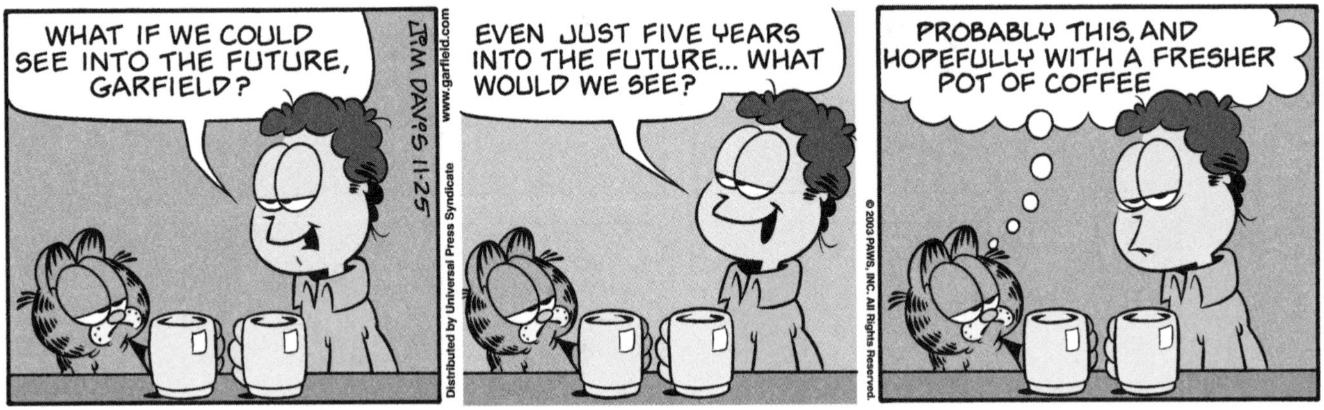
WHAT IF WE COULD SEE INTO THE FUTURE, GARFIELD?
EVEN JUST FIVE YEARS INTO THE FUTURE... WHAT WOULD WE SEE?
PROBABLY THIS, AND HOPEFULLY WITH A FRESHER POT OF COFFEE
JIM DAVIS 11-25
www.garfield.com
Distributed by Universal Press Syndicate
© 2003 PAWS, INC. All Rights Reserved.

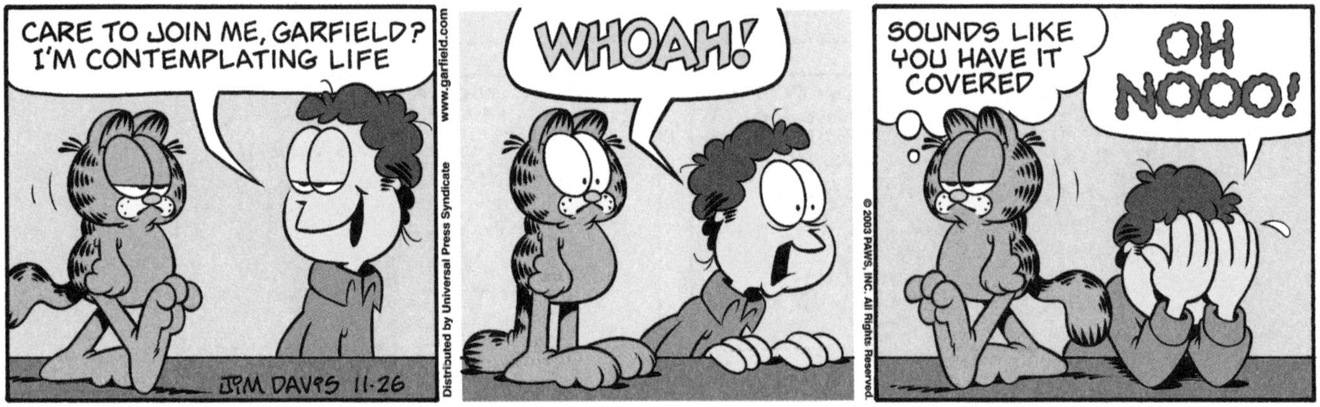
CARE TO JOIN ME, GARFIELD? I'M CONTEMPLATING LIFE
WHOAH!
SOUNDS LIKE YOU HAVE IT COVERED
OH NOOO!
JIM DAVIS 11-26
www.garfield.com
Distributed by Universal Press Syndicate
© 2003 PAWS, INC. All Rights Reserved.

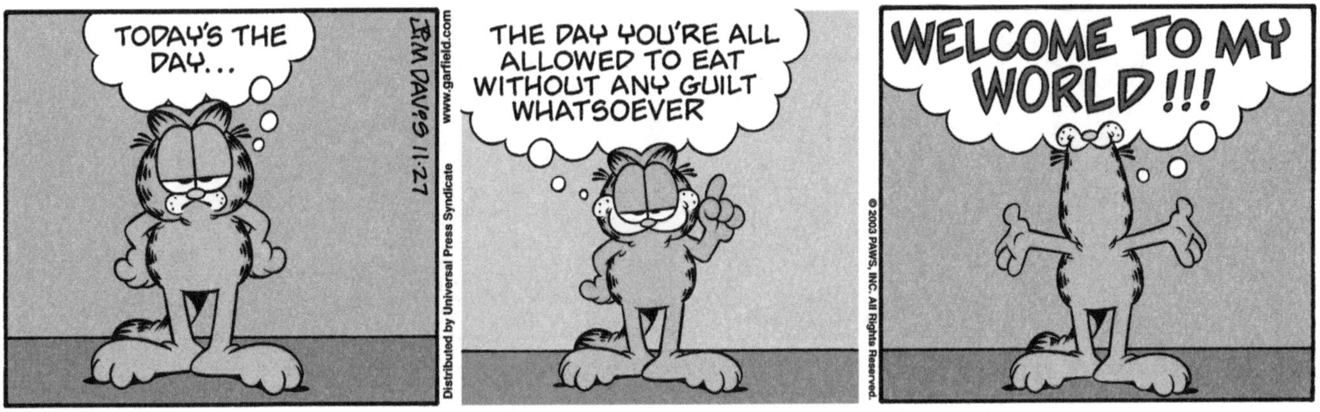
TODAY'S THE DAY...
JIM DAVIS 11-27
www.garfield.com
Distributed by Universal Press Syndicate
THE DAY YOU'RE ALL ALLOWED TO EAT WITHOUT ANY GUILT WHATSOEVER
© 2003 PAWS, INC. All Rights Reserved.
WELCOME TO MY WORLD!!!

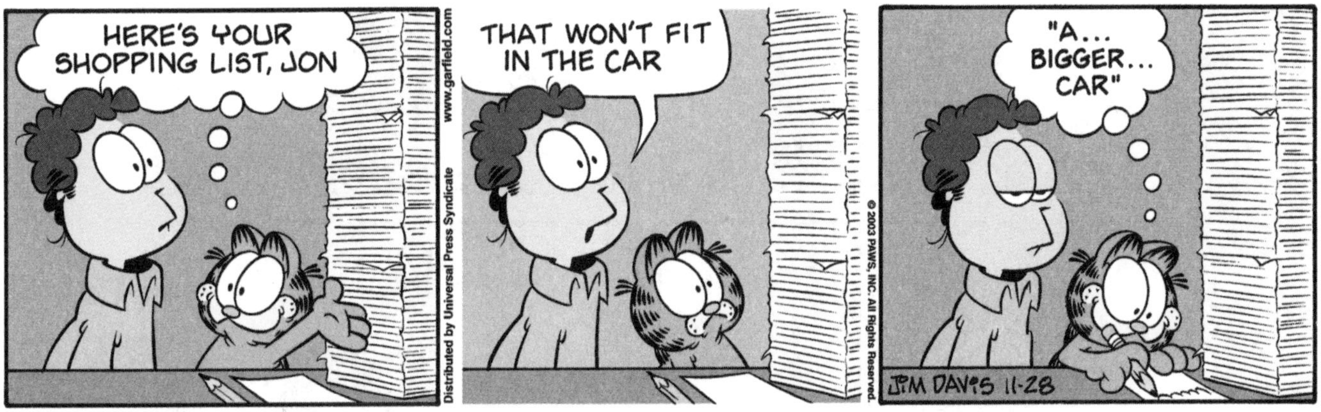
HERE'S YOUR SHOPPING LIST, JON
www.garfield.com
Distributed by Universal Press Syndicate
THAT WON'T FIT IN THE CAR
© 2003 PAWS, INC. All Rights Reserved.
"A... BIGGER... CAR"
JIM DAVIS 11-28

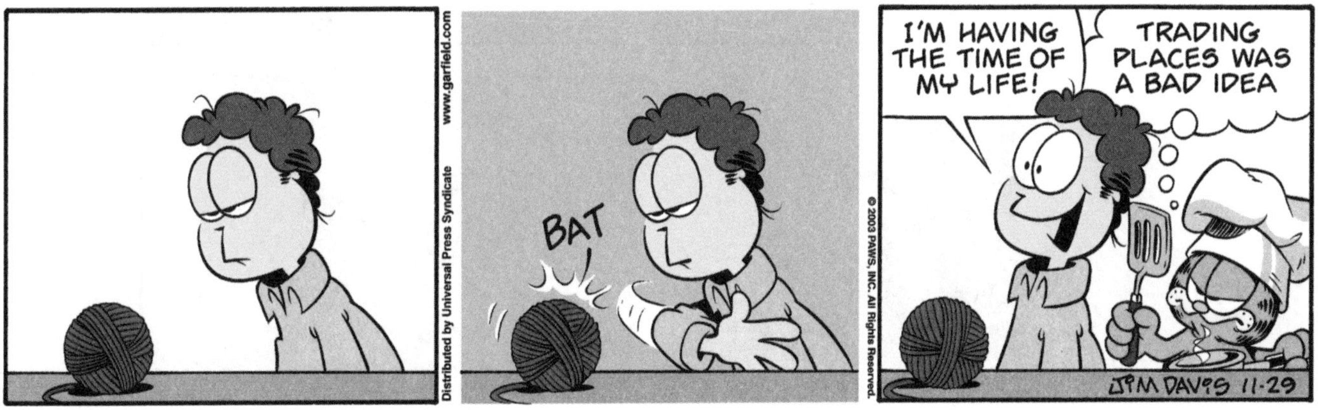
www.garfield.com
Distributed by Universal Press Syndicate
BAT
© 2003 PAWS, INC. All Rights Reserved.
I'M HAVING THE TIME OF MY LIFE!
TRADING PLACES WAS A BAD IDEA
JIM DAVIS 11-29

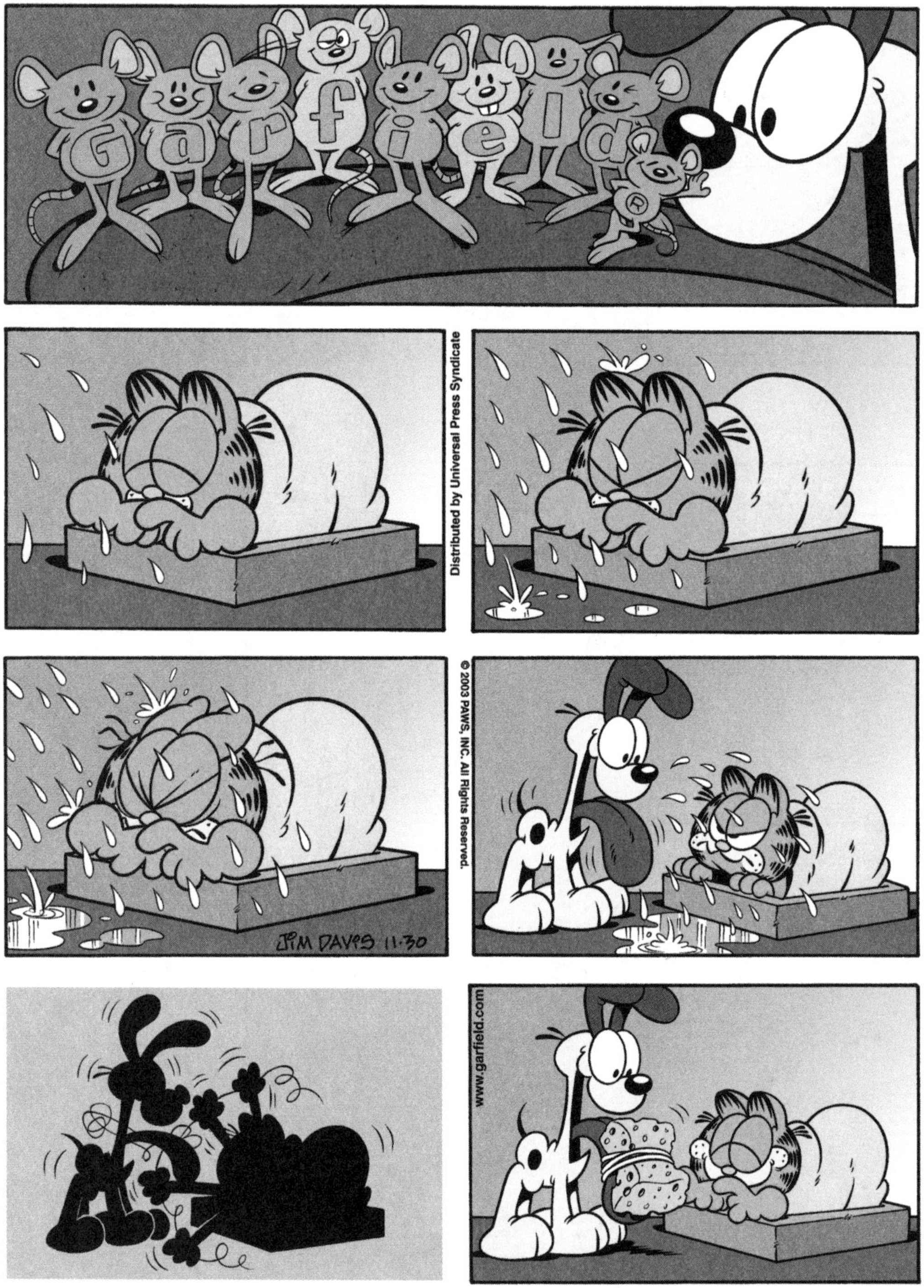
Garfield®
Distributed by Universal Press Syndicate
© 2003 PAWS, INC. All Rights Reserved.
JIM DAVIS 11-30
www.garfield.com

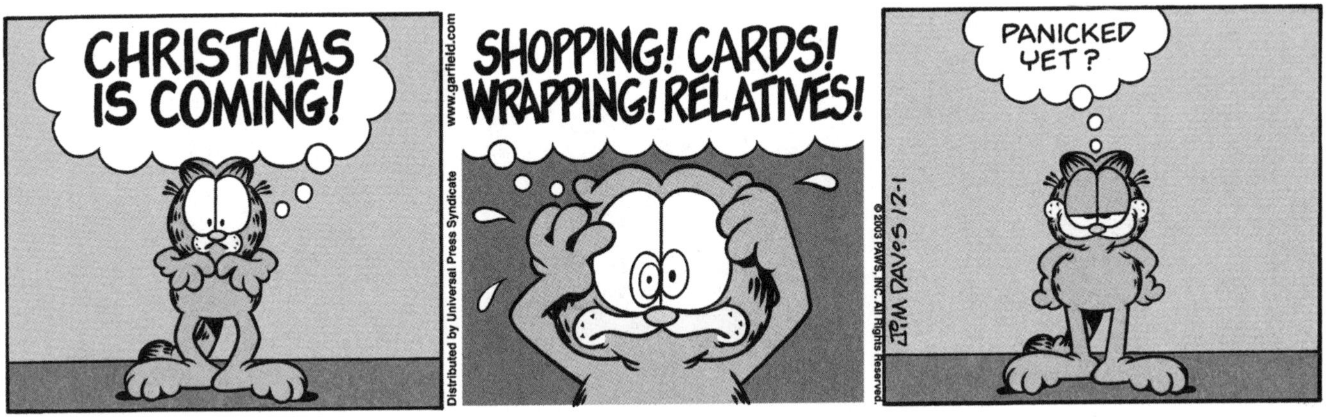
CHRISTMAS IS COMING!
www.garfield.com
Distributed by Universal Press Syndicate
SHOPPING! CARDS! WRAPPING! RELATIVES!
© 2003 PAWS, INC. All Rights Reserved.
JIM DAVIS 12-1
PANICKED YET?

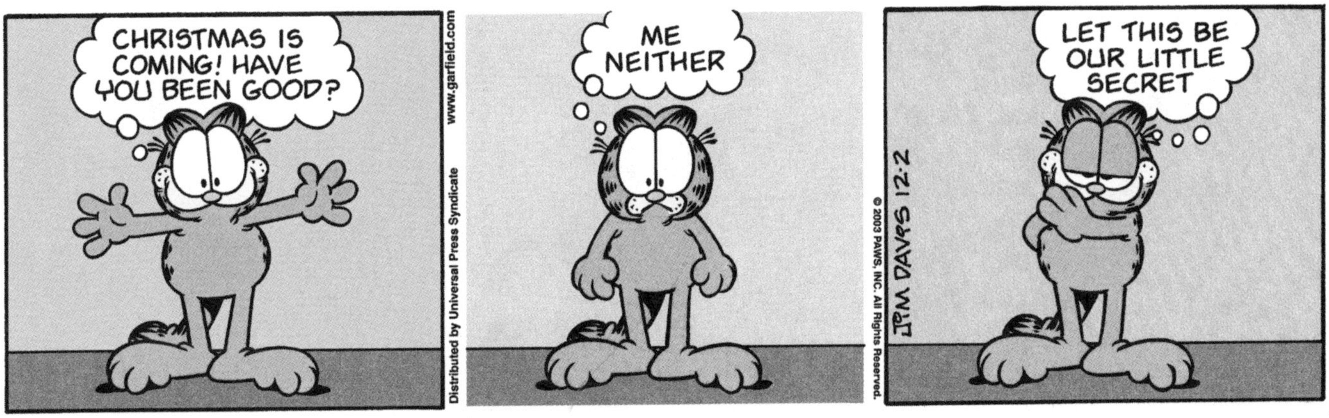
CHRISTMAS IS COMING! HAVE YOU BEEN GOOD?
www.garfield.com
Distributed by Universal Press Syndicate
ME NEITHER
© 2003 PAWS, INC. All Rights Reserved.
JIM DAVIS 12-2
LET THIS BE OUR LITTLE SECRET

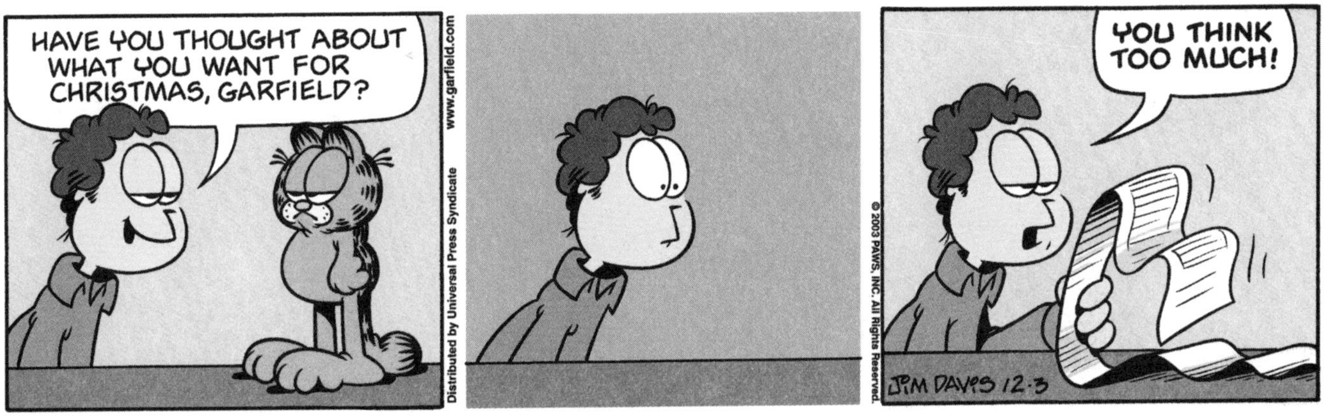
HAVE YOU THOUGHT ABOUT WHAT YOU WANT FOR CHRISTMAS, GARFIELD?
www.garfield.com
Distributed by Universal Press Syndicate
© 2003 PAWS, INC. All Rights Reserved.
YOU THINK TOO MUCH!
JIM DAVIS 12-3

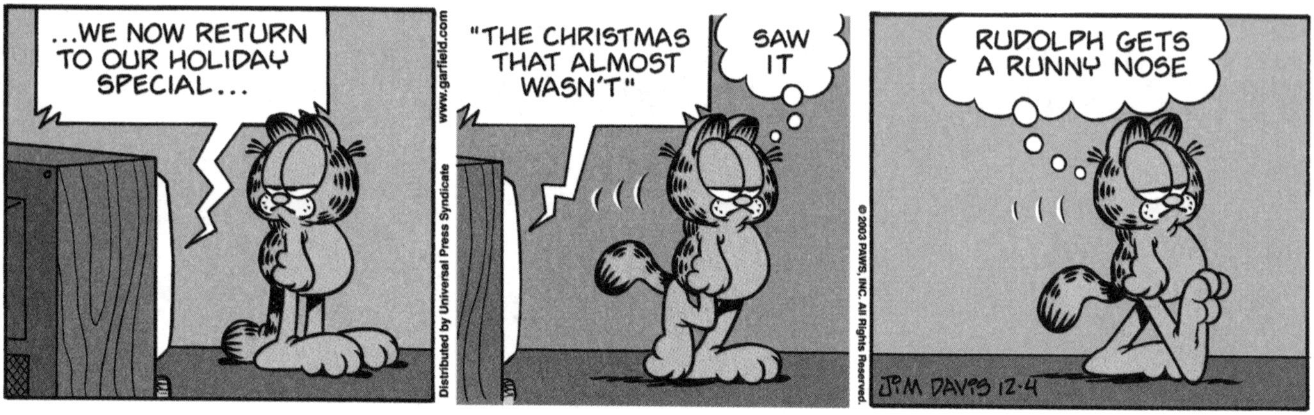
...WE NOW RETURN TO OUR HOLIDAY SPECIAL...
www.garfield.com
Distributed by Universal Press Syndicate
"THE CHRISTMAS THAT ALMOST WASN'T"
SAW IT
© 2003 PAWS, INC. All Rights Reserved.
RUDOLPH GETS A RUNNY NOSE
JIM DAVIS 12-4

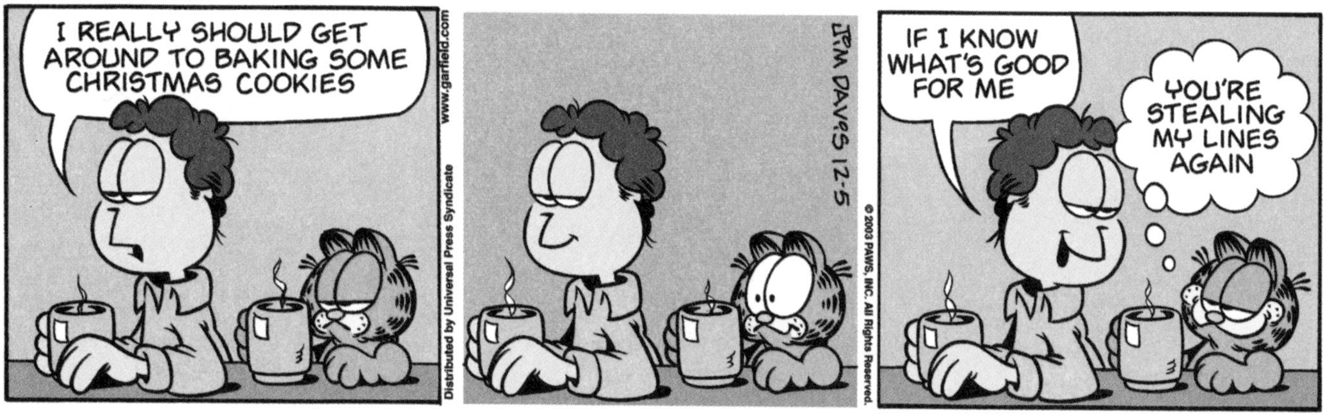
I REALLY SHOULD GET AROUND TO BAKING SOME CHRISTMAS COOKIES
www.garfield.com
Distributed by Universal Press Syndicate
JIM DAVIS 12-5
© 2003 PAWS, INC. All Rights Reserved.
IF I KNOW WHAT'S GOOD FOR ME
YOU'RE STEALING MY LINES AGAIN

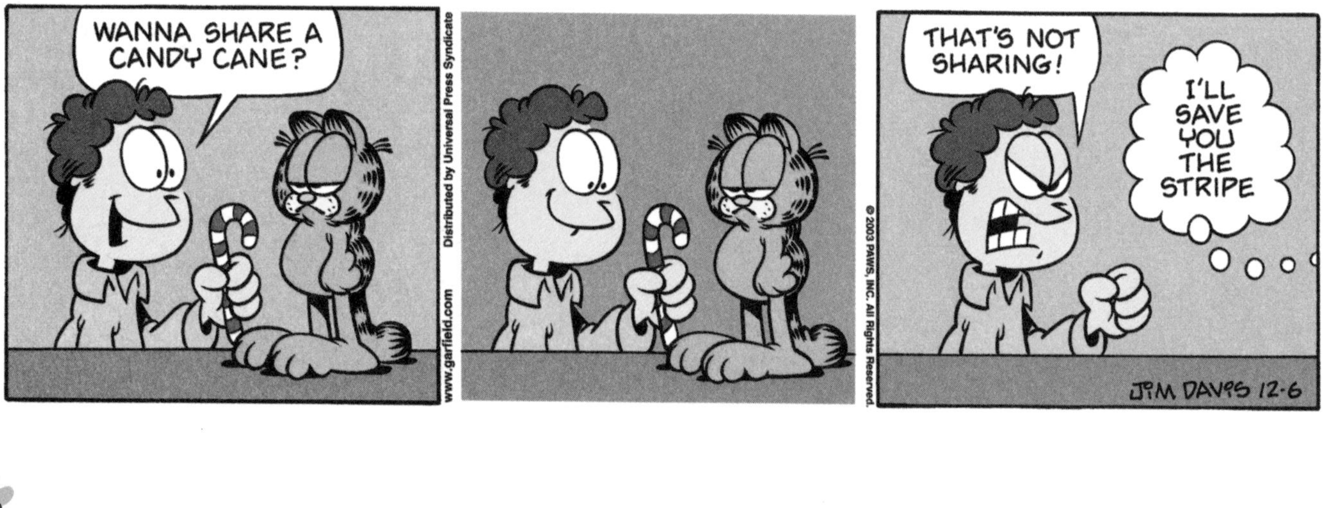
WANNA SHARE A CANDY CANE?
Distributed by Universal Press Syndicate
www.garfield.com
© 2003 PAWS, INC. All Rights Reserved.
THAT'S NOT SHARING!
I'LL SAVE YOU THE STRIPE
JIM DAVIS 12-6

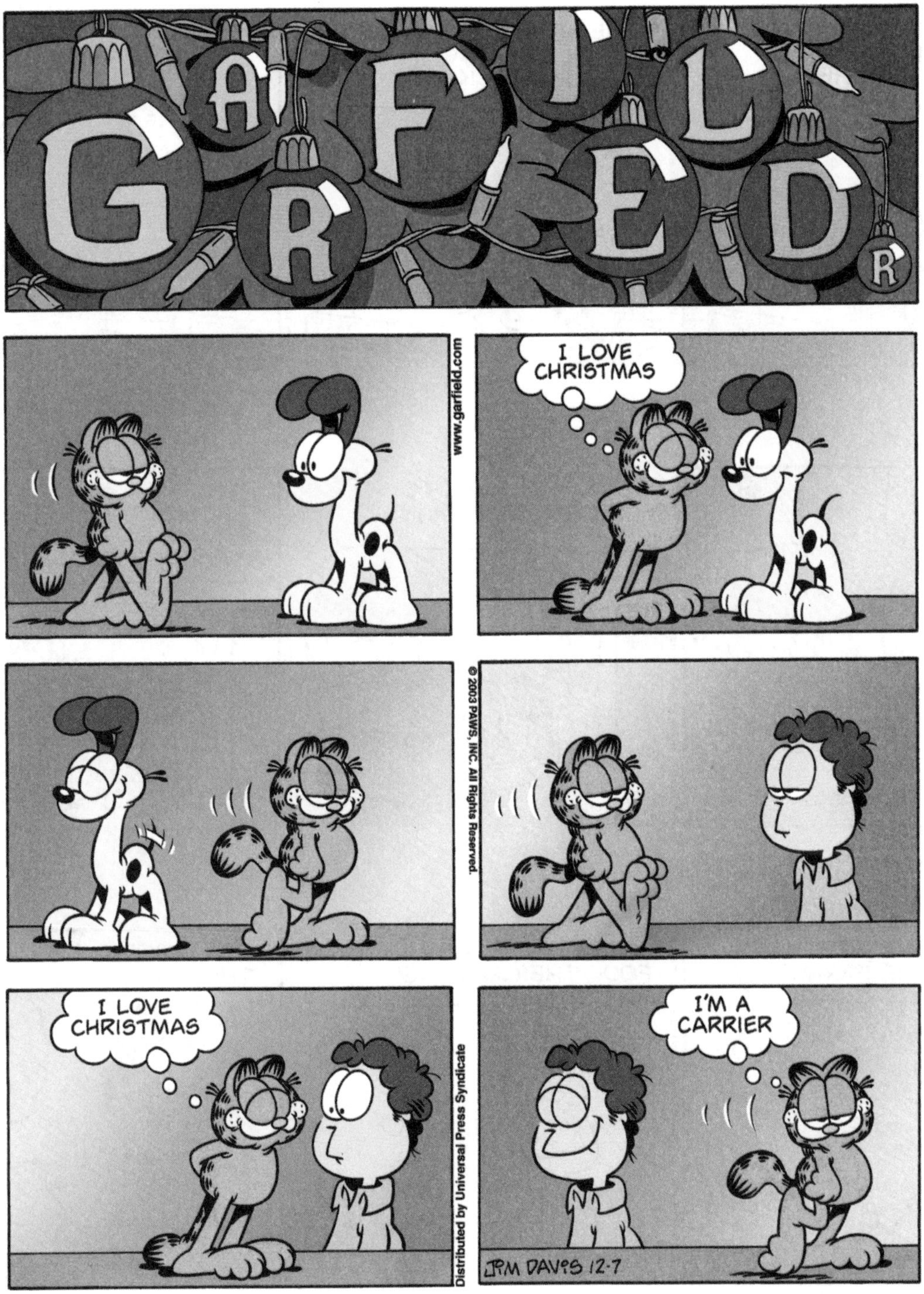
GARFIELD®
www.garfield.com
I LOVE CHRISTMAS
© 2003 PAWS, INC. All Rights Reserved.
I LOVE CHRISTMAS
I'M A CARRIER
Distributed by Universal Press Syndicate
JPM DAVIS 12-7

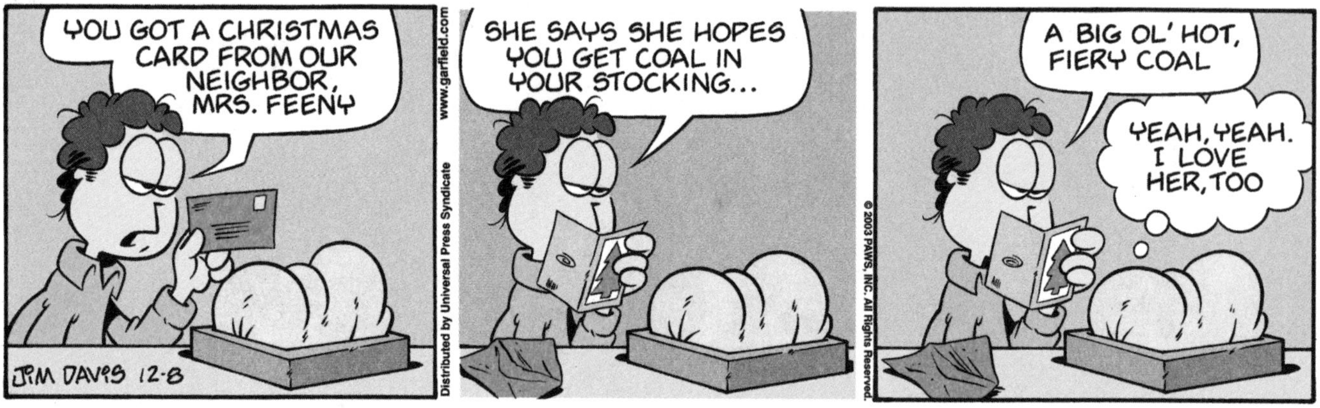
YOU GOT A CHRISTMAS CARD FROM OUR NEIGHBOR, MRS. FEENY
JIM DAVIS 12-8
www.garfield.com
Distributed by Universal Press Syndicate
SHE SAYS SHE HOPES YOU GET COAL IN YOUR STOCKING...
© 2003 PAWS, INC. All Rights Reserved.
A BIG OL' HOT, FIERY COAL
YEAH, YEAH. I LOVE HER, TOO

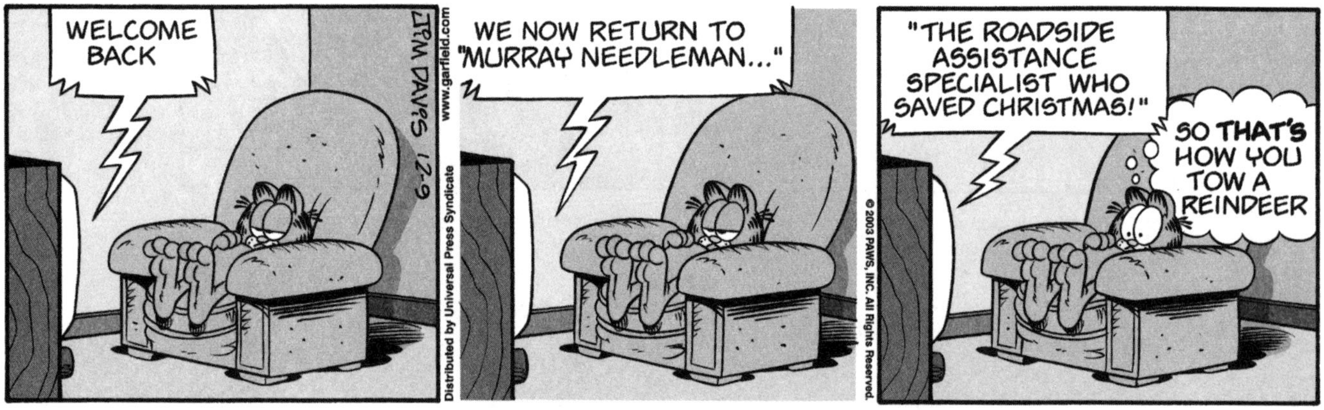
WELCOME BACK
JIM DAVIS 12-9
www.garfield.com
Distributed by Universal Press Syndicate
WE NOW RETURN TO "MURRAY NEEDLEMAN..."
© 2003 PAWS, INC. All Rights Reserved.
"THE ROADSIDE ASSISTANCE SPECIALIST WHO SAVED CHRISTMAS!"
SO **THAT'S** HOW YOU TOW A REINDEER

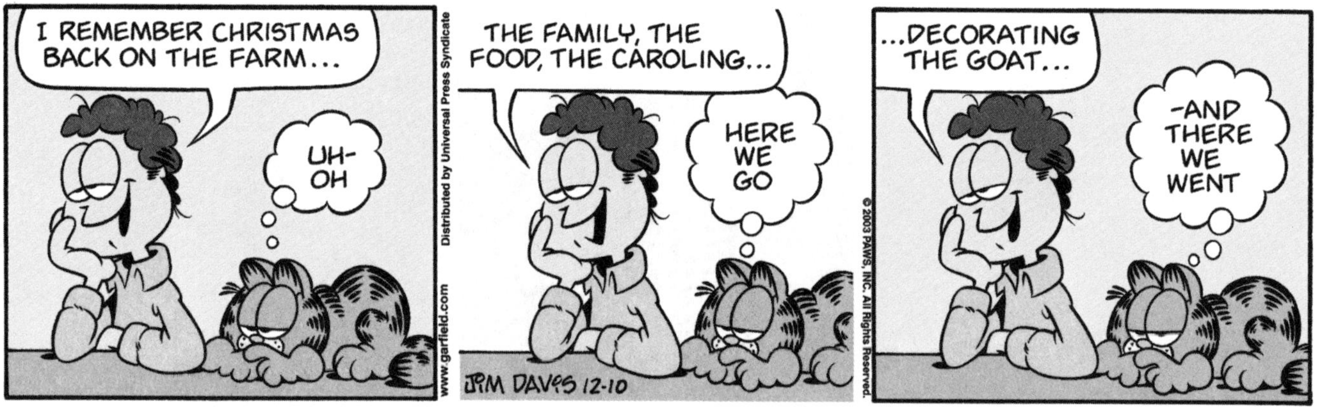
I REMEMBER CHRISTMAS BACK ON THE FARM...
UH-OH
Distributed by Universal Press Syndicate
www.garfield.com
THE FAMILY, THE FOOD, THE CAROLING...
HERE WE GO
JIM DAVIS 12-10
© 2003 PAWS, INC. All Rights Reserved.
...DECORATING THE GOAT...
-AND THERE WE WENT

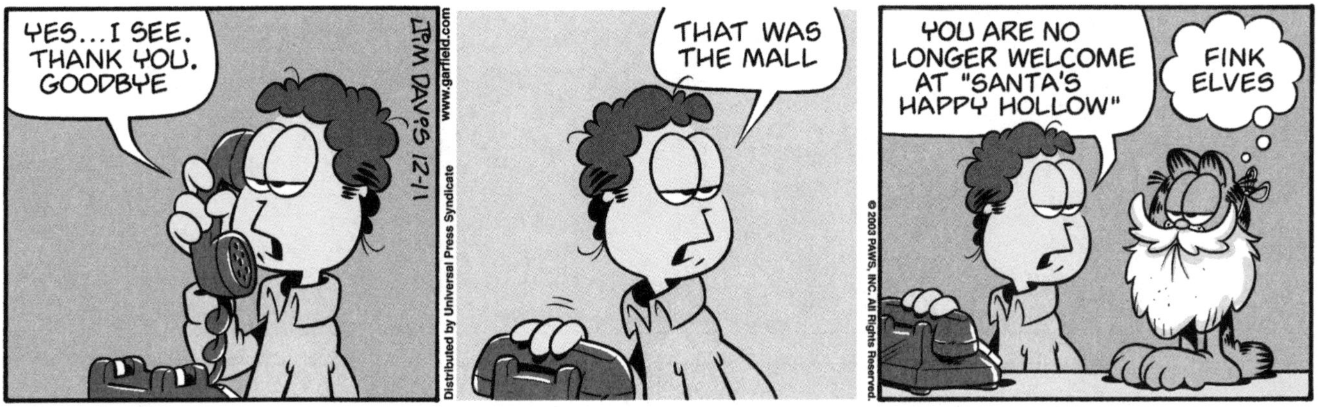
YES... I SEE. THANK YOU. GOODBYE
JIM DAVIS 12-11
www.garfield.com
Distributed by Universal Press Syndicate
THAT WAS THE MALL
YOU ARE NO LONGER WELCOME AT "SANTA'S HAPPY HOLLOW"
FINK ELVES
© 2003 PAWS, INC. All Rights Reserved.

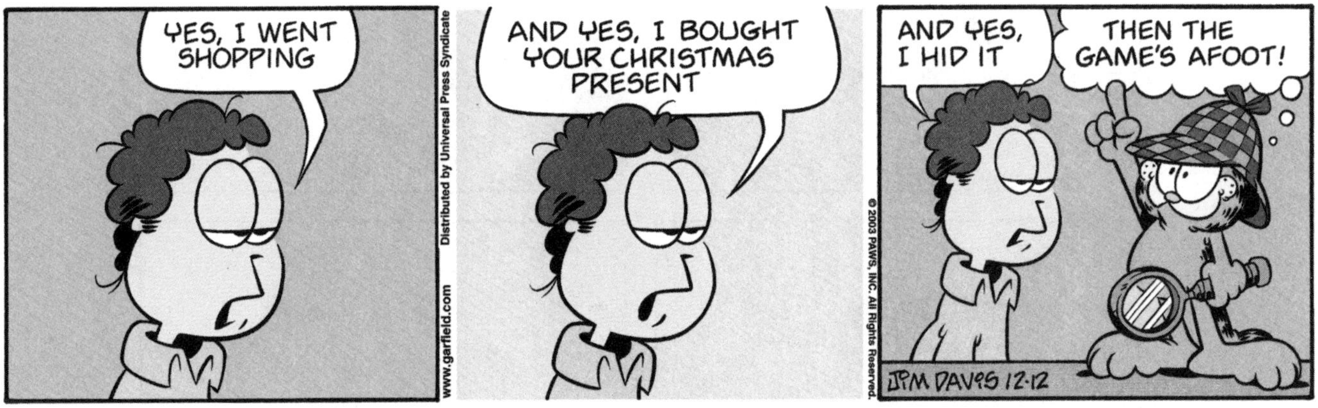
YES, I WENT SHOPPING
Distributed by Universal Press Syndicate
www.garfield.com
AND YES, I BOUGHT YOUR CHRISTMAS PRESENT
AND YES, I HID IT
THEN THE GAME'S AFOOT!
© 2003 PAWS, INC. All Rights Reserved.
JIM DAVIS 12-12

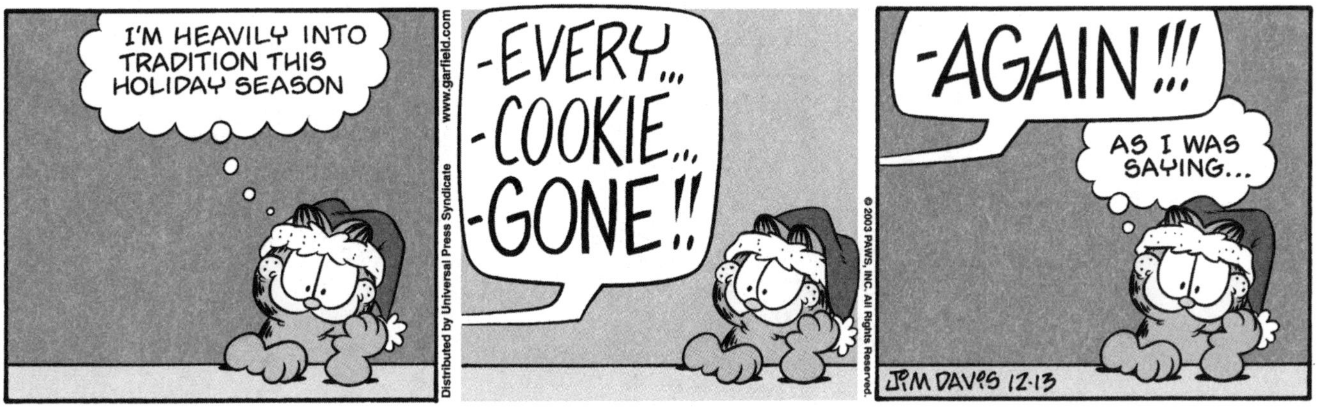
I'M HEAVILY INTO TRADITION THIS HOLIDAY SEASON
www.garfield.com
Distributed by Universal Press Syndicate
-EVERY...
-COOKIE...
-GONE!!
© 2003 PAWS, INC. All Rights Reserved.
-AGAIN!!!
AS I WAS SAYING...
JIM DAVIS 12-13

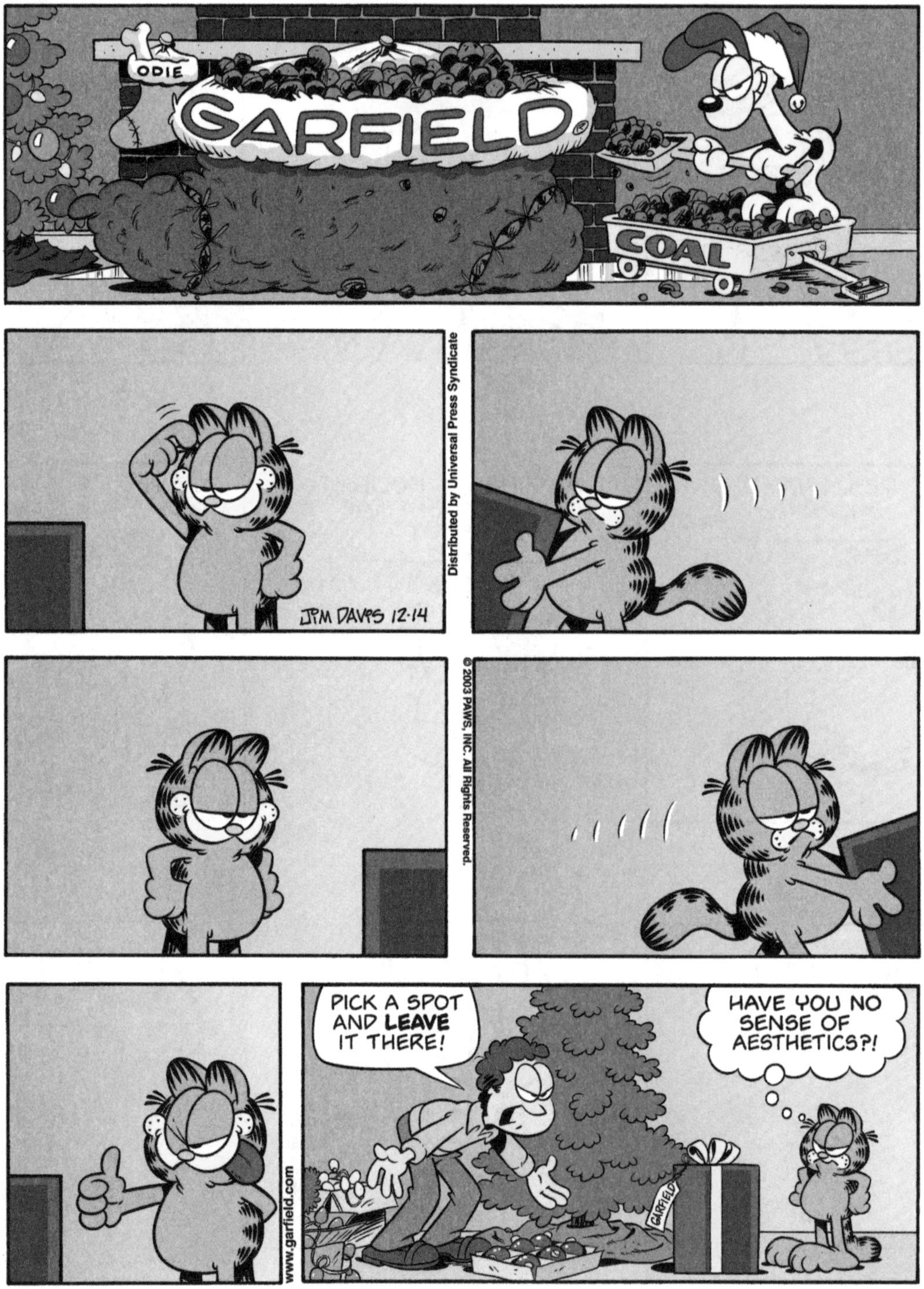

ODIE
GARFIELD
COAL
JPM DAVPS 12·14
Distributed by Universal Press Syndicate
© 2003 PAWS, INC. All Rights Reserved.
www.garfield.com
PICK A SPOT AND **LEAVE** IT THERE!
HAVE YOU NO SENSE OF AESTHETICS?!
GARFIELD

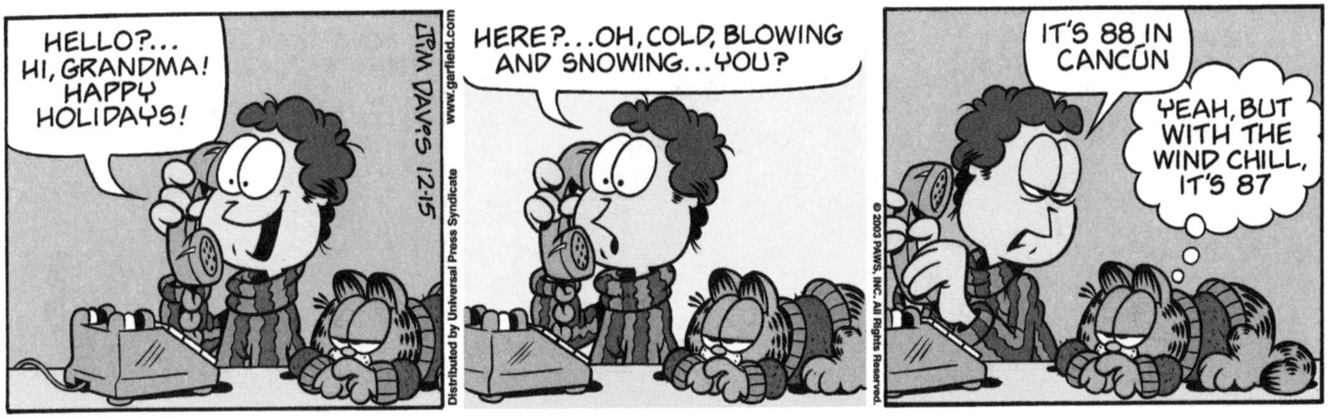
HELLO?... HI, GRANDMA! HAPPY HOLIDAYS!
JIM DAVIS 12-15
www.garfield.com
Distributed by Universal Press Syndicate
HERE?...OH, COLD, BLOWING AND SNOWING...YOU?
© 2003 PAWS, INC. All Rights Reserved.
IT'S 88 IN CANCÚN
YEAH, BUT WITH THE WIND CHILL, IT'S 87

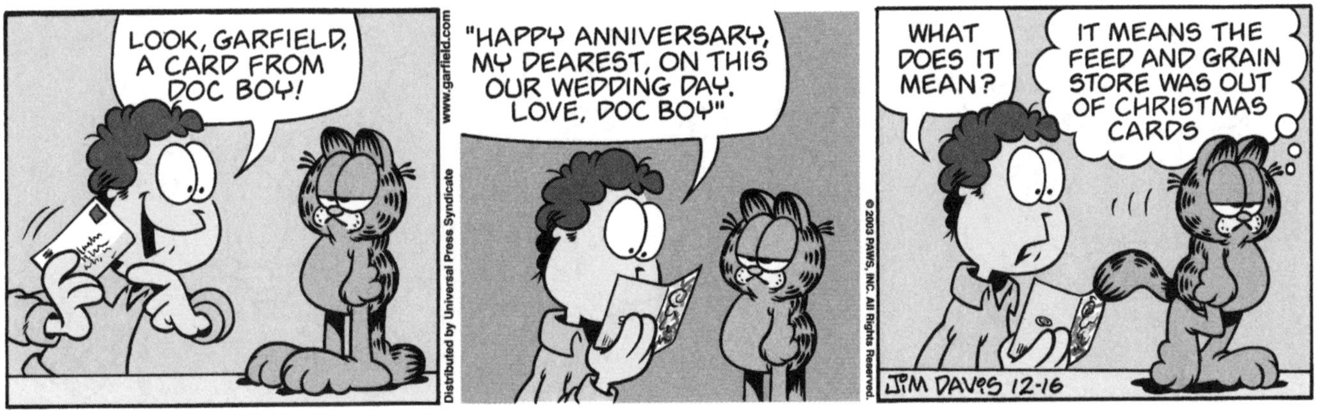
LOOK, GARFIELD, A CARD FROM DOC BOY!
www.garfield.com
Distributed by Universal Press Syndicate
"HAPPY ANNIVERSARY, MY DEAREST, ON THIS OUR WEDDING DAY. LOVE, DOC BOY"
© 2003 PAWS, INC. All Rights Reserved.
WHAT DOES IT MEAN?
IT MEANS THE FEED AND GRAIN STORE WAS OUT OF CHRISTMAS CARDS
JIM DAVIS 12-16

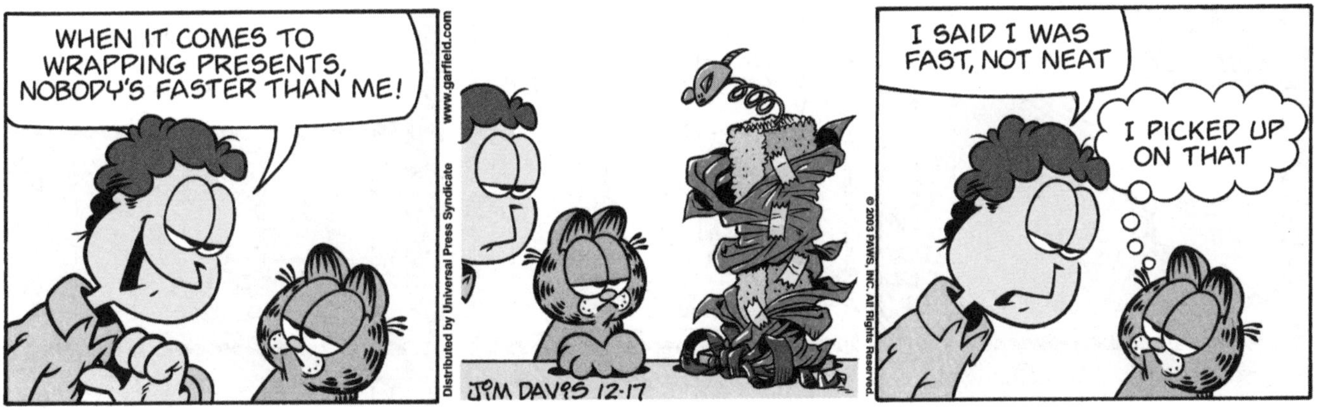
WHEN IT COMES TO WRAPPING PRESENTS, NOBODY'S FASTER THAN ME!
www.garfield.com
Distributed by Universal Press Syndicate
JIM DAVIS 12-17
© 2003 PAWS, INC. All Rights Reserved.
I SAID I WAS FAST, NOT NEAT
I PICKED UP ON THAT

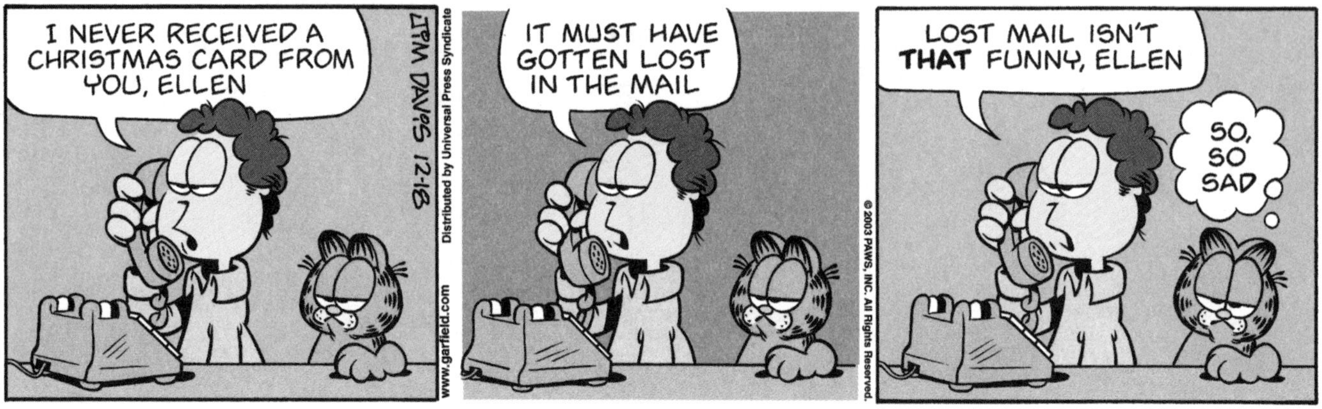
I NEVER RECEIVED A CHRISTMAS CARD FROM YOU, ELLEN
JIM DAVIS 12-18
Distributed by Universal Press Syndicate www.garfield.com
IT MUST HAVE GOTTEN LOST IN THE MAIL
© 2003 PAWS, INC. All Rights Reserved.
LOST MAIL ISN'T **THAT** FUNNY, ELLEN
SO, SO SAD

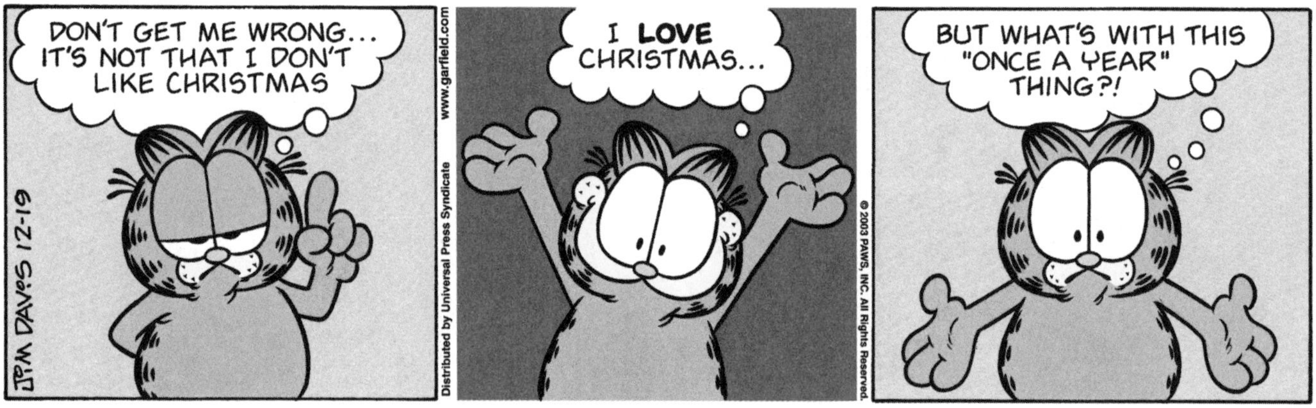
DON'T GET ME WRONG... IT'S NOT THAT I DON'T LIKE CHRISTMAS
JIM DAVIS 12-19
Distributed by Universal Press Syndicate www.garfield.com
I **LOVE** CHRISTMAS...
© 2003 PAWS, INC. All Rights Reserved.
BUT WHAT'S WITH THIS "ONCE A YEAR" THING?!

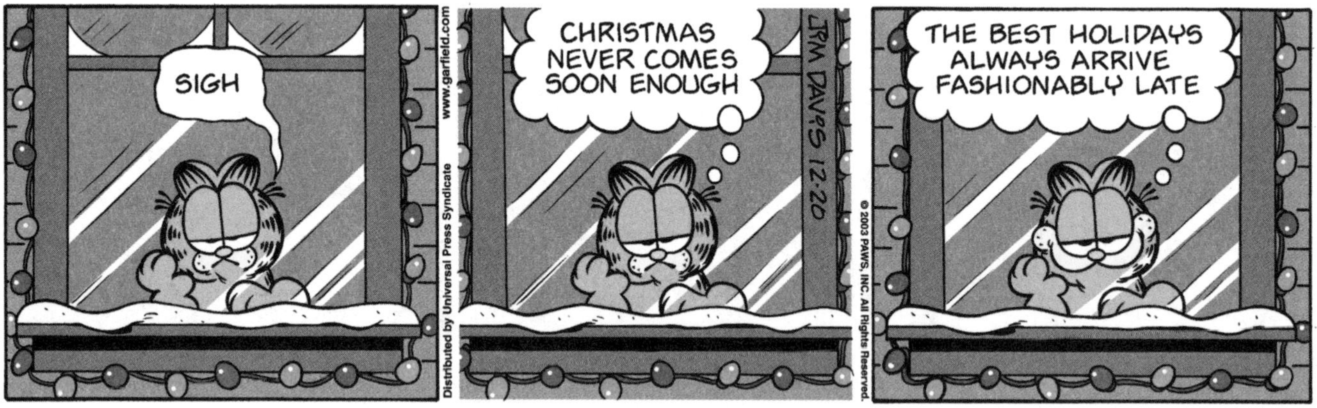
SIGH
Distributed by Universal Press Syndicate www.garfield.com
CHRISTMAS NEVER COMES SOON ENOUGH
JIM DAVIS 12-20
© 2003 PAWS, INC. All Rights Reserved.
THE BEST HOLIDAYS ALWAYS ARRIVE FASHIONABLY LATE

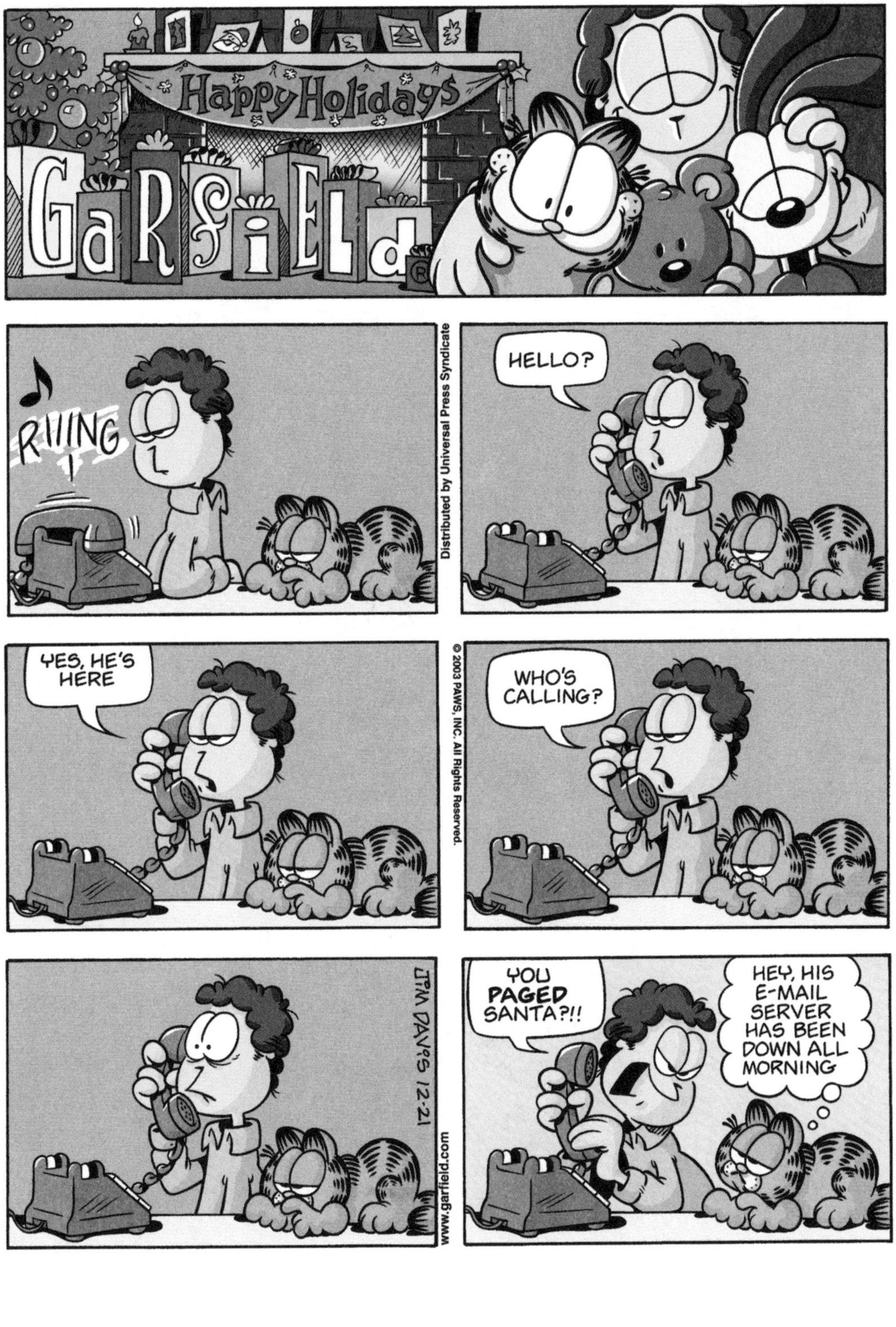
Happy Holidays
GARFIELD
RIIING
HELLO?
YES, HE'S HERE
WHO'S CALLING?
YOU PAGED SANTA?!!
HEY, HIS E-MAIL SERVER HAS BEEN DOWN ALL MORNING
JPM DAVPS 12-21
www.garfield.com

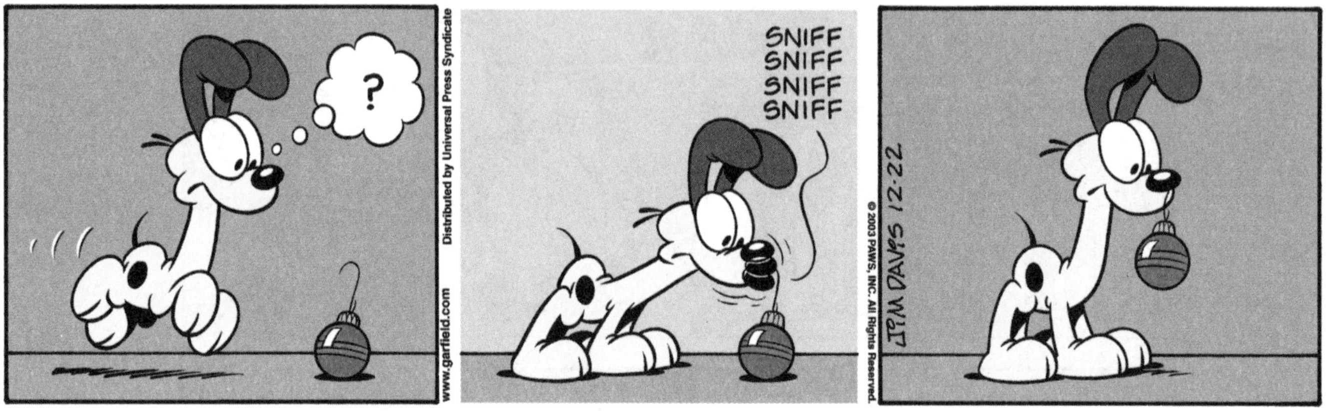
?
Distributed by Universal Press Syndicate
www.garfield.com
SNIFF
SNIFF
SNIFF
SNIFF
© 2003 PAWS, INC. All Rights Reserved.
JIM DAVIS 12-22

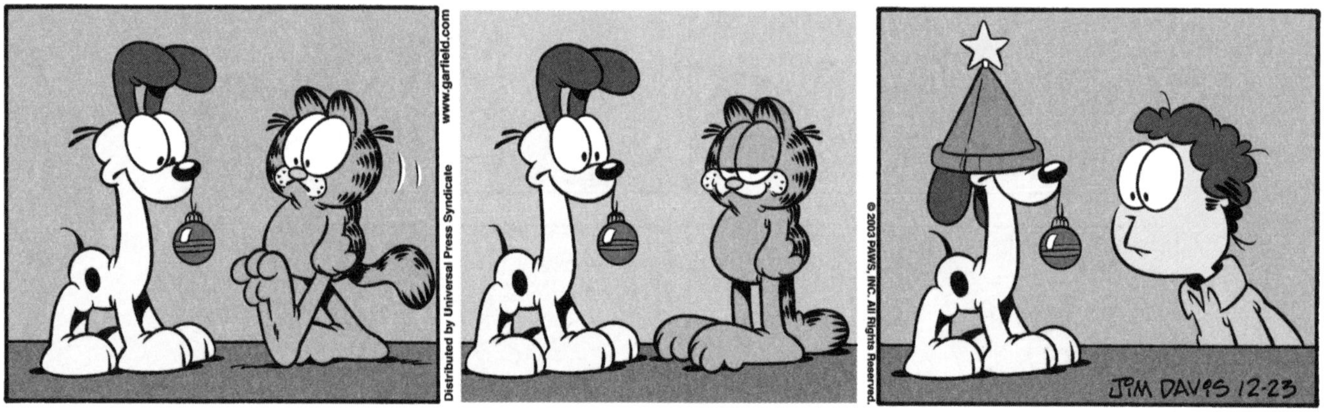
Distributed by Universal Press Syndicate
www.garfield.com
© 2003 PAWS, INC. All Rights Reserved.
JIM DAVIS 12-23

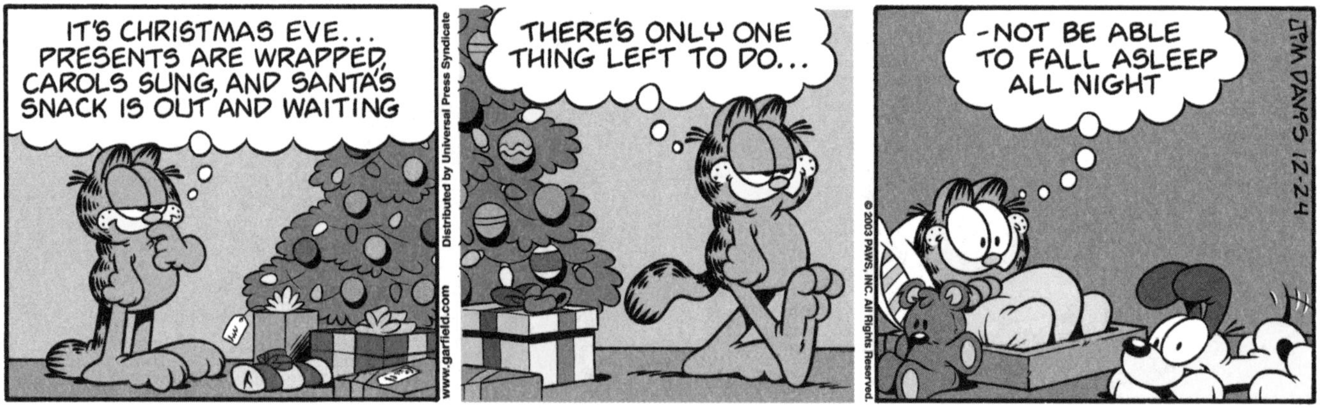
IT'S CHRISTMAS EVE... PRESENTS ARE WRAPPED, CAROLS SUNG, AND SANTA'S SNACK IS OUT AND WAITING
Distributed by Universal Press Syndicate
www.garfield.com
THERE'S ONLY ONE THING LEFT TO DO...
-NOT BE ABLE TO FALL ASLEEP ALL NIGHT
© 2003 PAWS, INC. All Rights Reserved.
JIM DAVIS 12-24

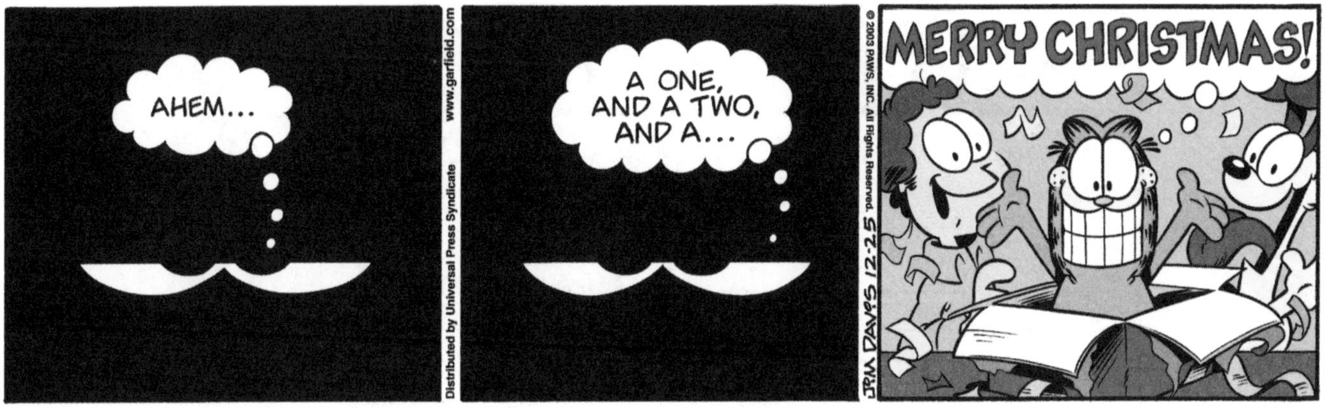
AHEM...
www.garfield.com
Distributed by Universal Press Syndicate
A ONE, AND A TWO, AND A...
© 2003 PAWS, INC. All Rights Reserved.
JIM DAVIS 12-25
MERRY CHRISTMAS!

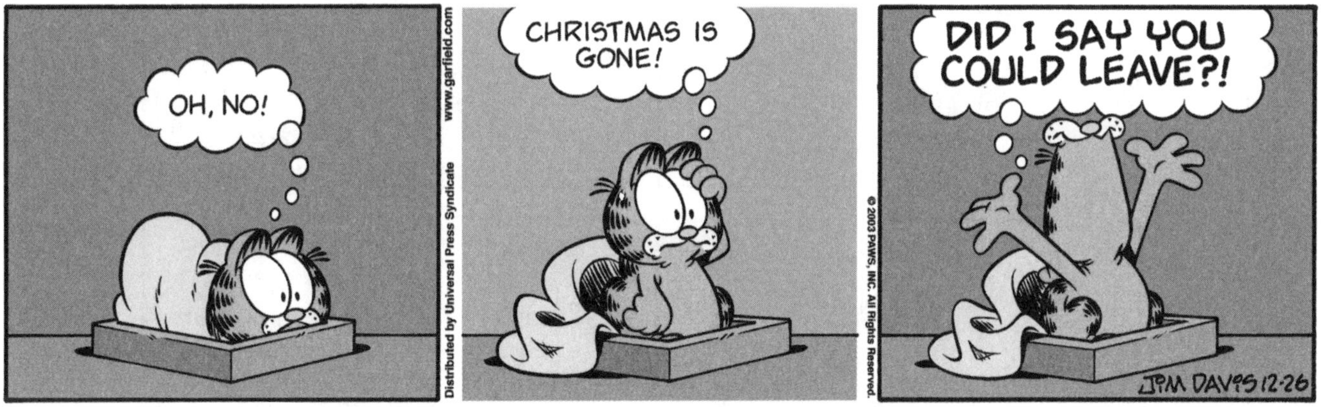
OH, NO!
www.garfield.com
Distributed by Universal Press Syndicate
CHRISTMAS IS GONE!
© 2003 PAWS, INC. All Rights Reserved.
DID I SAY YOU COULD LEAVE?!
JIM DAVIS 12-26

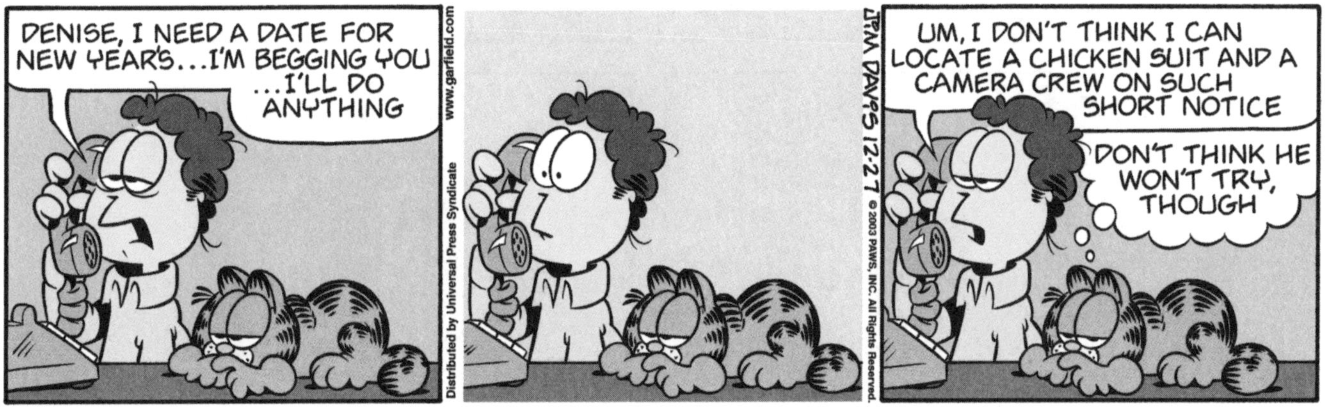
DENISE, I NEED A DATE FOR NEW YEAR'S...I'M BEGGING YOU ...I'LL DO ANYTHING
www.garfield.com
Distributed by Universal Press Syndicate
JIM DAVIS 12-27
© 2003 PAWS, INC. All Rights Reserved.
UM, I DON'T THINK I CAN LOCATE A CHICKEN SUIT AND A CAMERA CREW ON SUCH SHORT NOTICE
DON'T THINK HE WON'T TRY, THOUGH

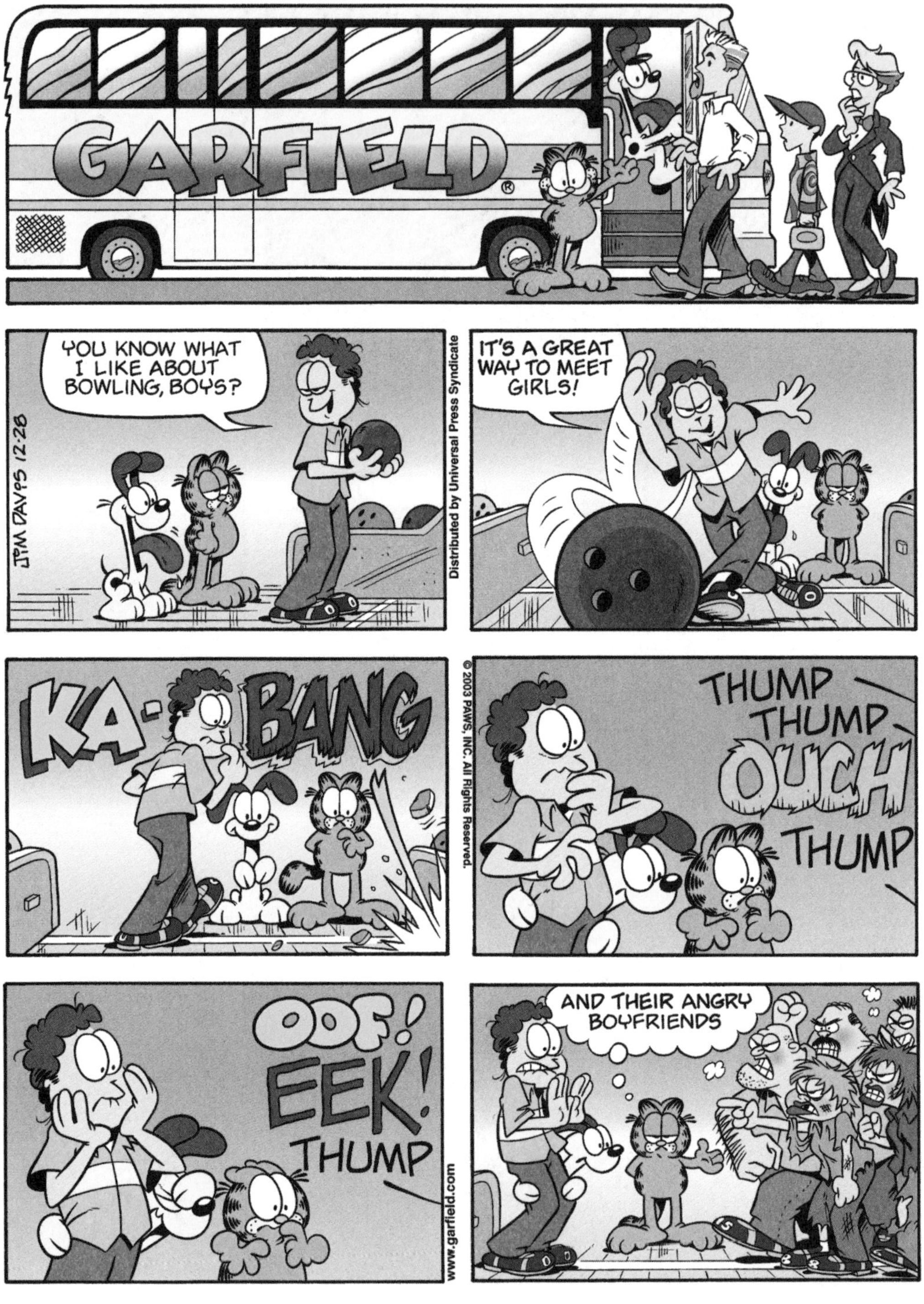
GARFIELD®
YOU KNOW WHAT I LIKE ABOUT BOWLING, BOYS?
JIM DAVIS 12-28
Distributed by Universal Press Syndicate
IT'S A GREAT WAY TO MEET GIRLS!
KA-BANG
© 2003 PAWS, INC. All Rights Reserved.
THUMP
THUMP
OUCH
THUMP
OOF!
EEK!
THUMP
www.garfield.com
AND THEIR ANGRY BOYFRIENDS

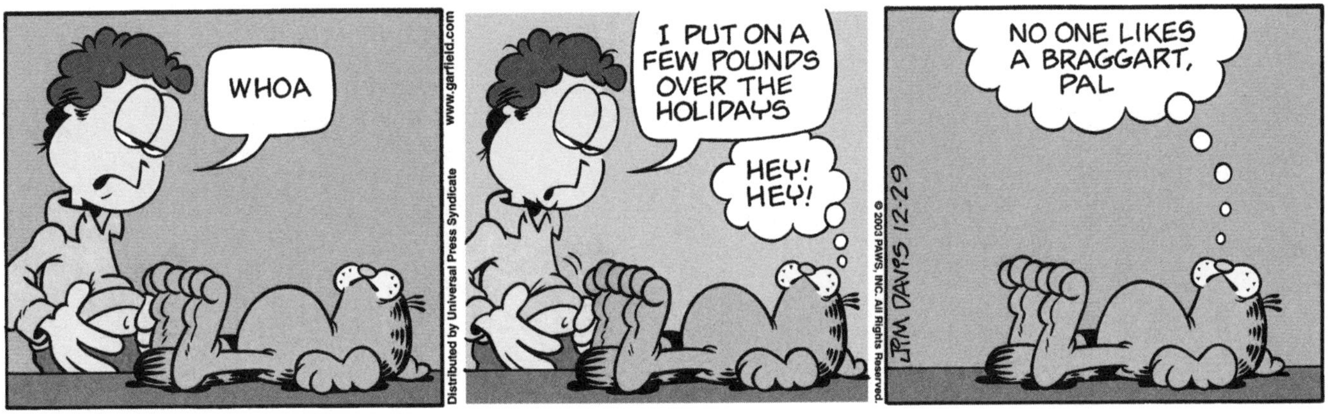
WHOA
I PUT ON A FEW POUNDS OVER THE HOLIDAYS
HEY! HEY!
NO ONE LIKES A BRAGGART, PAL
JIM DAVIS 12-29
www.garfield.com
Distributed by Universal Press Syndicate
© 2003 PAWS, INC. All Rights Reserved.

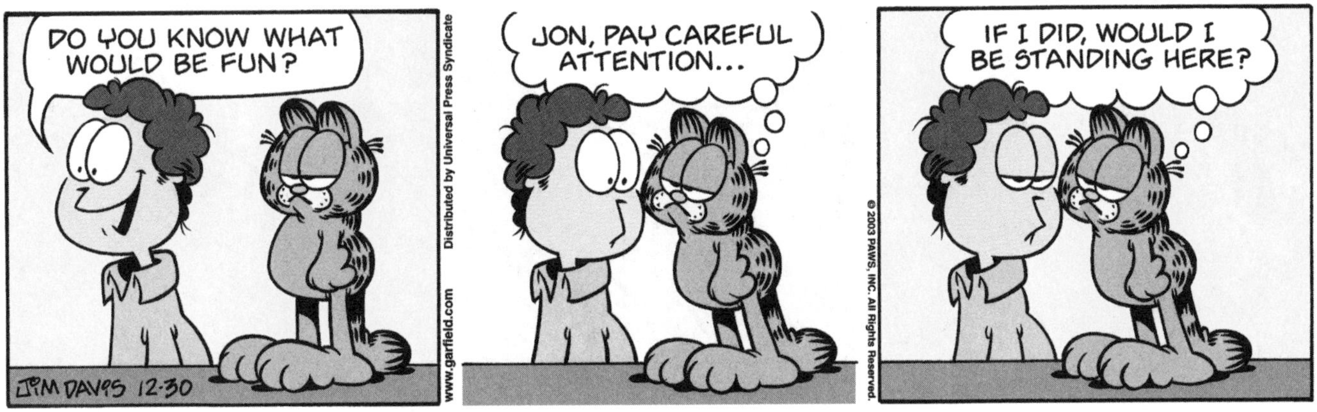
DO YOU KNOW WHAT WOULD BE FUN?
JON, PAY CAREFUL ATTENTION...
IF I DID, WOULD I BE STANDING HERE?
JIM DAVIS 12-30
www.garfield.com
Distributed by Universal Press Syndicate
© 2003 PAWS, INC. All Rights Reserved.

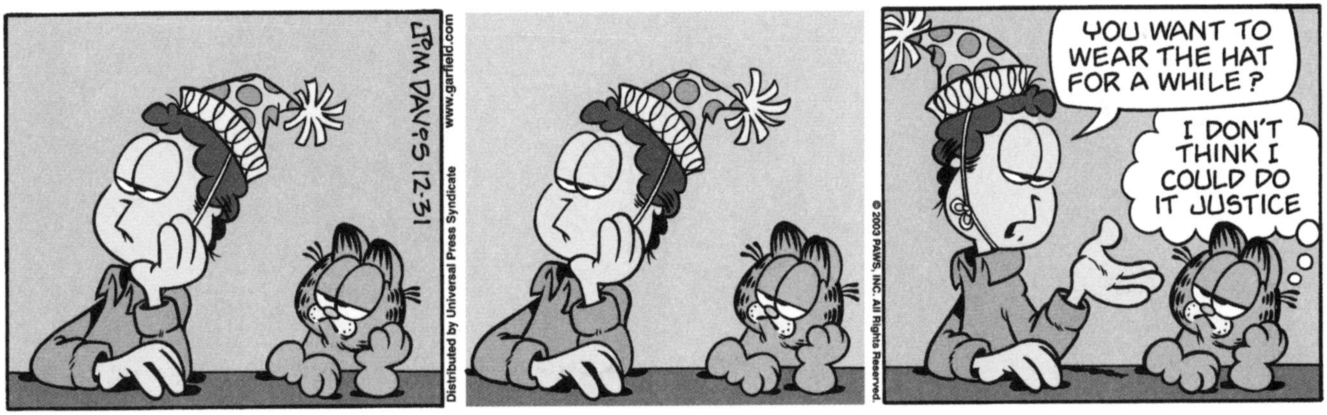
JIM DAVIS 12-31
www.garfield.com
Distributed by Universal Press Syndicate
YOU WANT TO WEAR THE HAT FOR A WHILE?
I DON'T THINK I COULD DO IT JUSTICE
© 2003 PAWS, INC. All Rights Reserved.

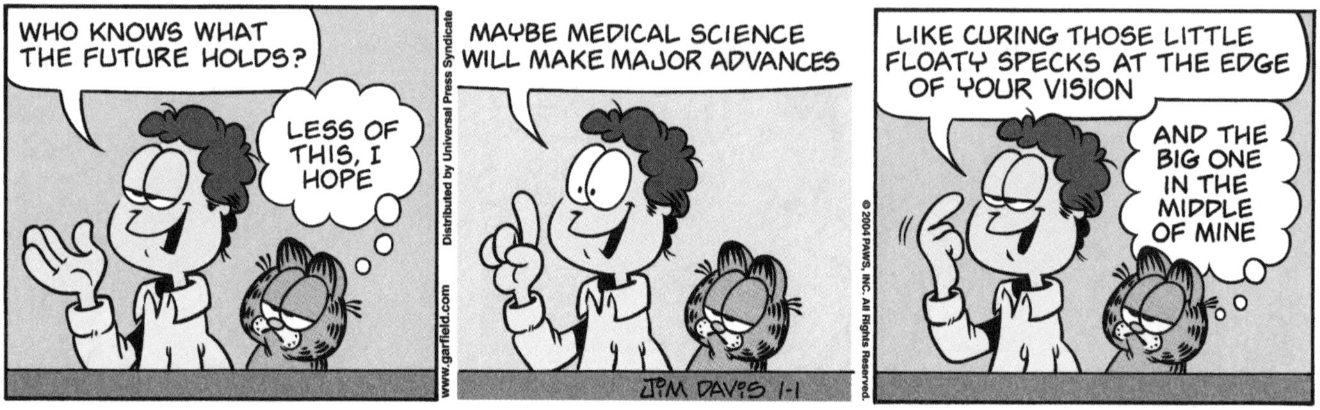
WHO KNOWS WHAT THE FUTURE HOLDS?
LESS OF THIS, I HOPE
www.garfield.com Distributed by Universal Press Syndicate
MAYBE MEDICAL SCIENCE WILL MAKE MAJOR ADVANCES
JIM DAVIS 1-1
© 2004 PAWS, INC. All Rights Reserved.
LIKE CURING THOSE LITTLE FLOATY SPECKS AT THE EDGE OF YOUR VISION
AND THE BIG ONE IN THE MIDDLE OF MINE

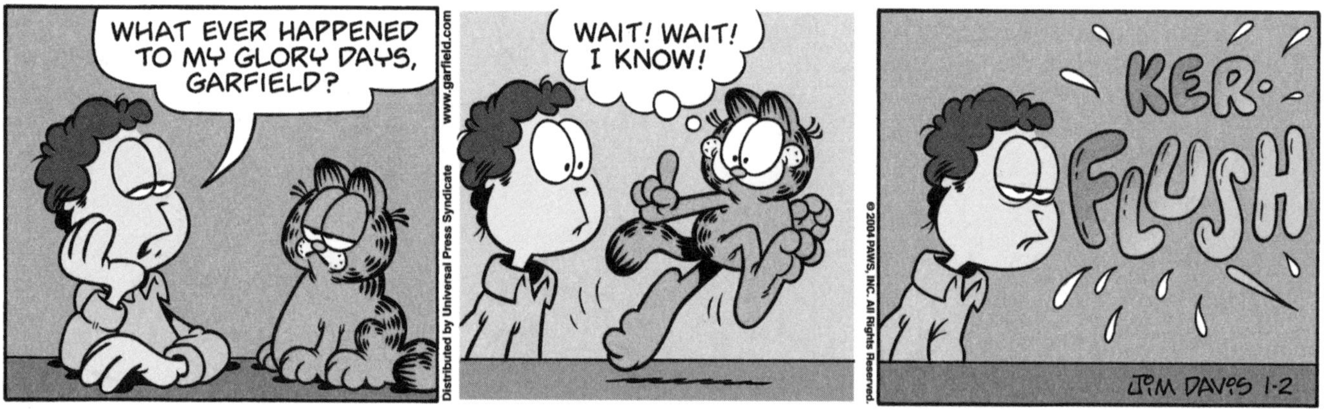
WHAT EVER HAPPENED TO MY GLORY DAYS, GARFIELD?
Distributed by Universal Press Syndicate www.garfield.com
WAIT! WAIT! I KNOW!
© 2004 PAWS, INC. All Rights Reserved.
KER-FLUSH
JIM DAVIS 1-2

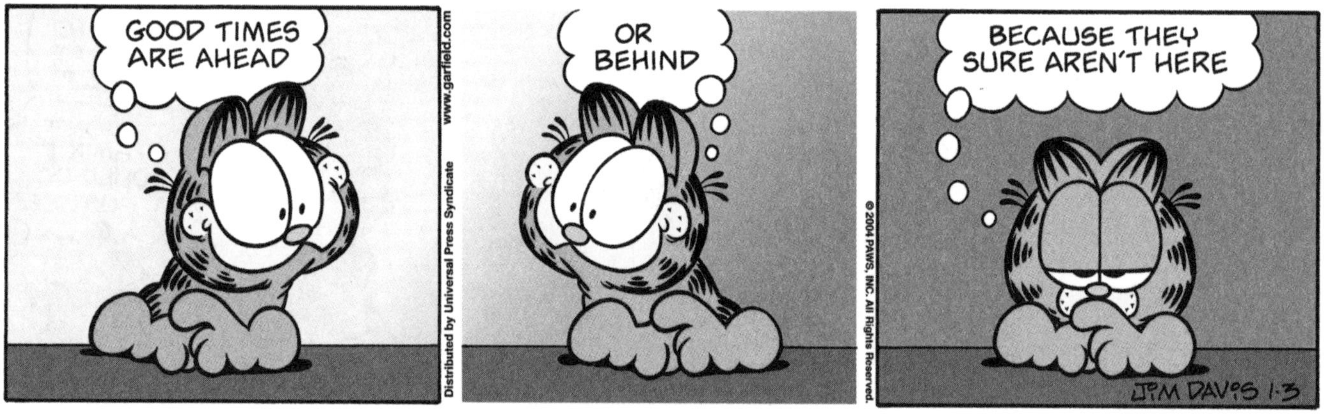
GOOD TIMES ARE AHEAD
Distributed by Universal Press Syndicate www.garfield.com
OR BEHIND
© 2004 PAWS, INC. All Rights Reserved.
BECAUSE THEY SURE AREN'T HERE
JIM DAVIS 1-3

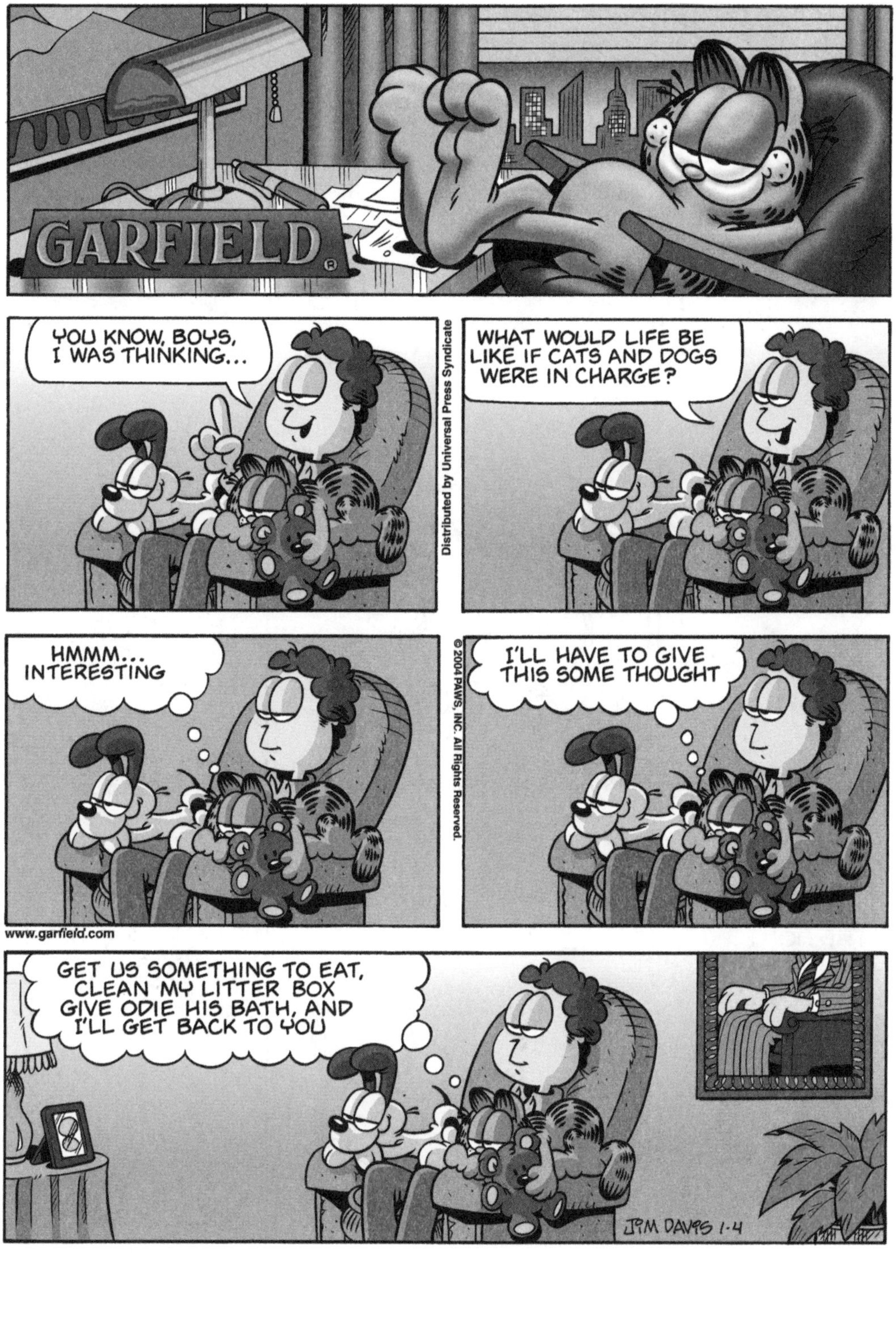
GARFIELD®
YOU KNOW, BOYS, I WAS THINKING...
WHAT WOULD LIFE BE LIKE IF CATS AND DOGS WERE IN CHARGE?
HMMM... INTERESTING
I'LL HAVE TO GIVE THIS SOME THOUGHT
GET US SOMETHING TO EAT, CLEAN MY LITTER BOX GIVE ODIE HIS BATH, AND I'LL GET BACK TO YOU
JIM DAVIS 1-4
Distributed by Universal Press Syndicate
© 2004 PAWS, INC. All Rights Reserved.
www.garfield.com

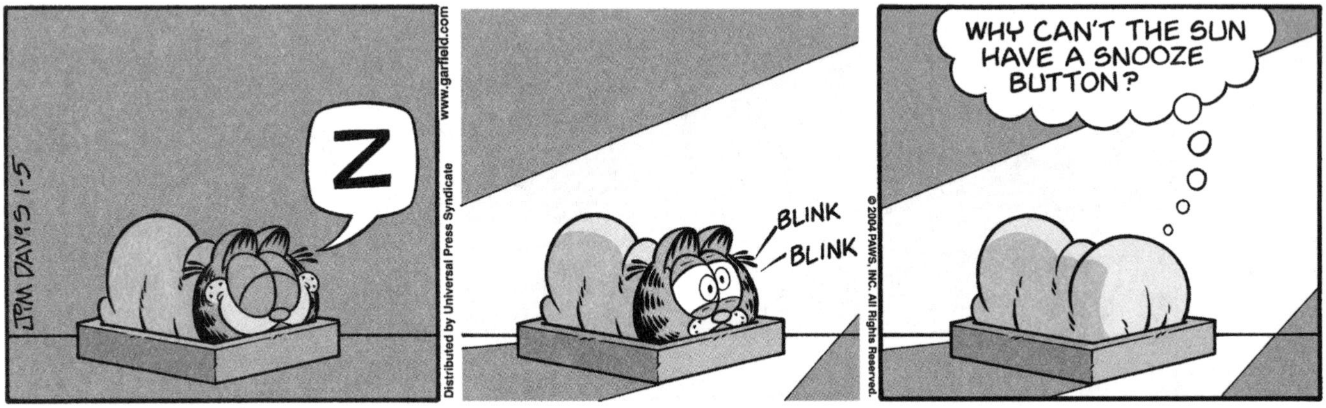
JIM DAVIS 1-5
Z
Distributed by Universal Press Syndicate www.garfield.com
BLINK
BLINK
© 2004 PAWS, INC. All Rights Reserved.
WHY CAN'T THE SUN HAVE A SNOOZE BUTTON?

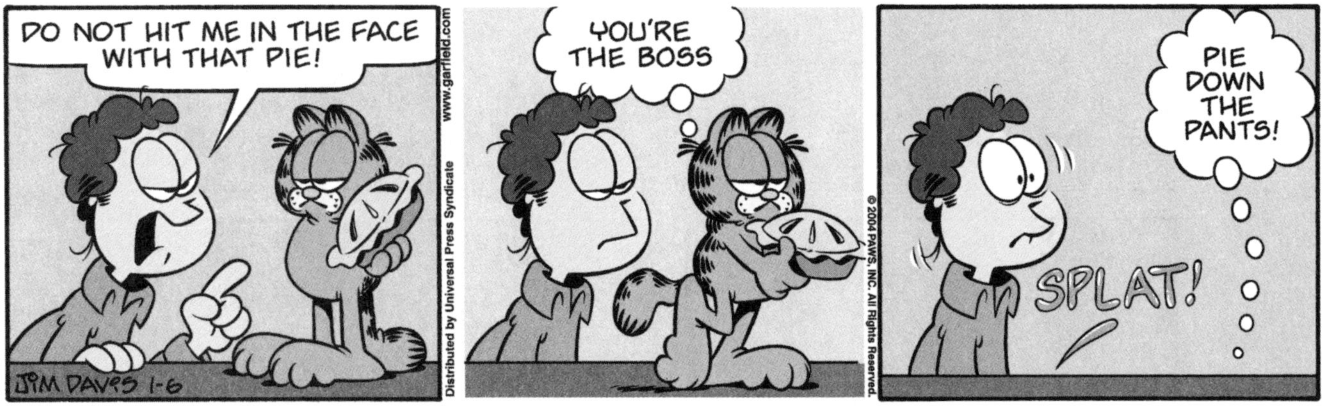
DO NOT HIT ME IN THE FACE WITH THAT PIE!
JIM DAVIS 1-6
Distributed by Universal Press Syndicate www.garfield.com
YOU'RE THE BOSS
© 2004 PAWS, INC. All Rights Reserved.
PIE DOWN THE PANTS!
SPLAT!

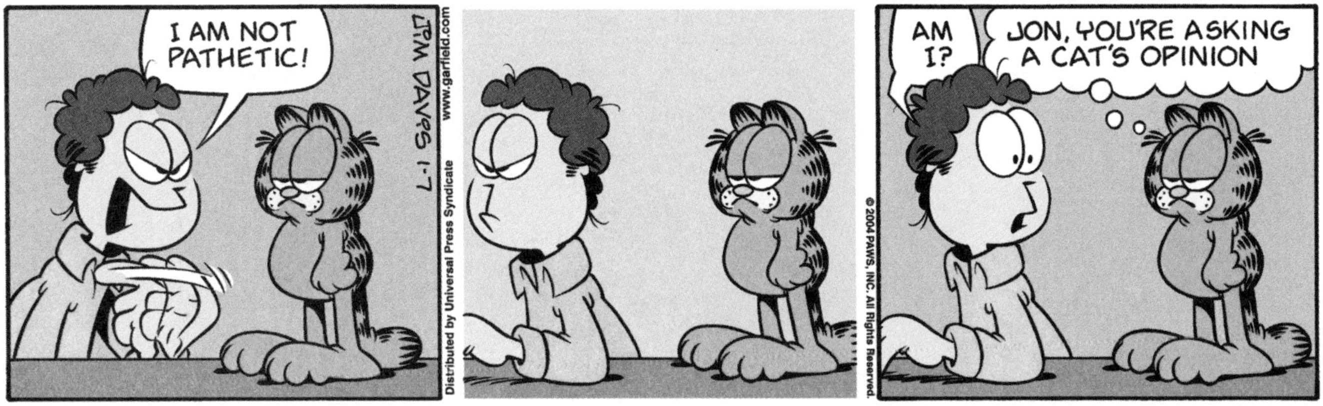
I AM NOT PATHETIC!
JIM DAVIS 1-7
Distributed by Universal Press Syndicate www.garfield.com
© 2004 PAWS, INC. All Rights Reserved.
AM I?
JON, YOU'RE ASKING A CAT'S OPINION

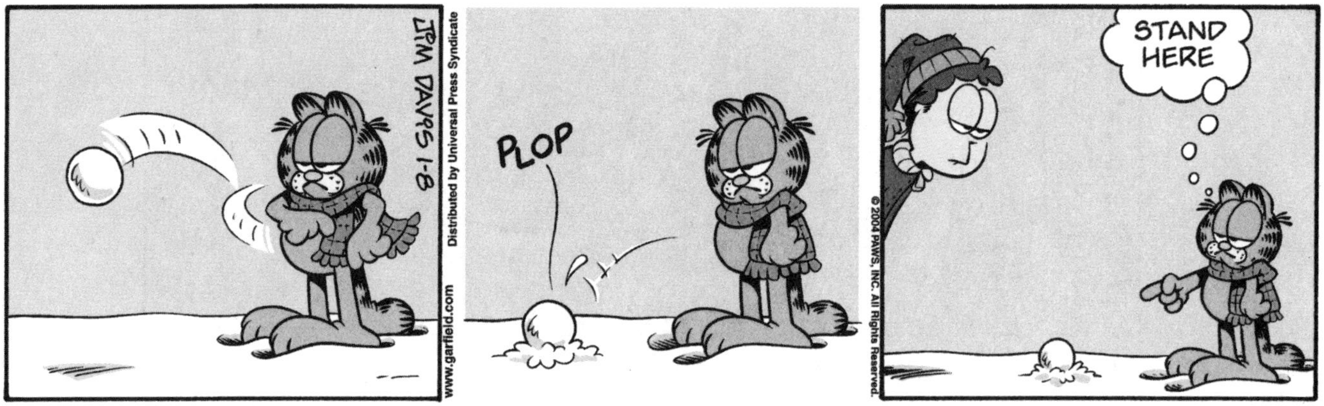
PLOP
STAND HERE

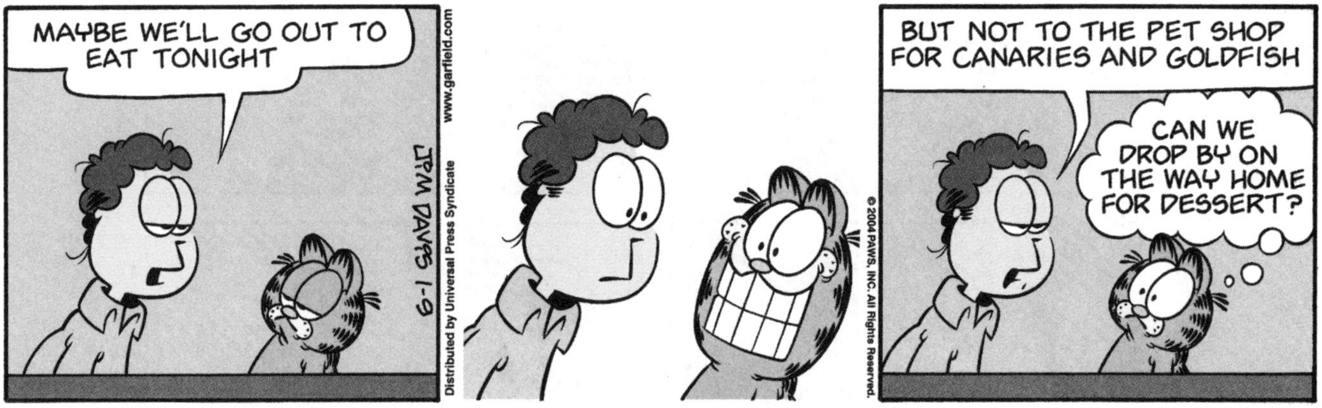
MAYBE WE'LL GO OUT TO EAT TONIGHT
BUT NOT TO THE PET SHOP FOR CANARIES AND GOLDFISH
CAN WE DROP BY ON THE WAY HOME FOR DESSERT?

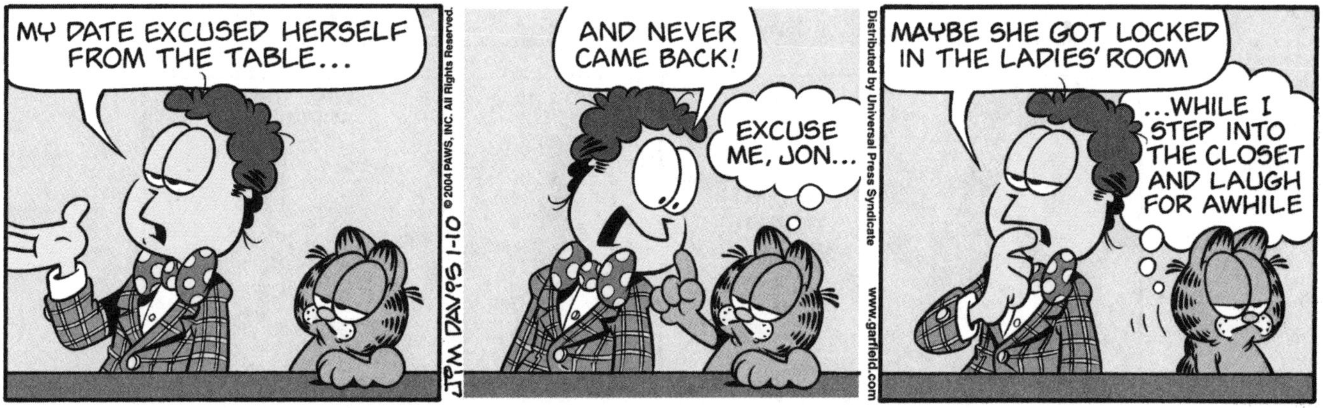
MY DATE EXCUSED HERSELF FROM THE TABLE...
AND NEVER CAME BACK!
EXCUSE ME, JON...
MAYBE SHE GOT LOCKED IN THE LADIES' ROOM
...WHILE I STEP INTO THE CLOSET AND LAUGH FOR AWHILE

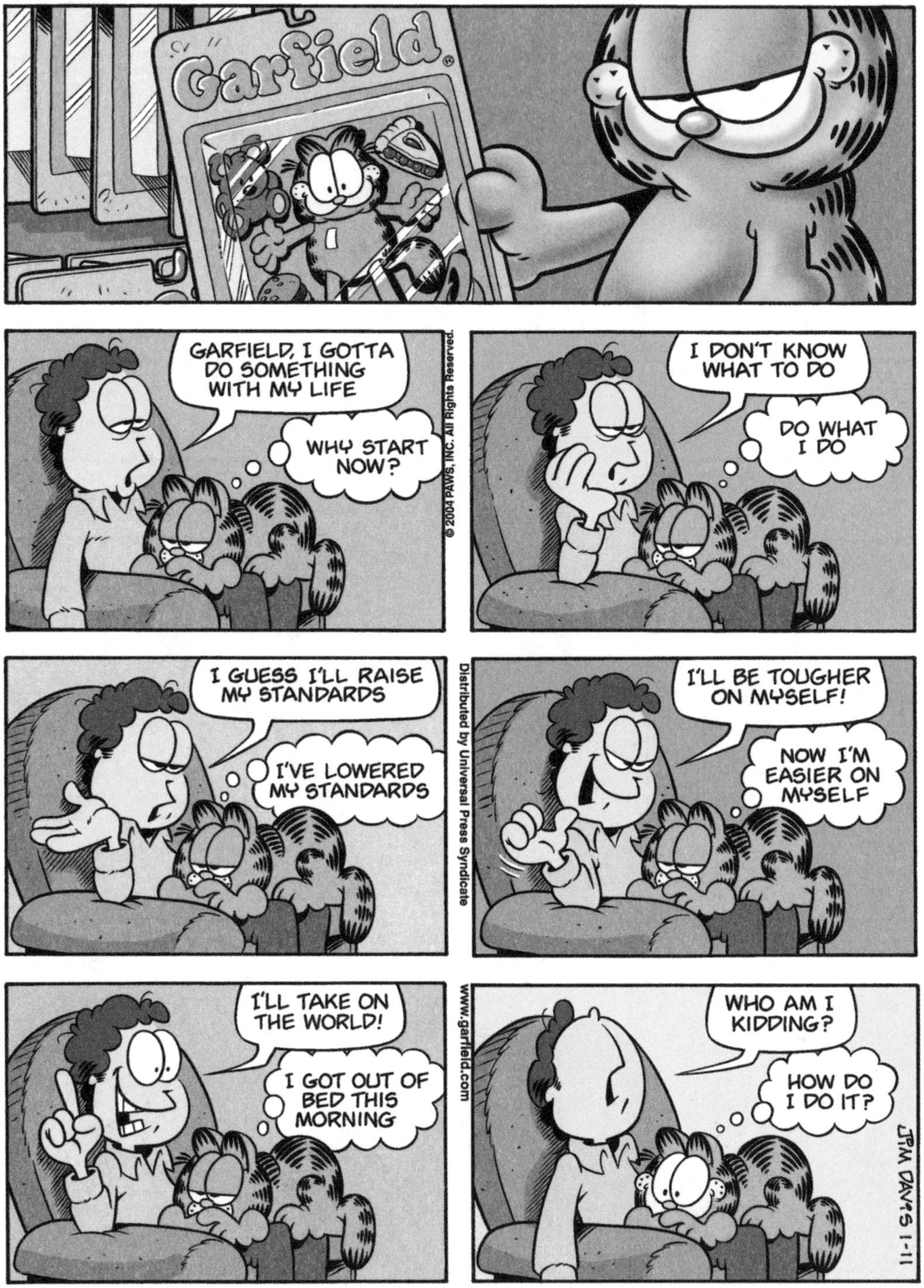
Garfield
GARFIELD, I GOTTA DO SOMETHING WITH MY LIFE
WHY START NOW?
I DON'T KNOW WHAT TO DO
DO WHAT I DO
I GUESS I'LL RAISE MY STANDARDS
I'VE LOWERED MY STANDARDS
I'LL BE TOUGHER ON MYSELF!
NOW I'M EASIER ON MYSELF
I'LL TAKE ON THE WORLD!
I GOT OUT OF BED THIS MORNING
WHO AM I KIDDING?
HOW DO I DO IT?
JIM DAVIS 1-11
© 2004 PAWS, INC. All Rights Reserved.
Distributed by Universal Press Syndicate
www.garfield.com

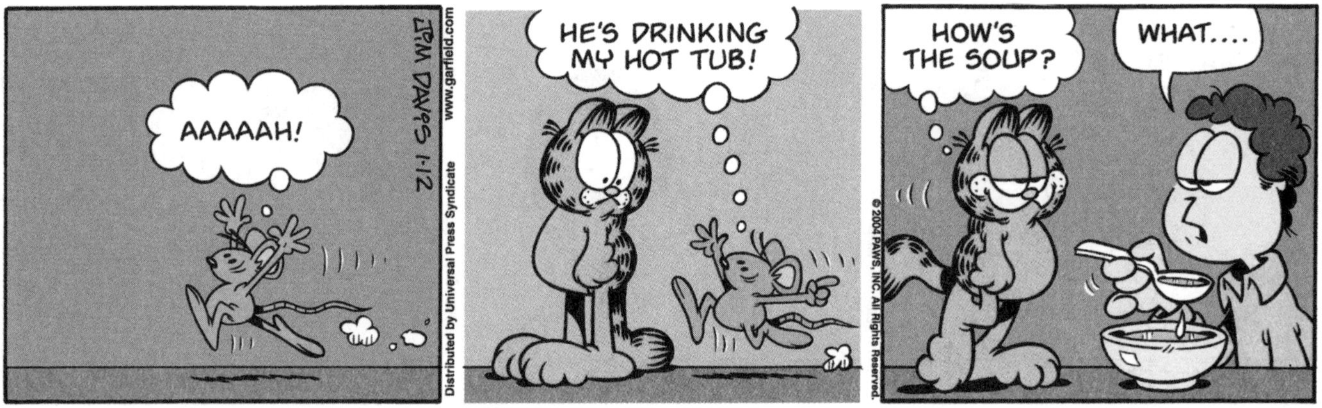
JIM DAVIS 1-12
www.garfield.com
Distributed by Universal Press Syndicate
AAAAAH!
HE'S DRINKING MY HOT TUB!
HOW'S THE SOUP?
WHAT....
© 2004 PAWS, INC. All Rights Reserved.

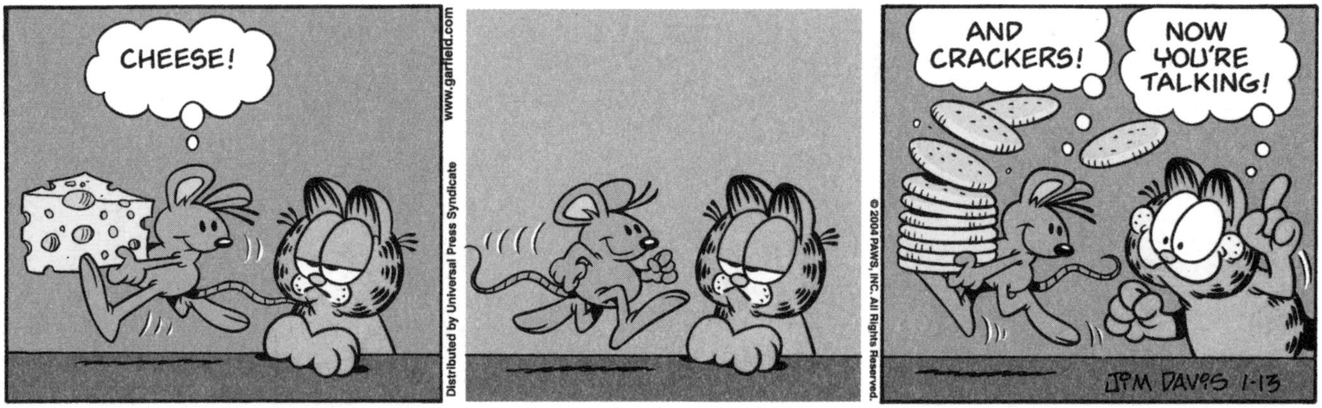
CHEESE!
www.garfield.com
Distributed by Universal Press Syndicate
© 2004 PAWS, INC. All Rights Reserved.
AND CRACKERS!
NOW YOU'RE TALKING!
JIM DAVIS 1-13

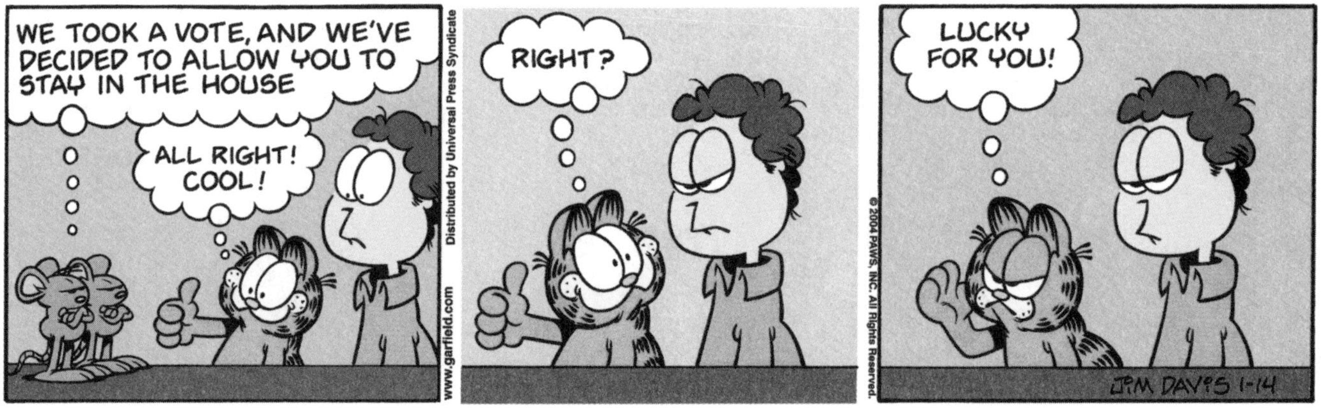
WE TOOK A VOTE, AND WE'VE DECIDED TO ALLOW YOU TO STAY IN THE HOUSE
ALL RIGHT! COOL!
Distributed by Universal Press Syndicate
www.garfield.com
RIGHT?
© 2004 PAWS, INC. All Rights Reserved.
LUCKY FOR YOU!
JIM DAVIS 1-14

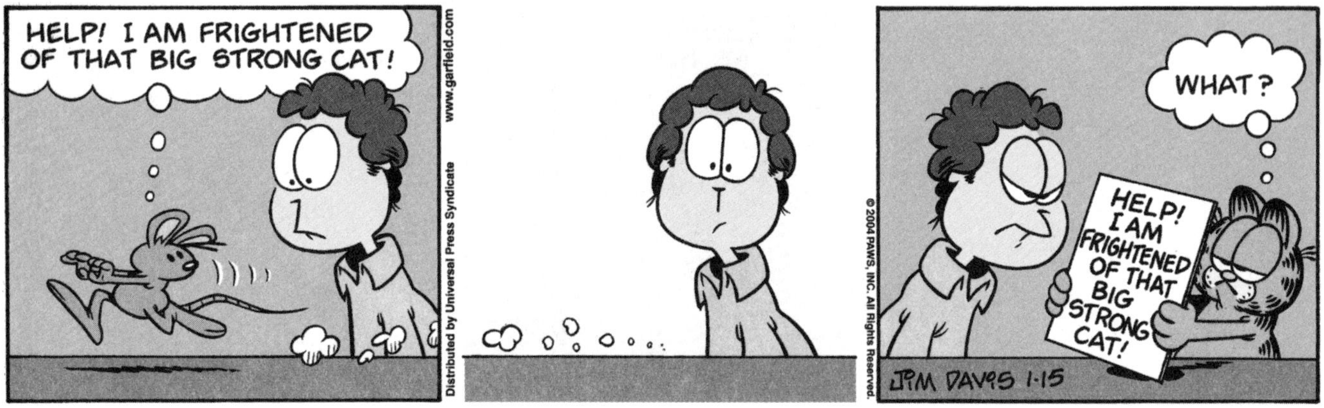
HELP! I AM FRIGHTENED OF THAT BIG STRONG CAT!
WHAT?
HELP! I AM FRIGHTENED OF THAT BIG STRONG CAT!
JIM DAVIS 1-15
www.garfield.com
Distributed by Universal Press Syndicate
© 2004 PAWS, INC. All Rights Reserved.

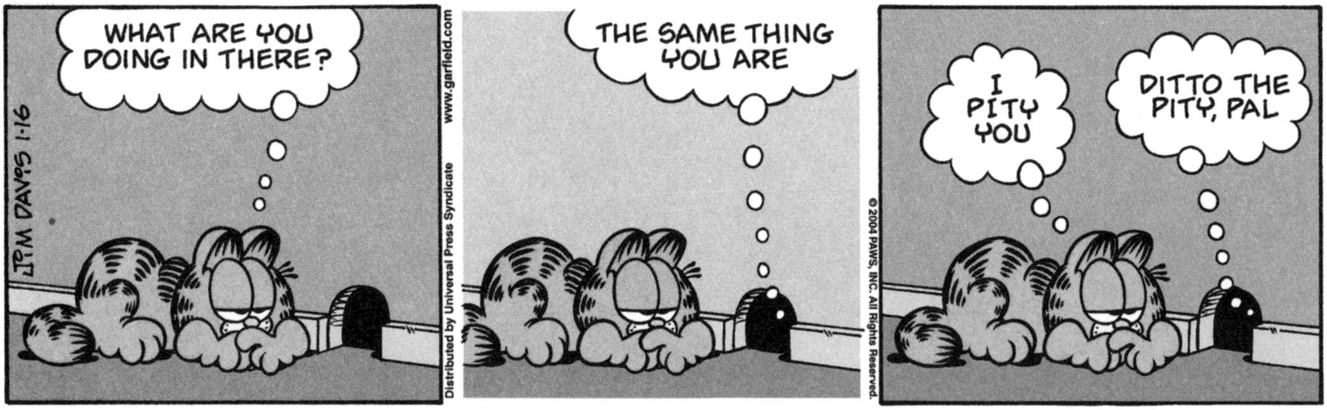
JIM DAVIS 1-16
WHAT ARE YOU DOING IN THERE?
THE SAME THING YOU ARE
I PITY YOU
DITTO THE PITY, PAL
www.garfield.com
Distributed by Universal Press Syndicate
© 2004 PAWS, INC. All Rights Reserved.

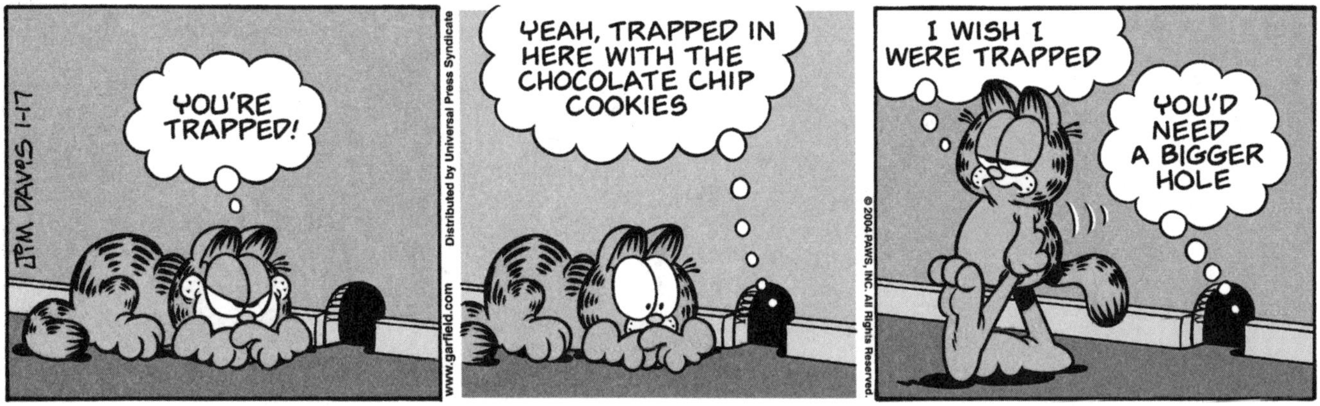
JIM DAVIS 1-17
YOU'RE TRAPPED!
YEAH, TRAPPED IN HERE WITH THE CHOCOLATE CHIP COOKIES
I WISH I WERE TRAPPED
YOU'D NEED A BIGGER HOLE
Distributed by Universal Press Syndicate
www.garfield.com
© 2004 PAWS, INC. All Rights Reserved.

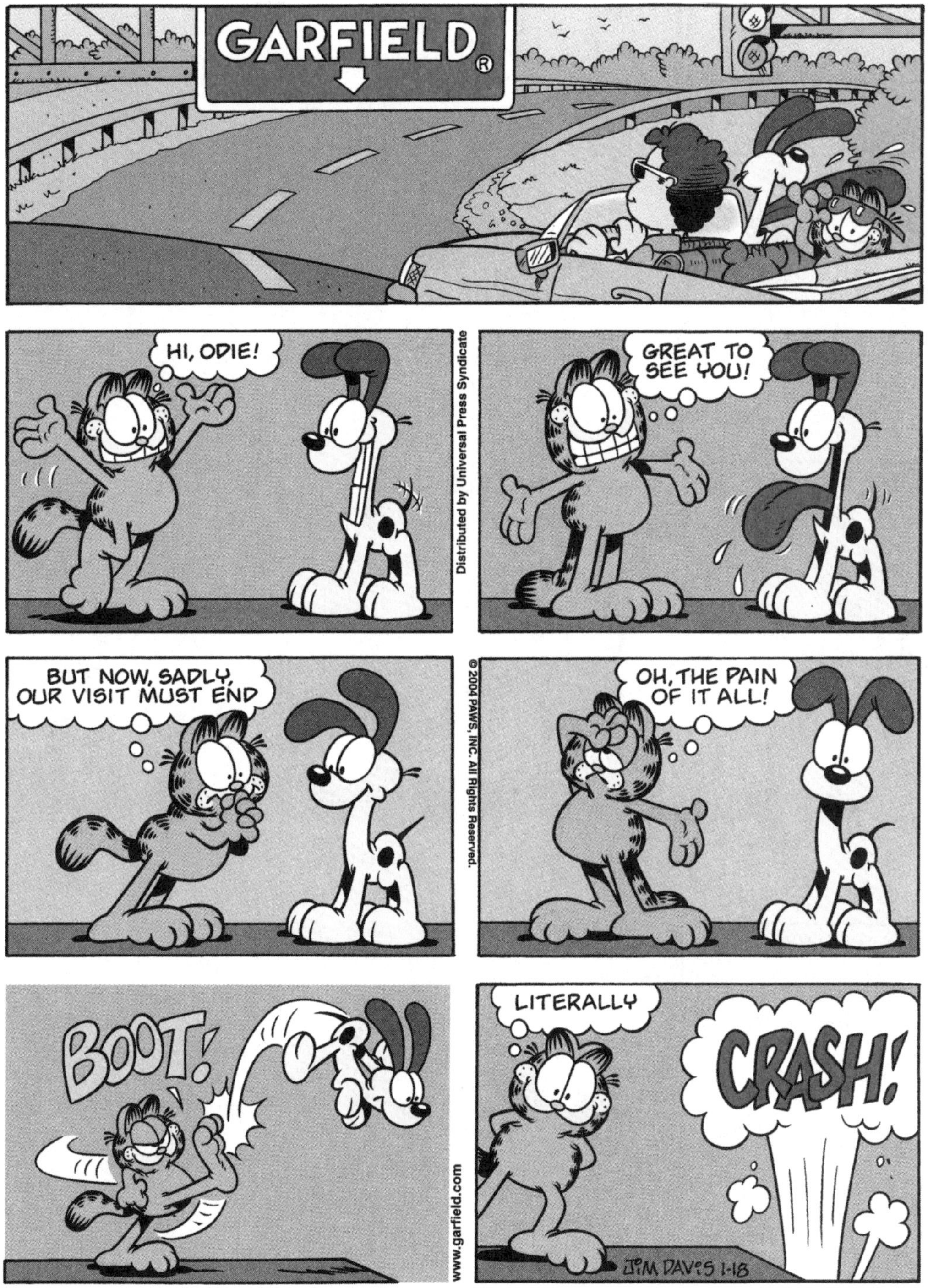
GARFIELD®
HI, ODIE!
GREAT TO SEE YOU!
BUT NOW, SADLY, OUR VISIT MUST END
OH, THE PAIN OF IT ALL!
BOOT!
LITERALLY
CRASH!
JIM DAVIS 1-18
Distributed by Universal Press Syndicate
© 2004 PAWS, INC. All Rights Reserved.
www.garfield.com

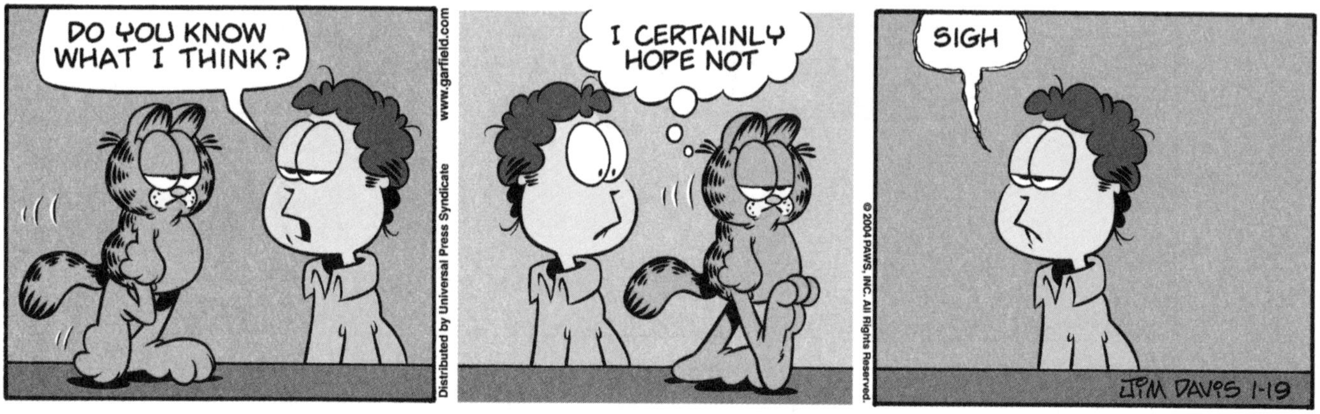
DO YOU KNOW WHAT I THINK?
Distributed by Universal Press Syndicate www.garfield.com
I CERTAINLY HOPE NOT
© 2004 PAWS, INC. All Rights Reserved.
SIGH
JIM DAVIS 1-19

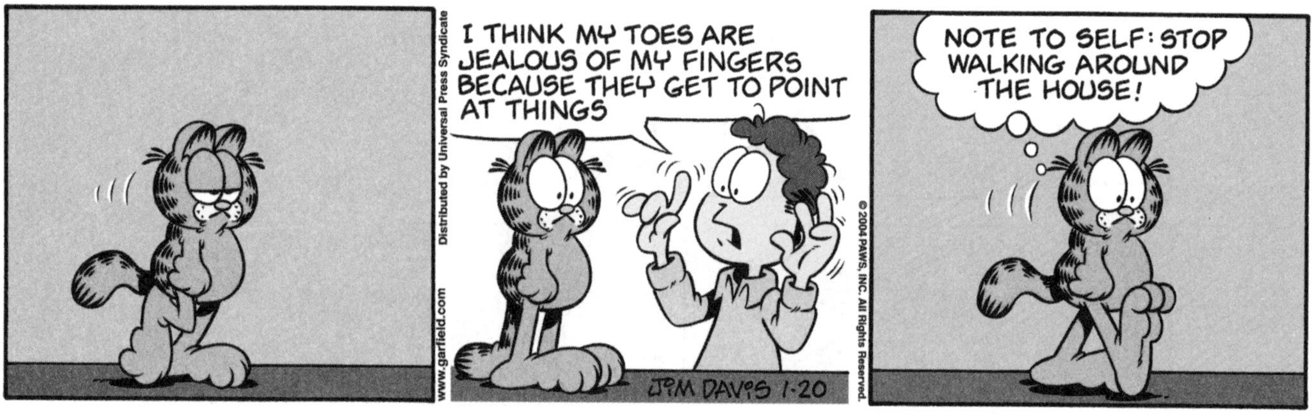
Distributed by Universal Press Syndicate www.garfield.com
I THINK MY TOES ARE JEALOUS OF MY FINGERS BECAUSE THEY GET TO POINT AT THINGS
JIM DAVIS 1-20
© 2004 PAWS, INC. All Rights Reserved.
NOTE TO SELF: STOP WALKING AROUND THE HOUSE!

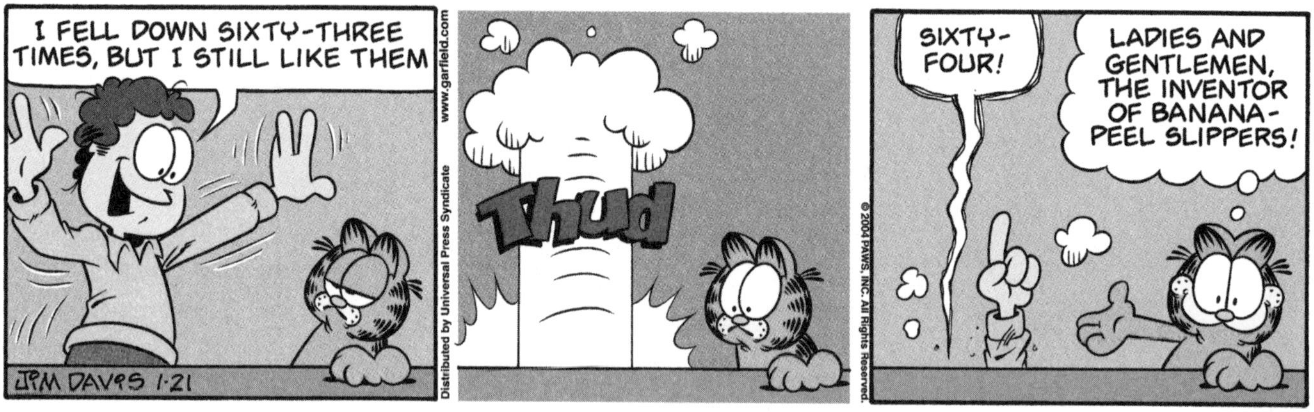
I FELL DOWN SIXTY-THREE TIMES, BUT I STILL LIKE THEM
JIM DAVIS 1-21
Distributed by Universal Press Syndicate www.garfield.com
Thud
© 2004 PAWS, INC. All Rights Reserved.
SIXTY-FOUR!
LADIES AND GENTLEMEN, THE INVENTOR OF BANANA-PEEL SLIPPERS!

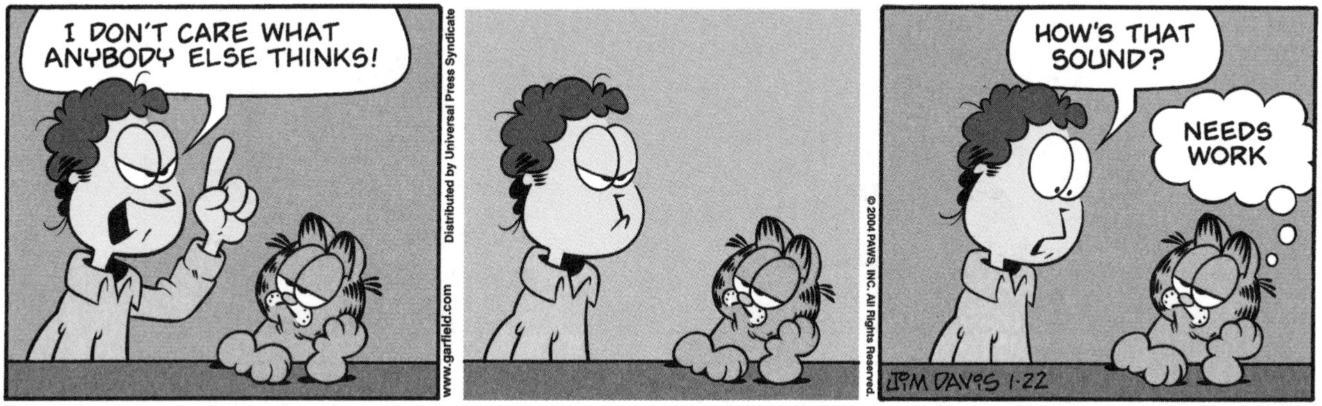
I DON'T CARE WHAT ANYBODY ELSE THINKS!
HOW'S THAT SOUND?
NEEDS WORK
www.garfield.com Distributed by Universal Press Syndicate
© 2004 PAWS, INC. All Rights Reserved.
JIM DAVIS 1-22

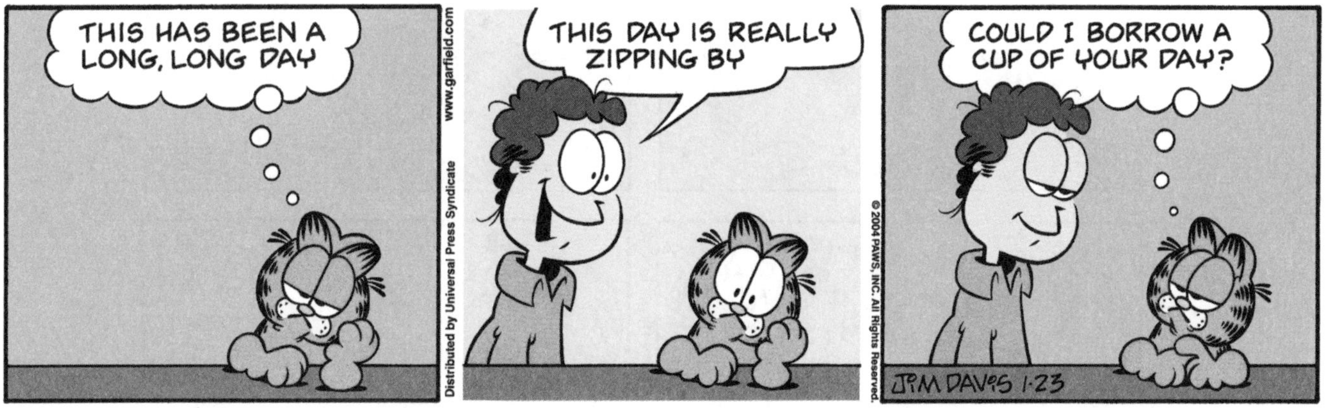
THIS HAS BEEN A LONG, LONG DAY
THIS DAY IS REALLY ZIPPING BY
COULD I BORROW A CUP OF YOUR DAY?
Distributed by Universal Press Syndicate www.garfield.com
© 2004 PAWS, INC. All Rights Reserved.
JIM DAVIS 1-23

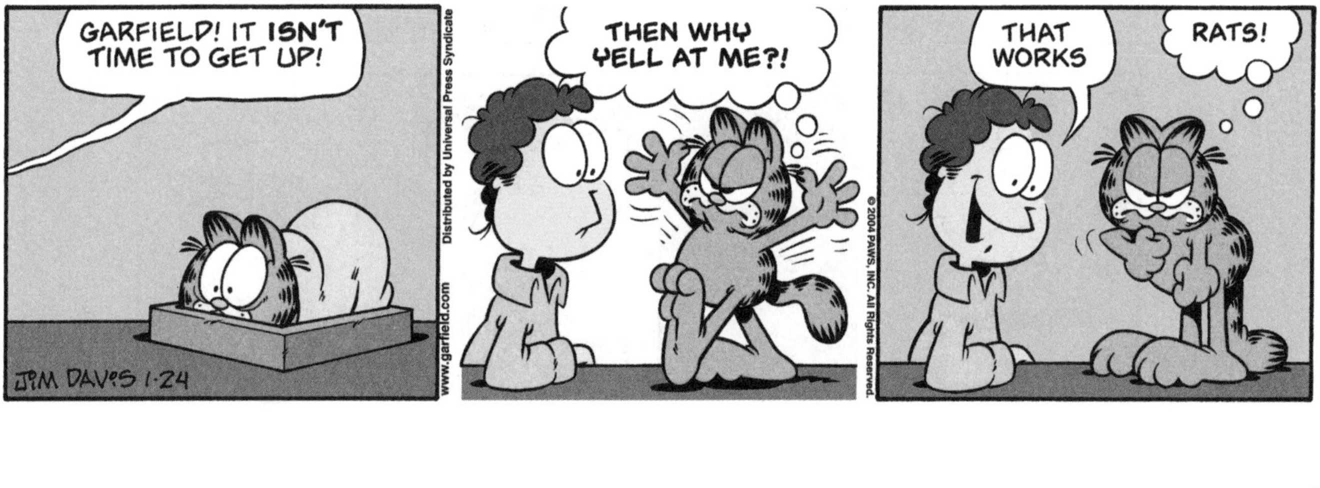
GARFIELD! IT **ISN'T** TIME TO GET UP!
JIM DAVIS 1-24
THEN WHY YELL AT ME?!
THAT WORKS
RATS!
www.garfield.com Distributed by Universal Press Syndicate
© 2004 PAWS, INC. All Rights Reserved.

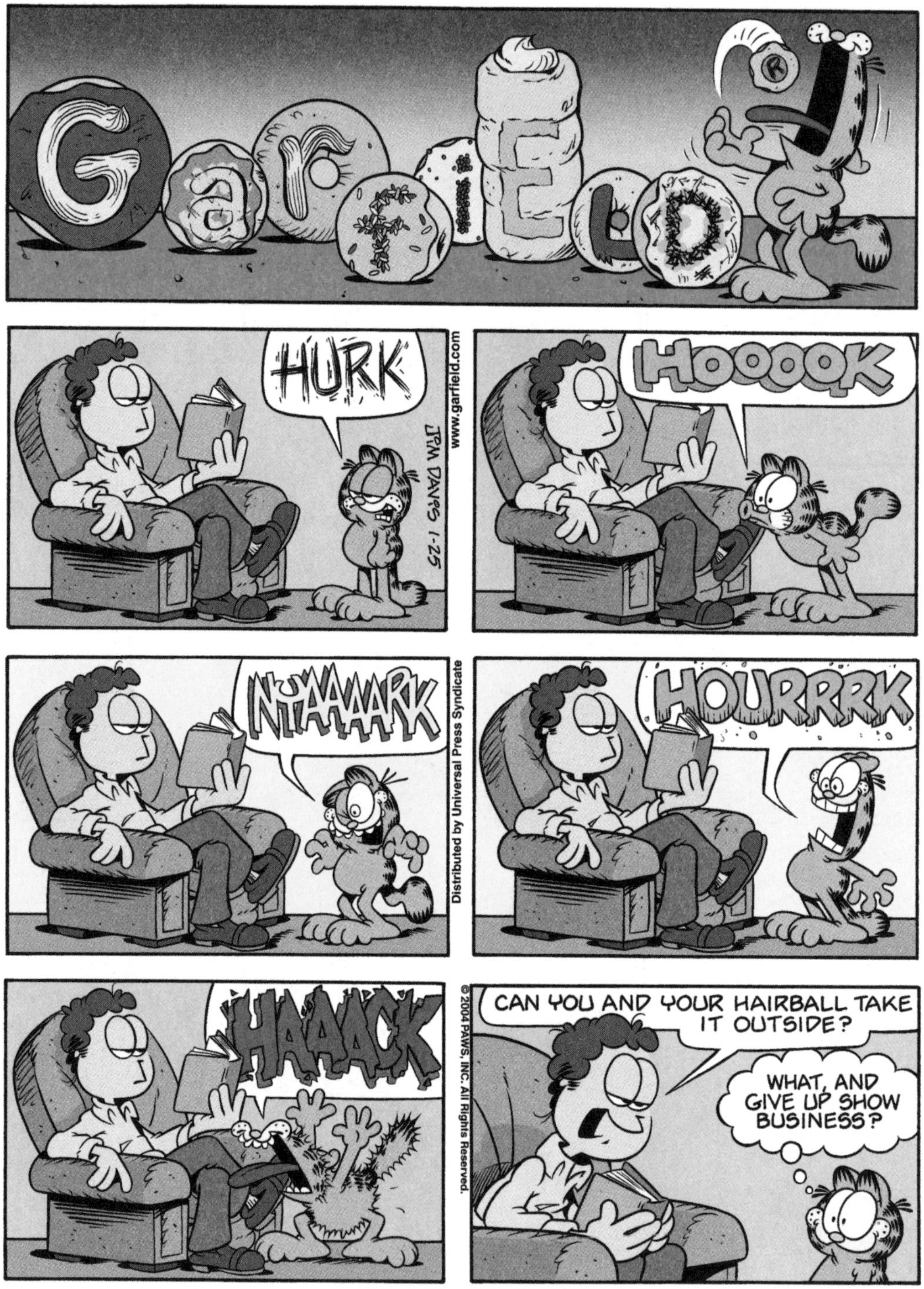
GARFIELD
HURK
JIM DAVIS 1-25
www.garfield.com
HOOOOK
NYAAAARK
Distributed by Universal Press Syndicate
HOURRRK
HAAACK
© 2004 PAWS, INC. All Rights Reserved.
CAN YOU AND YOUR HAIRBALL TAKE IT OUTSIDE?
WHAT, AND GIVE UP SHOW BUSINESS?

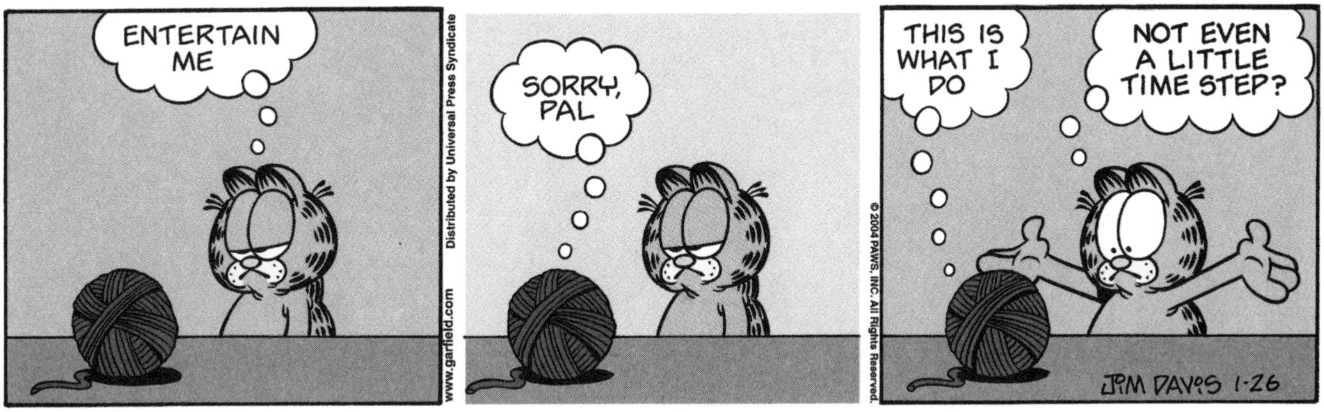
ENTERTAIN ME
SORRY, PAL
THIS IS WHAT I DO
NOT EVEN A LITTLE TIME STEP?
www.garfield.com Distributed by Universal Press Syndicate
© 2004 PAWS, INC. All Rights Reserved.
JIM DAVIS 1-26

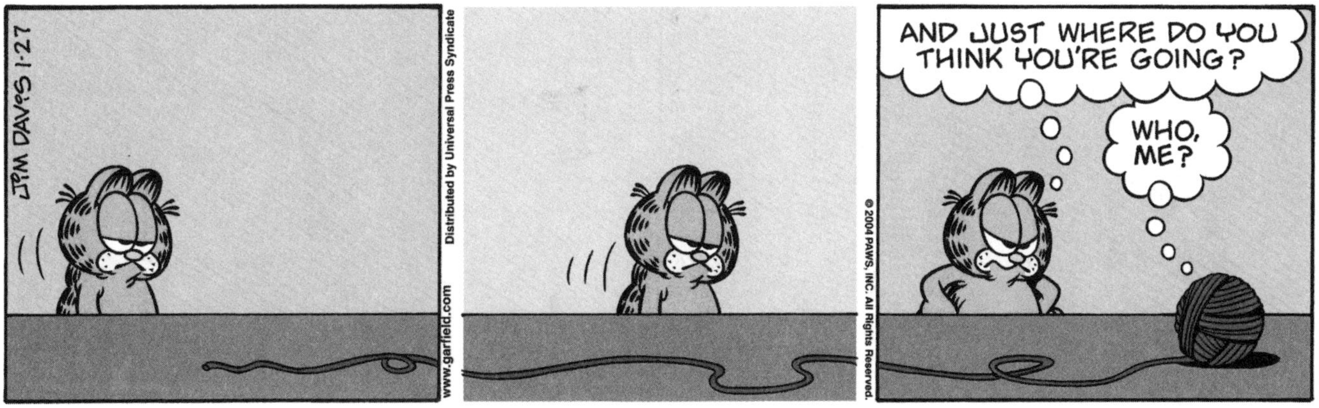
JIM DAVIS 1-27
AND JUST WHERE DO YOU THINK YOU'RE GOING?
WHO, ME?
www.garfield.com Distributed by Universal Press Syndicate
© 2004 PAWS, INC. All Rights Reserved.

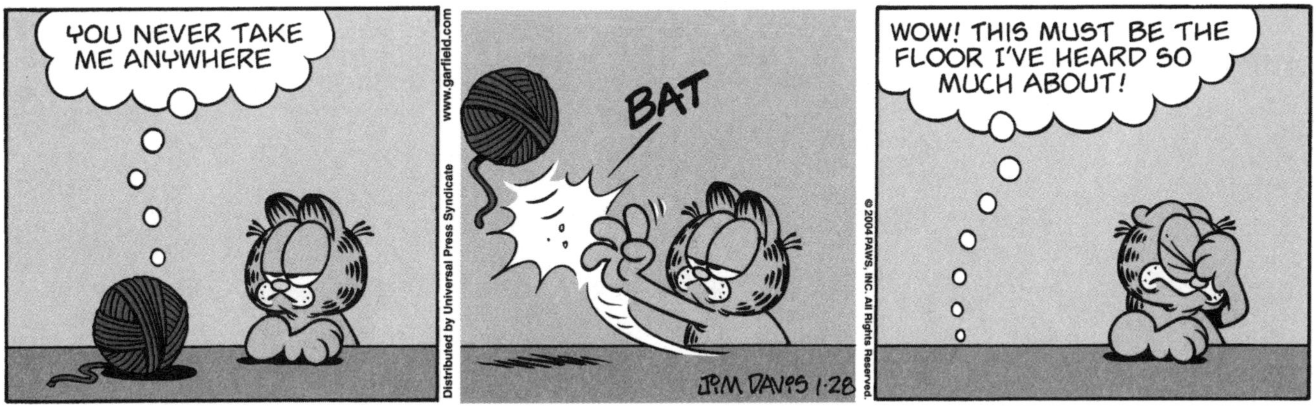
YOU NEVER TAKE ME ANYWHERE
BAT
WOW! THIS MUST BE THE FLOOR I'VE HEARD SO MUCH ABOUT!
www.garfield.com Distributed by Universal Press Syndicate
© 2004 PAWS, INC. All Rights Reserved.
JIM DAVIS 1-28

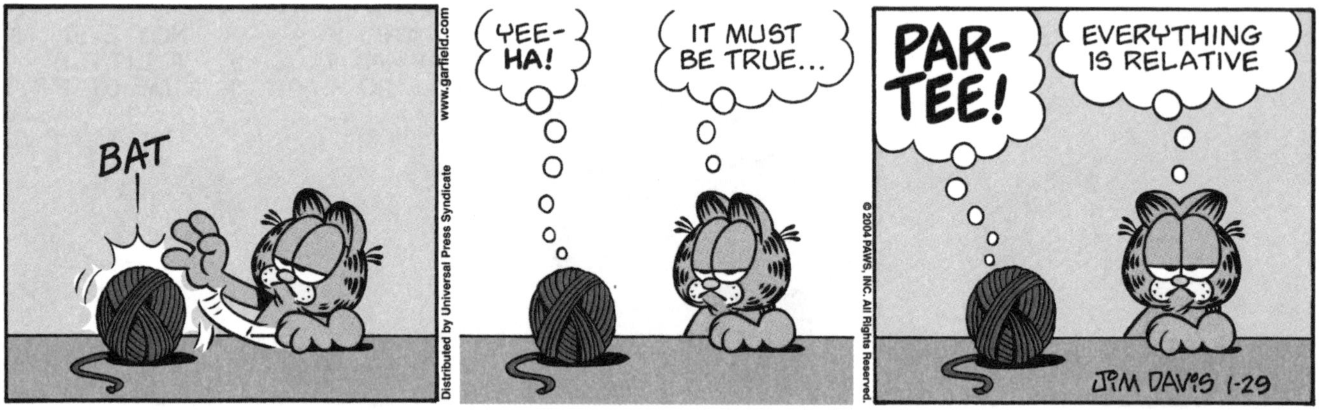
BAT
www.garfield.com
Distributed by Universal Press Syndicate
YEE-HA!
IT MUST BE TRUE...
© 2004 PAWS, INC. All Rights Reserved.
PAR-TEE!
EVERYTHING IS RELATIVE
JIM DAVIS 1-29

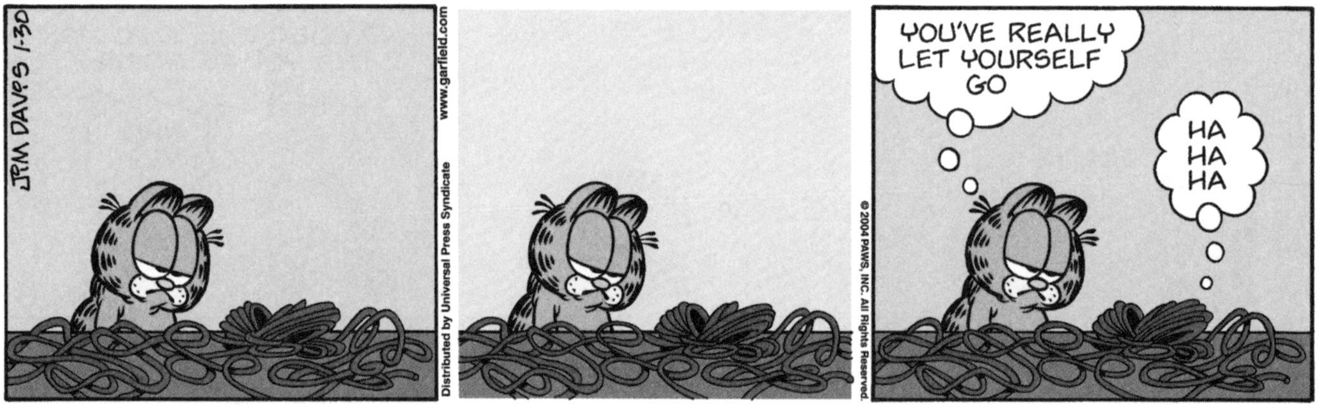
JIM DAVIS 1-30
www.garfield.com
Distributed by Universal Press Syndicate
© 2004 PAWS, INC. All Rights Reserved.
YOU'VE REALLY LET YOURSELF GO
HA HA HA

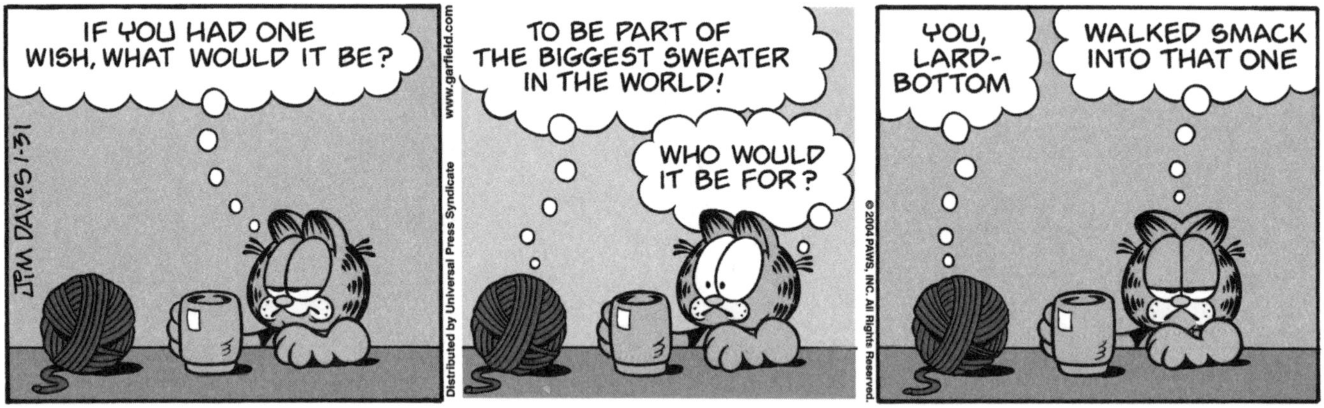
IF YOU HAD ONE WISH, WHAT WOULD IT BE?
JIM DAVIS 1-31
www.garfield.com
Distributed by Universal Press Syndicate
TO BE PART OF THE BIGGEST SWEATER IN THE WORLD!
WHO WOULD IT BE FOR?
© 2004 PAWS, INC. All Rights Reserved.
YOU, LARD-BOTTOM
WALKED SMACK INTO THAT ONE

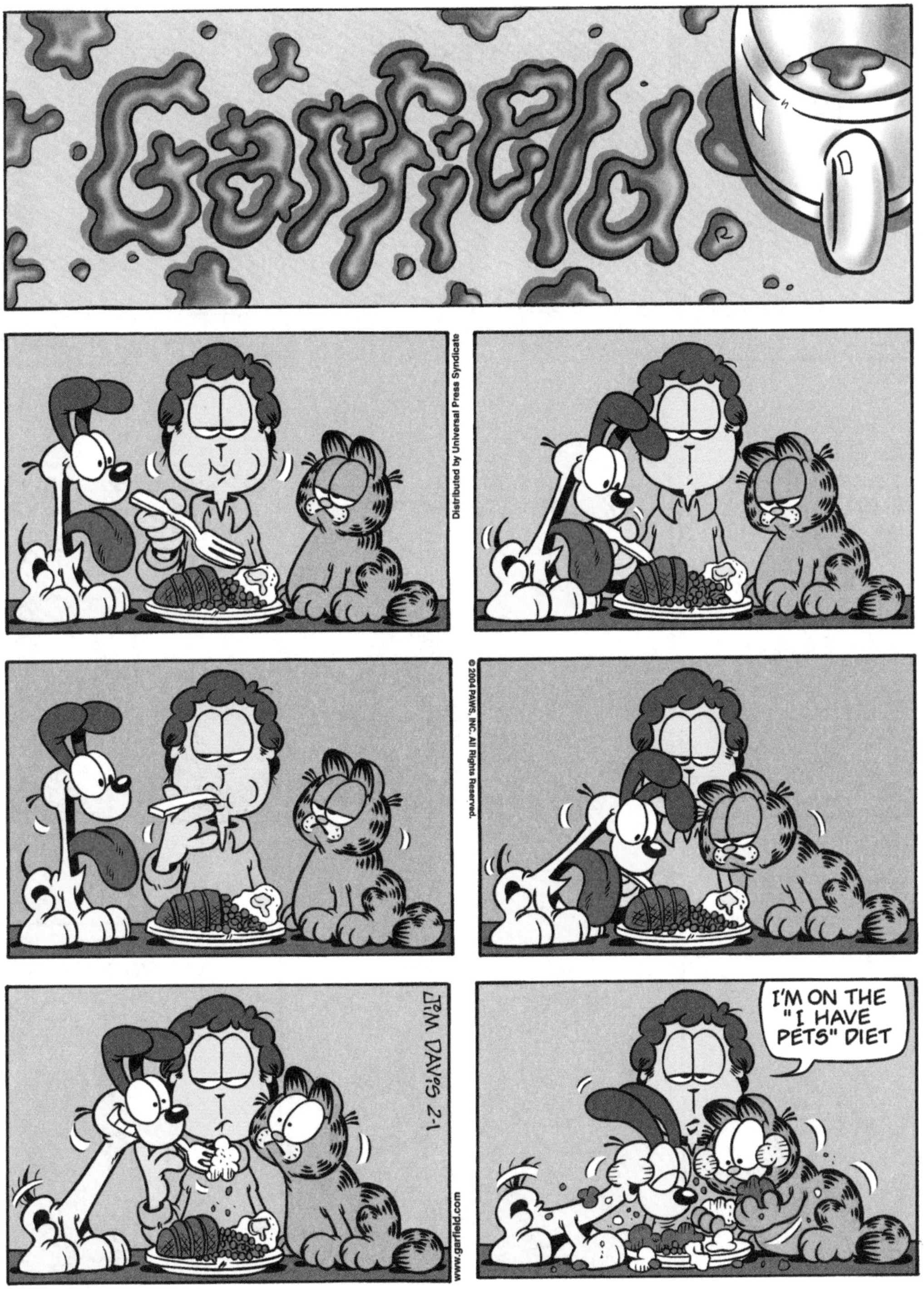
Garfield
Distributed by Universal Press Syndicate
© 2004 PAWS, INC. All Rights Reserved.
JIM DAVIS 2-1
www.garfield.com
I'M ON THE "I HAVE PETS" DIET

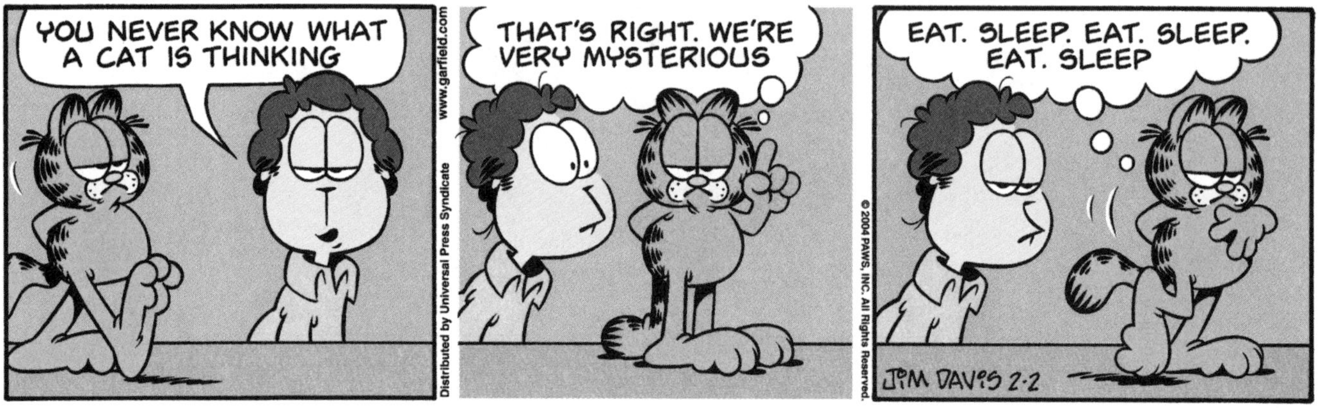

YOU NEVER KNOW WHAT A CAT IS THINKING
www.garfield.com
Distributed by Universal Press Syndicate
THAT'S RIGHT. WE'RE VERY MYSTERIOUS
© 2004 PAWS, INC. All Rights Reserved.
EAT. SLEEP. EAT. SLEEP. EAT. SLEEP
JIM DAVIS 2-2

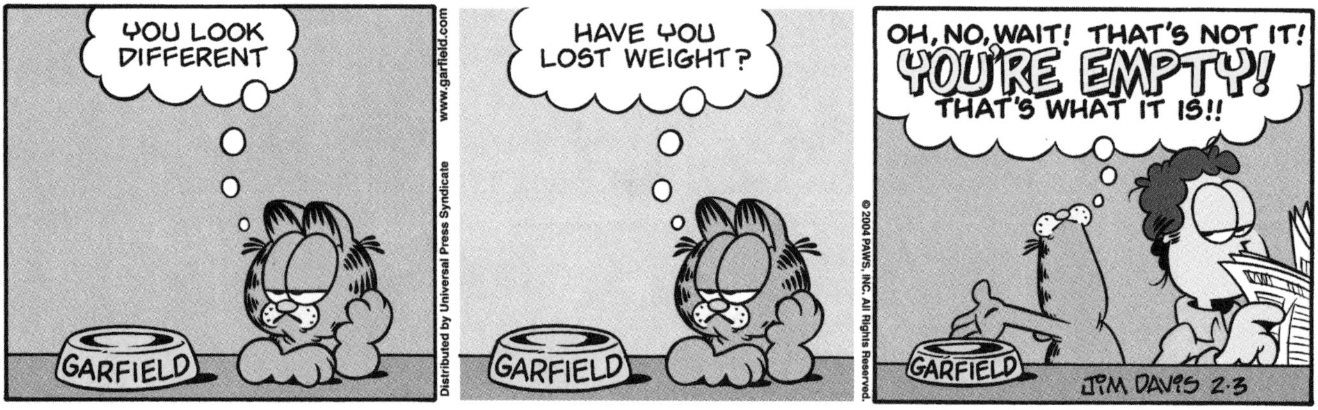

YOU LOOK DIFFERENT
GARFIELD
www.garfield.com
Distributed by Universal Press Syndicate
HAVE YOU LOST WEIGHT?
GARFIELD
© 2004 PAWS, INC. All Rights Reserved.
OH, NO, WAIT! THAT'S NOT IT! YOU'RE EMPTY! THAT'S WHAT IT IS!!
GARFIELD
JIM DAVIS 2-3

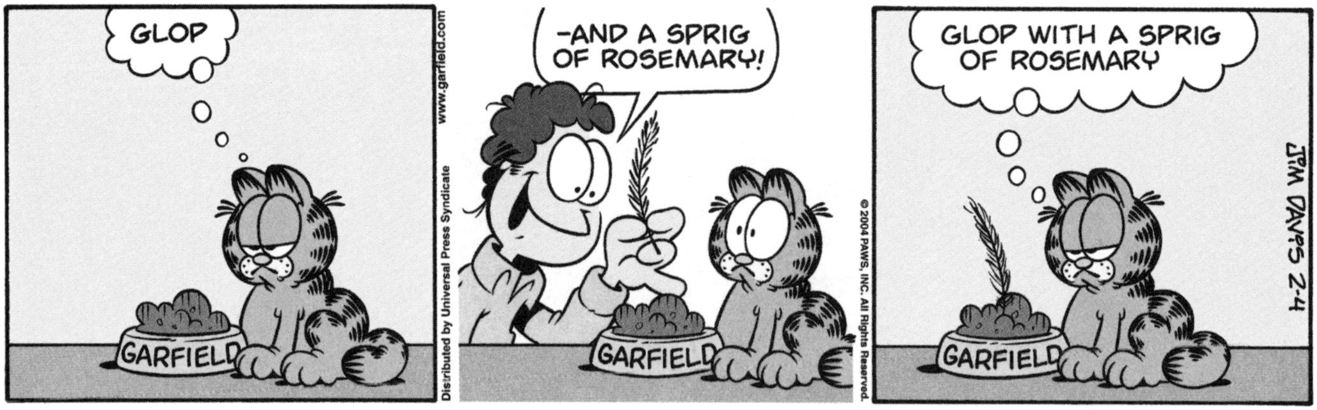

GLOP
GARFIELD
www.garfield.com
Distributed by Universal Press Syndicate
-AND A SPRIG OF ROSEMARY!
GARFIELD
© 2004 PAWS, INC. All Rights Reserved.
GLOP WITH A SPRIG OF ROSEMARY
GARFIELD
JIM DAVIS 2-4

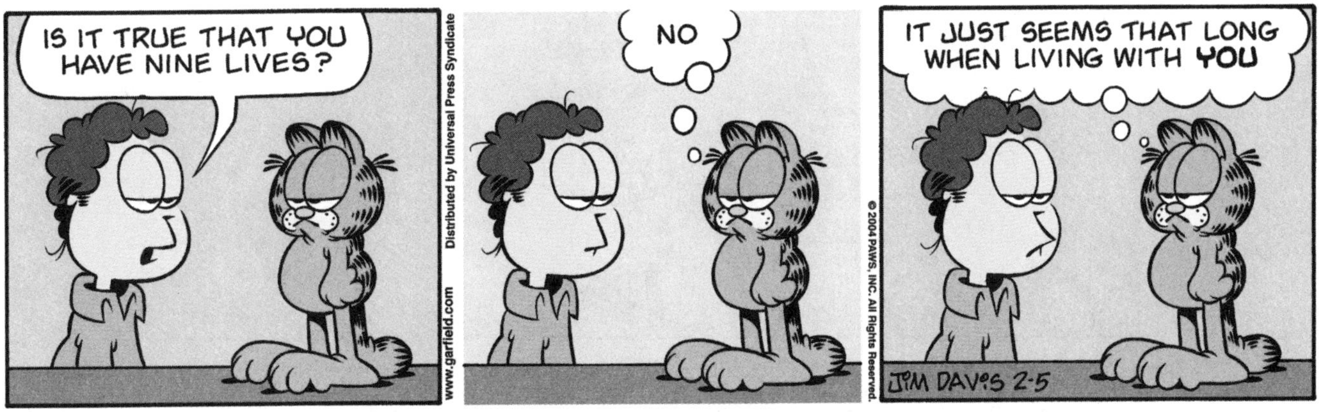
IS IT TRUE THAT YOU HAVE NINE LIVES?
NO
IT JUST SEEMS THAT LONG WHEN LIVING WITH **YOU**
www.garfield.com Distributed by Universal Press Syndicate
© 2004 PAWS, INC. All Rights Reserved.
JIM DAVIS 2-5

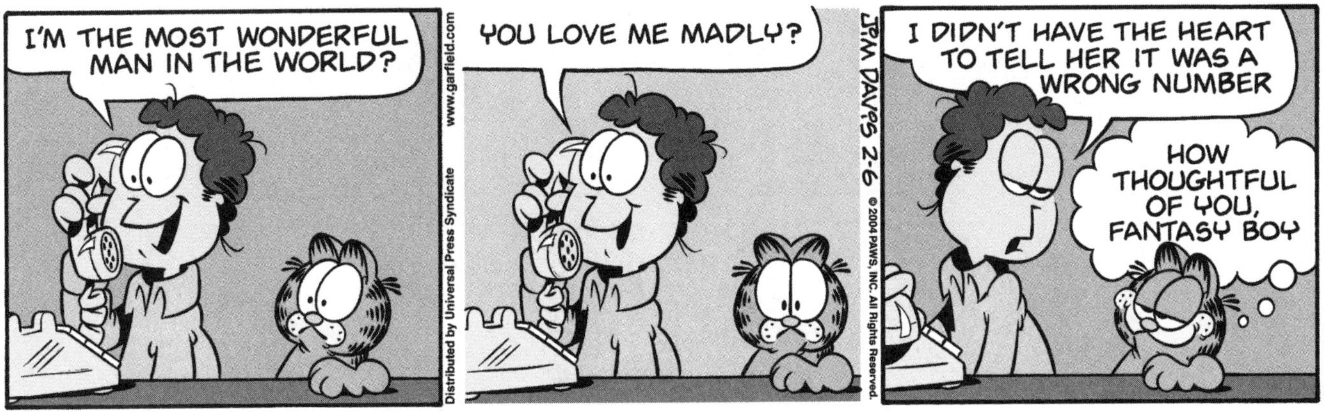
I'M THE MOST WONDERFUL MAN IN THE WORLD?
YOU LOVE ME MADLY?
I DIDN'T HAVE THE HEART TO TELL HER IT WAS A WRONG NUMBER
HOW THOUGHTFUL OF YOU, FANTASY BOY
Distributed by Universal Press Syndicate www.garfield.com
JIM DAVIS 2-6 © 2004 PAWS, INC. All Rights Reserved.

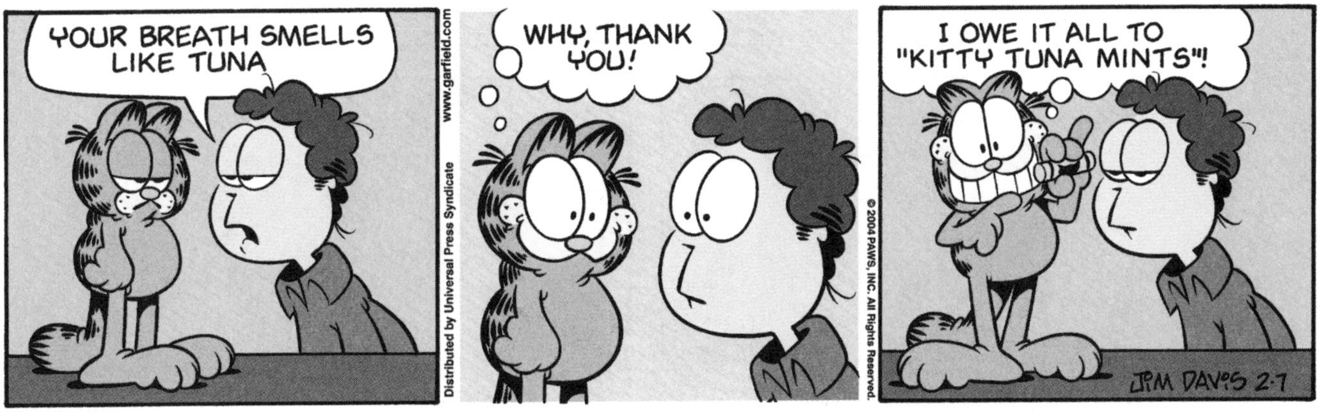
YOUR BREATH SMELLS LIKE TUNA
WHY, THANK YOU!
I OWE IT ALL TO "KITTY TUNA MINTS"!
Distributed by Universal Press Syndicate www.garfield.com
© 2004 PAWS, INC. All Rights Reserved.
JIM DAVIS 2-7

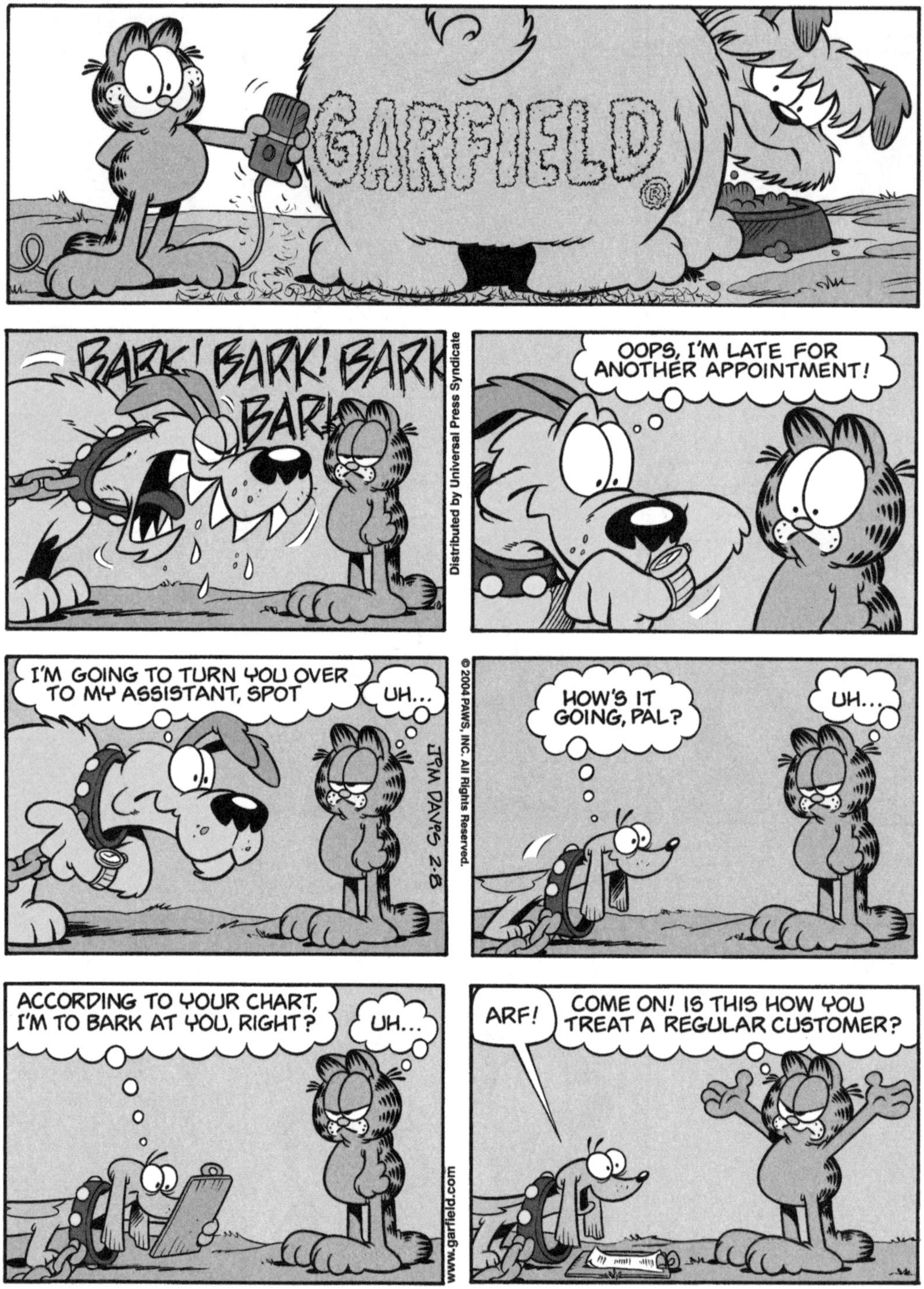
GARFIELD®
BARK! BARK! BARK
BARK
Distributed by Universal Press Syndicate
OOPS, I'M LATE FOR ANOTHER APPOINTMENT!
I'M GOING TO TURN YOU OVER TO MY ASSISTANT, SPOT
UH...
JIM DAVIS 2-8
© 2004 PAWS, INC. All Rights Reserved.
HOW'S IT GOING, PAL?
UH...
ACCORDING TO YOUR CHART, I'M TO BARK AT YOU, RIGHT?
UH...
www.garfield.com
ARF!
COME ON! IS THIS HOW YOU TREAT A REGULAR CUSTOMER?

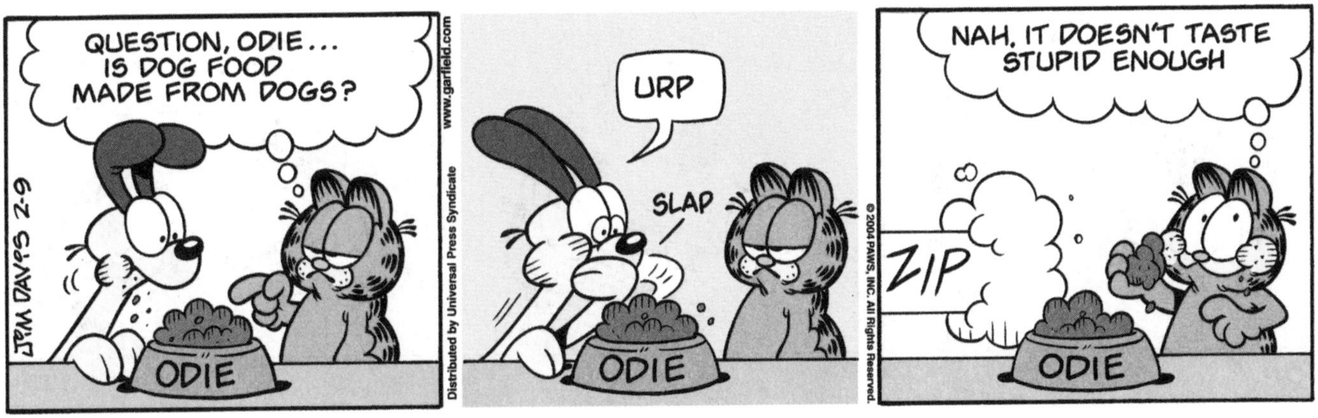
QUESTION, ODIE... IS DOG FOOD MADE FROM DOGS?
JIM DAVIS 2-9
ODIE
www.garfield.com
Distributed by Universal Press Syndicate
URP
SLAP
ODIE
© 2004 PAWS, INC. All Rights Reserved.
NAH, IT DOESN'T TASTE STUPID ENOUGH
ZIP
ODIE

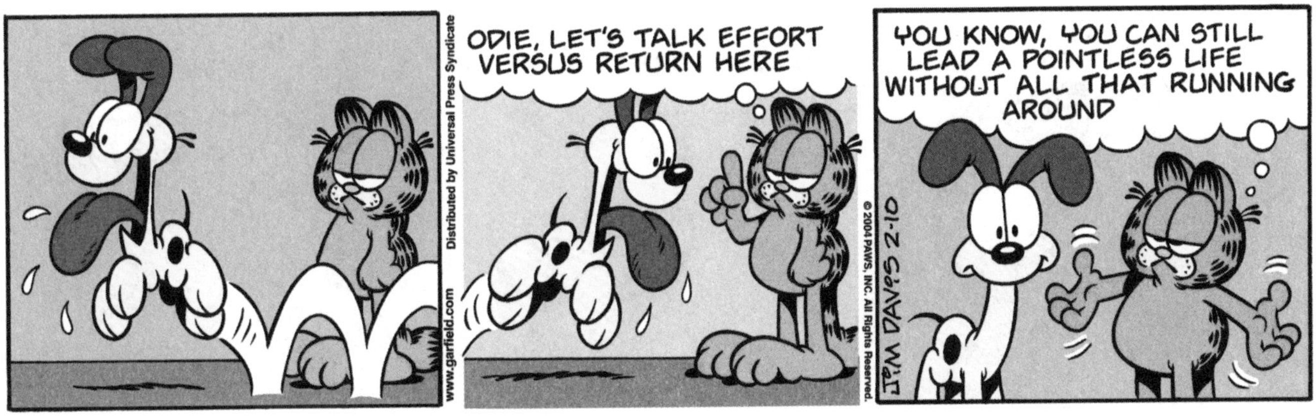
Distributed by Universal Press Syndicate
www.garfield.com
ODIE, LET'S TALK EFFORT VERSUS RETURN HERE
© 2004 PAWS, INC. All Rights Reserved.
YOU KNOW, YOU CAN STILL LEAD A POINTLESS LIFE WITHOUT ALL THAT RUNNING AROUND
JIM DAVIS 2-10

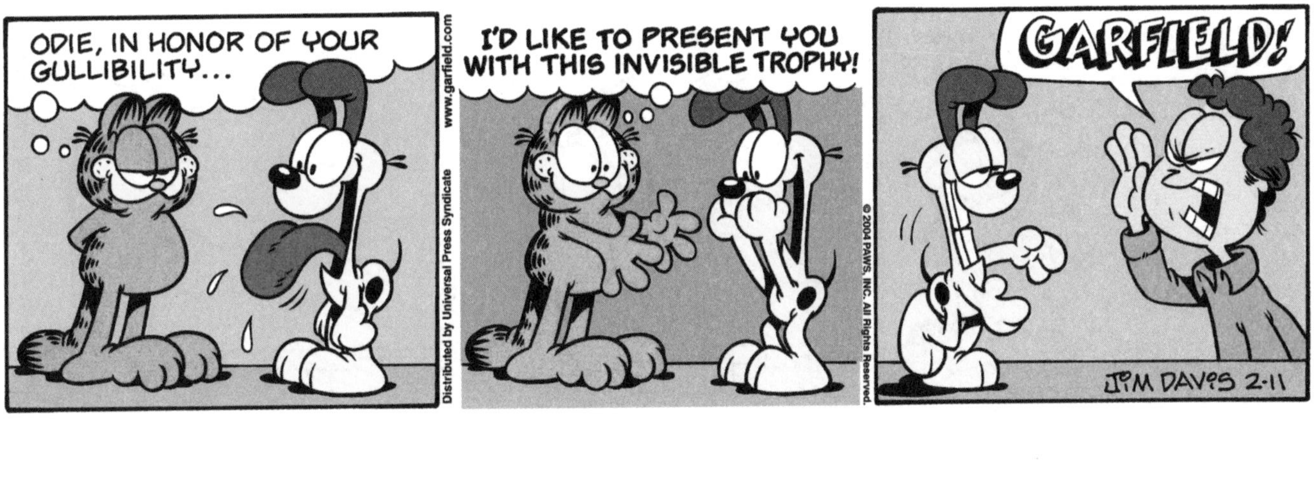
ODIE, IN HONOR OF YOUR GULLIBILITY...
www.garfield.com
Distributed by Universal Press Syndicate
I'D LIKE TO PRESENT YOU WITH THIS INVISIBLE TROPHY!
© 2004 PAWS, INC. All Rights Reserved.
GARFIELD!
JIM DAVIS 2-11

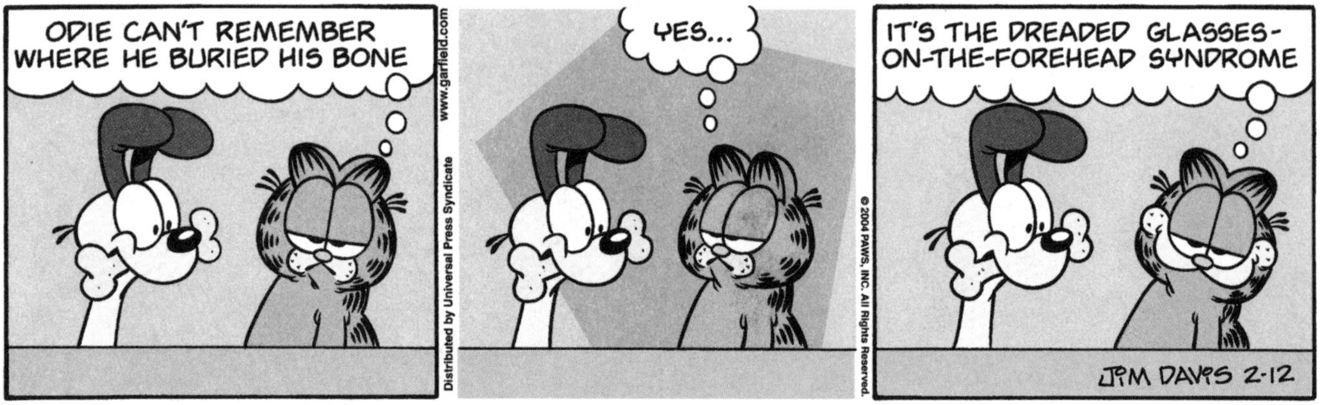
ODIE CAN'T REMEMBER WHERE HE BURIED HIS BONE
YES...
IT'S THE DREADED GLASSES-ON-THE-FOREHEAD SYNDROME
JIM DAVIS 2-12
www.garfield.com Distributed by Universal Press Syndicate
© 2004 PAWS, INC. All Rights Reserved.

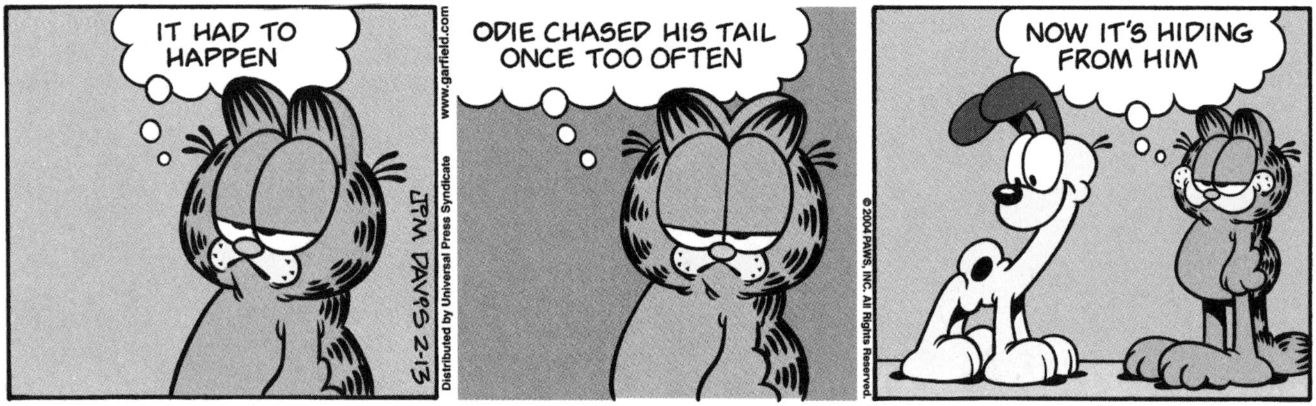
IT HAD TO HAPPEN
JIM DAVIS 2-13
ODIE CHASED HIS TAIL ONCE TOO OFTEN
NOW IT'S HIDING FROM HIM
www.garfield.com Distributed by Universal Press Syndicate
© 2004 PAWS, INC. All Rights Reserved.

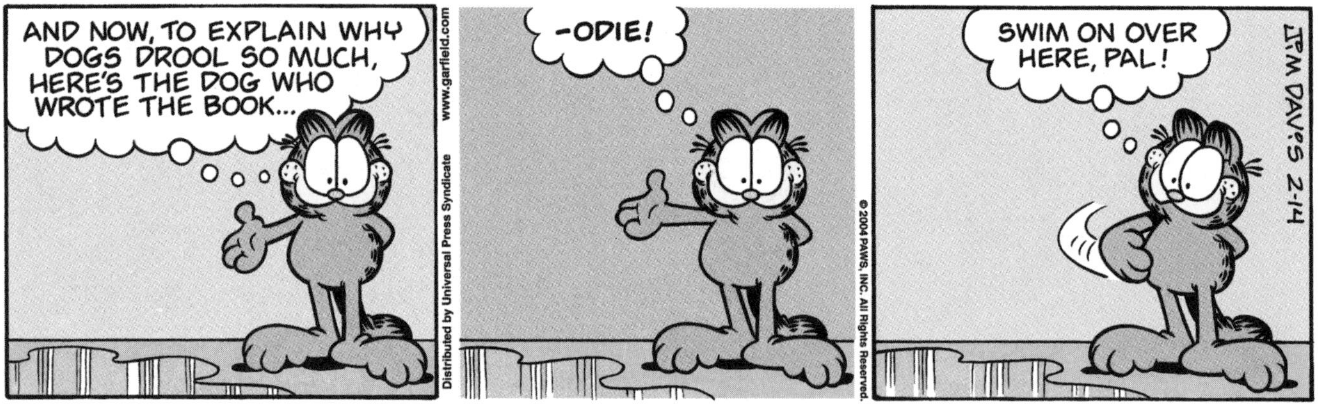
AND NOW, TO EXPLAIN WHY DOGS DROOL SO MUCH, HERE'S THE DOG WHO WROTE THE BOOK...
-ODIE!
SWIM ON OVER HERE, PAL!
JIM DAVIS 2-14
www.garfield.com Distributed by Universal Press Syndicate
© 2004 PAWS, INC. All Rights Reserved.

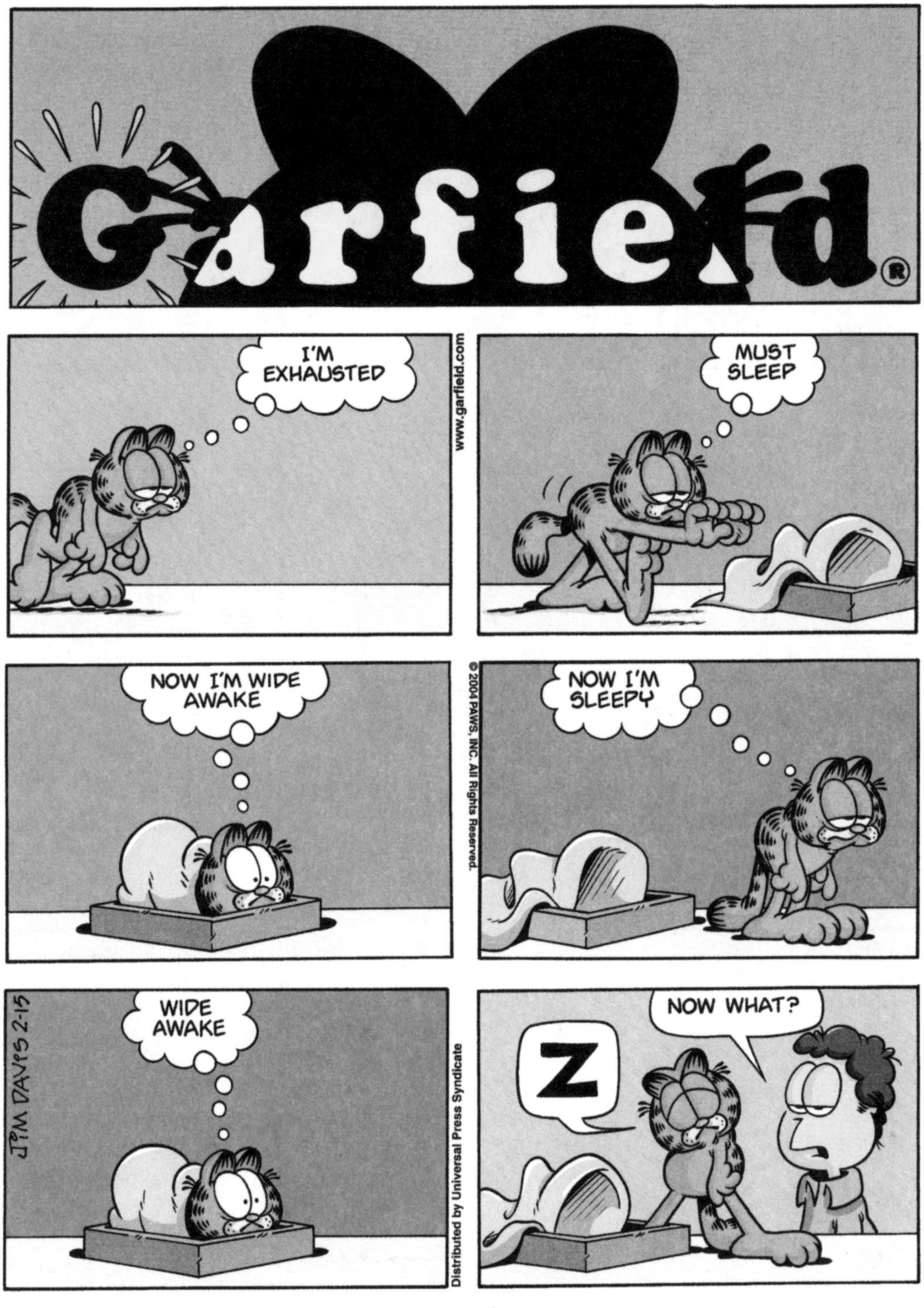
Garfield®
I'M EXHAUSTED
MUST SLEEP
NOW I'M WIDE AWAKE
NOW I'M SLEEPY
WIDE AWAKE
Z
NOW WHAT?
JIM DAVIS 2-15
www.garfield.com
© 2004 PAWS, INC. All Rights Reserved.
Distributed by Universal Press Syndicate

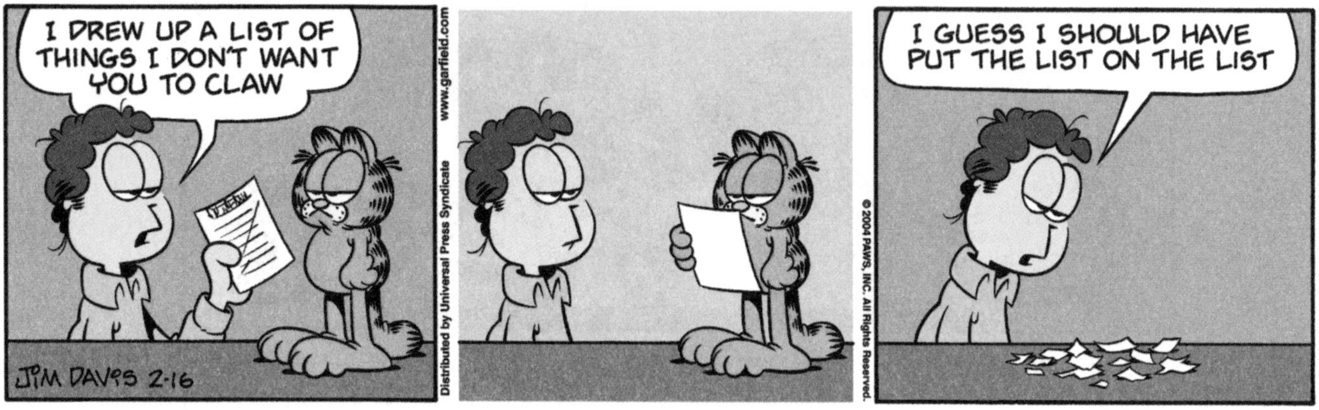
I DREW UP A LIST OF THINGS I DON'T WANT YOU TO CLAW
JIM DAVIS 2·16
www.garfield.com
Distributed by Universal Press Syndicate
© 2004 PAWS, INC. All Rights Reserved.
I GUESS I SHOULD HAVE PUT THE LIST ON THE LIST

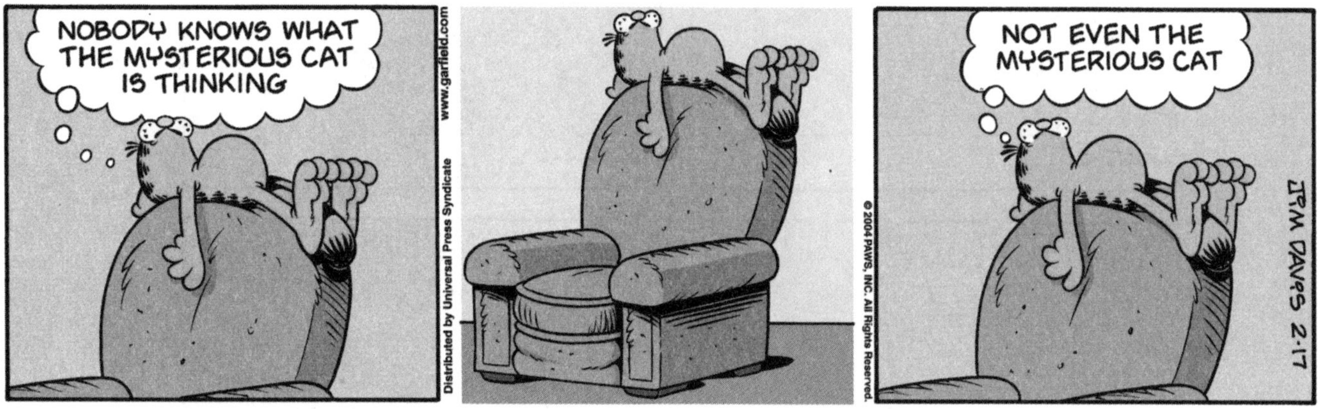
NOBODY KNOWS WHAT THE MYSTERIOUS CAT IS THINKING
www.garfield.com
Distributed by Universal Press Syndicate
© 2004 PAWS, INC. All Rights Reserved.
NOT EVEN THE MYSTERIOUS CAT
JIM DAVIS 2·17

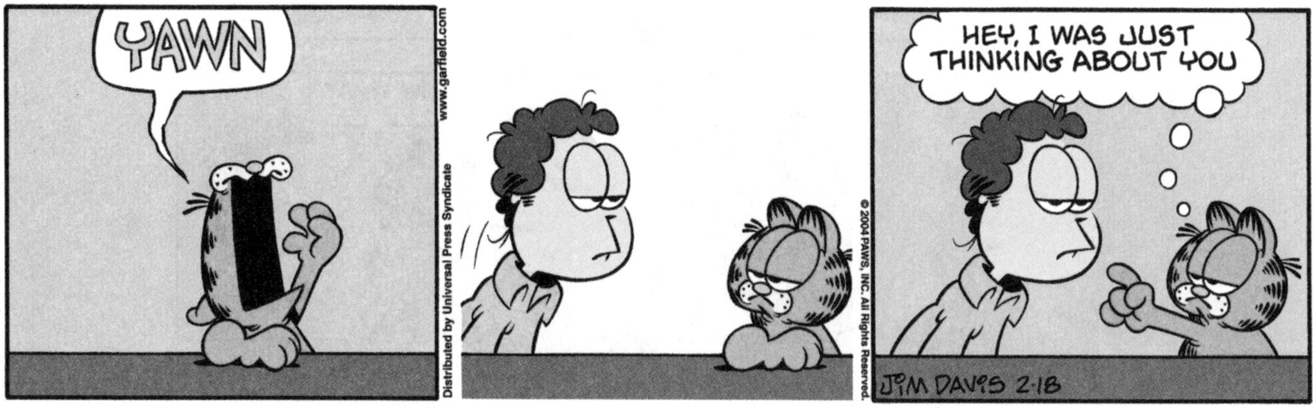
YAWN
www.garfield.com
Distributed by Universal Press Syndicate
© 2004 PAWS, INC. All Rights Reserved.
HEY, I WAS JUST THINKING ABOUT YOU
JIM DAVIS 2·18

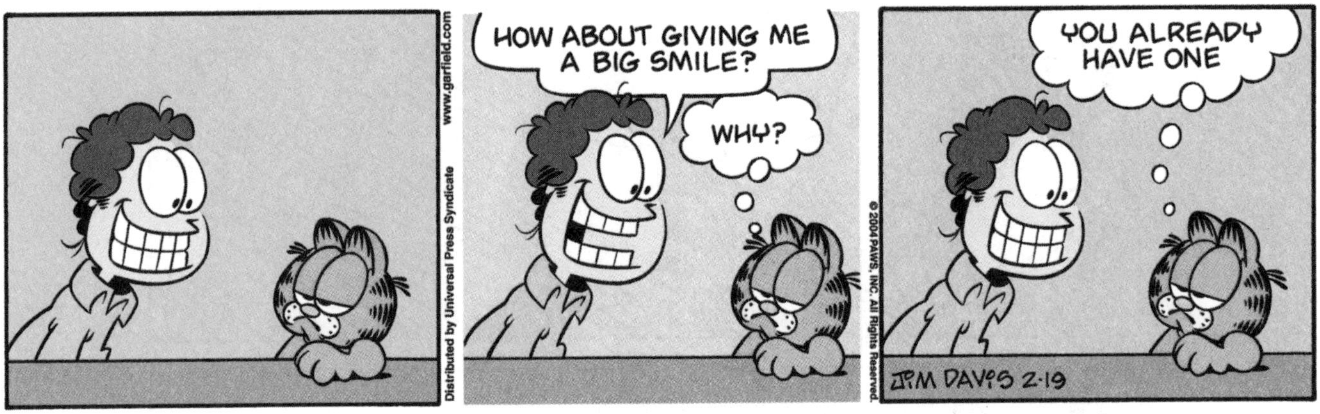
www.garfield.com
Distributed by Universal Press Syndicate
HOW ABOUT GIVING ME A BIG SMILE?
WHY?
© 2004 PAWS, INC. All Rights Reserved.
YOU ALREADY HAVE ONE
JIM DAVIS 2-19

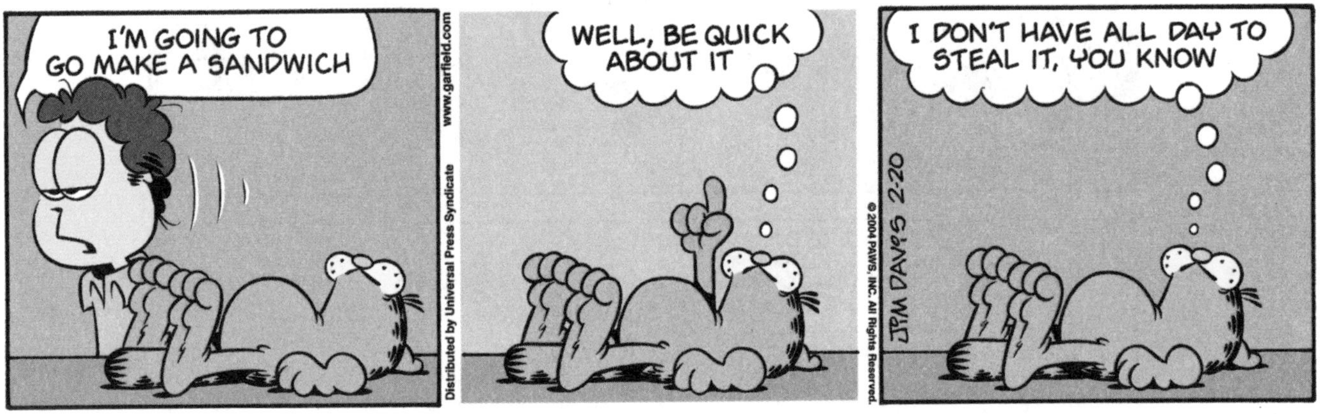
I'M GOING TO GO MAKE A SANDWICH
www.garfield.com
Distributed by Universal Press Syndicate
WELL, BE QUICK ABOUT IT
© 2004 PAWS, INC. All Rights Reserved.
JIM DAVIS 2-20
I DON'T HAVE ALL DAY TO STEAL IT, YOU KNOW

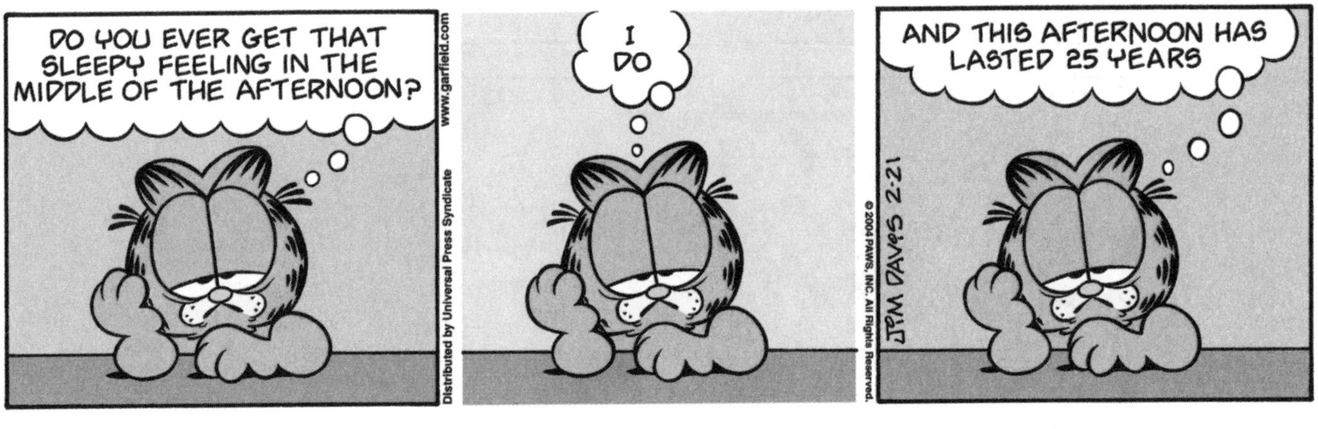
DO YOU EVER GET THAT SLEEPY FEELING IN THE MIDDLE OF THE AFTERNOON?
www.garfield.com
Distributed by Universal Press Syndicate
I DO
© 2004 PAWS, INC. All Rights Reserved.
JIM DAVIS 2-21
AND THIS AFTERNOON HAS LASTED 25 YEARS

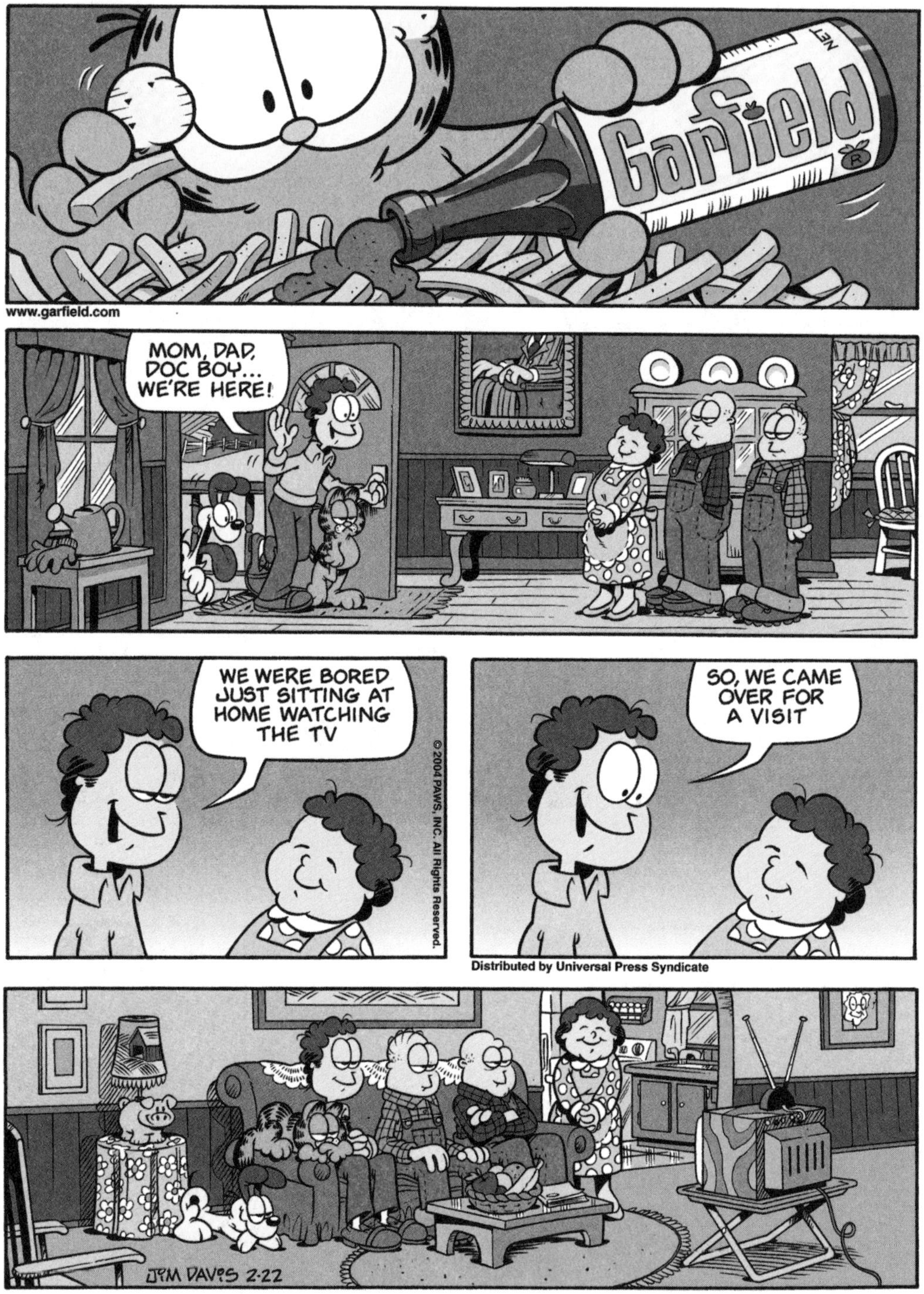
Garfield
NET
www.garfield.com
MOM, DAD, DOG BOY... WE'RE HERE!
WE WERE BORED JUST SITTING AT HOME WATCHING THE TV
© 2004 PAWS, INC. All Rights Reserved.
SO, WE CAME OVER FOR A VISIT
Distributed by Universal Press Syndicate
JIM DAVIS 2·22

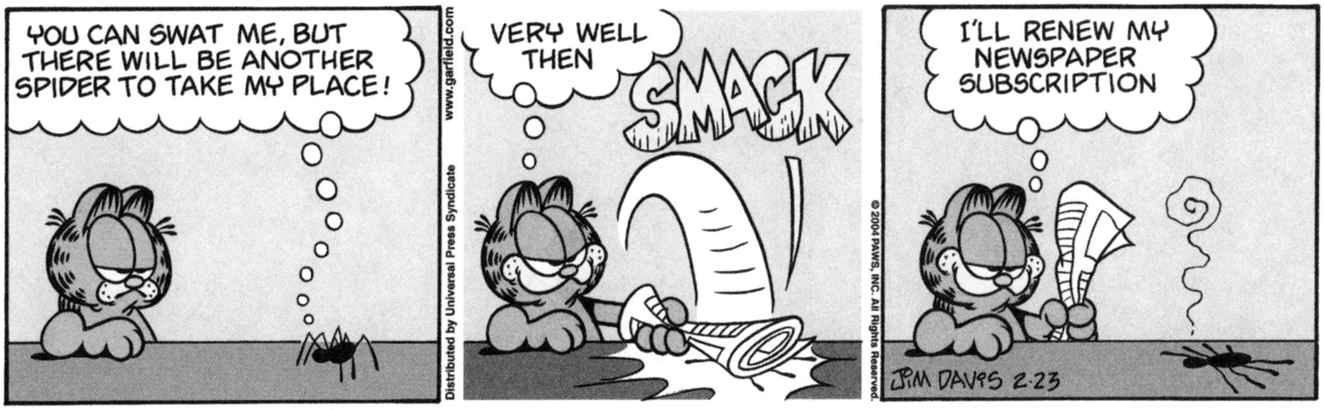
YOU CAN SWAT ME, BUT THERE WILL BE ANOTHER SPIDER TO TAKE MY PLACE!
www.garfield.com
Distributed by Universal Press Syndicate
VERY WELL THEN
SMACK
© 2004 PAWS, INC. All Rights Reserved.
I'LL RENEW MY NEWSPAPER SUBSCRIPTION
JIM DAVIS 2-23

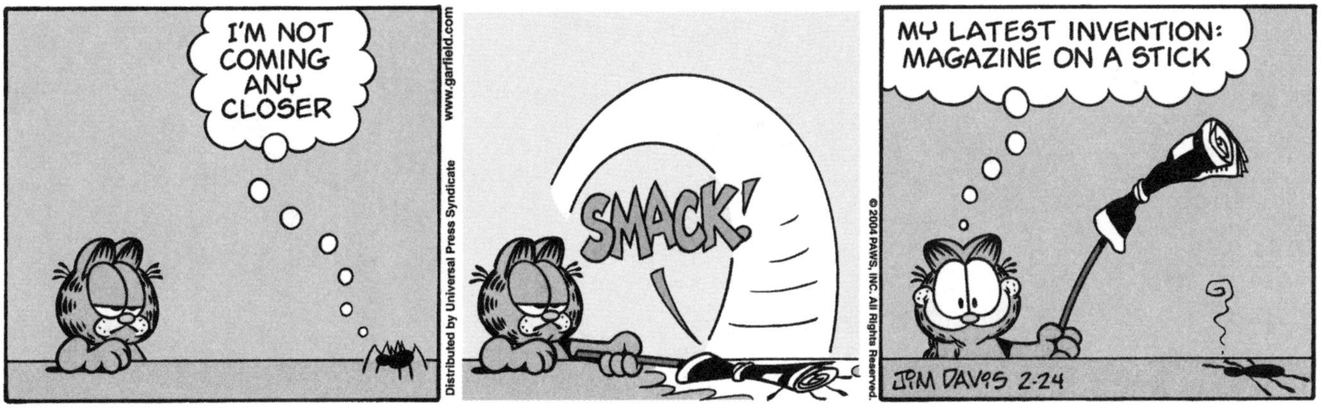
I'M NOT COMING ANY CLOSER
www.garfield.com
Distributed by Universal Press Syndicate
SMACK!
© 2004 PAWS, INC. All Rights Reserved.
MY LATEST INVENTION: MAGAZINE ON A STICK
JIM DAVIS 2-24

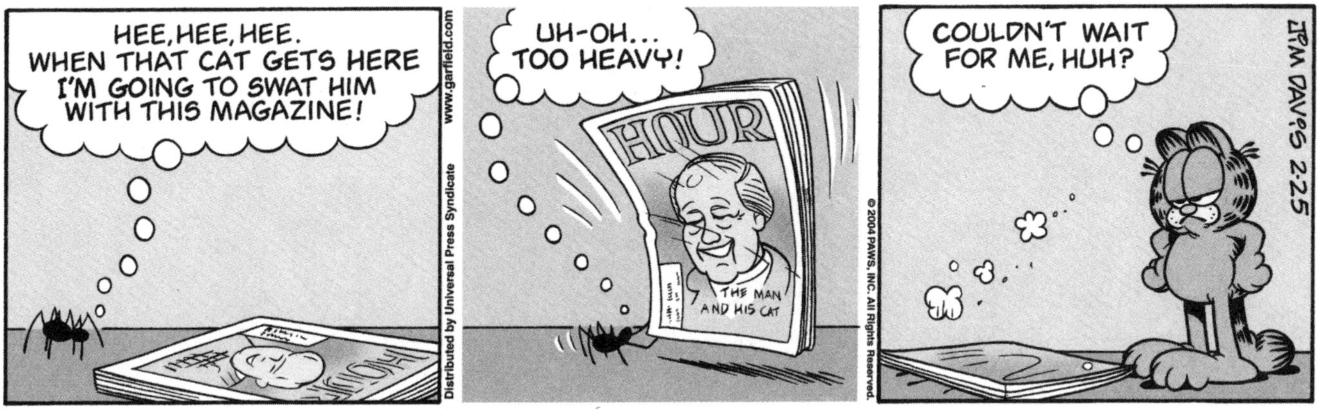
HEE, HEE, HEE. WHEN THAT CAT GETS HERE I'M GOING TO SWAT HIM WITH THIS MAGAZINE!
www.garfield.com
Distributed by Universal Press Syndicate
UH-OH... TOO HEAVY!
HOUR
THE MAN AND HIS CAT
© 2004 PAWS, INC. All Rights Reserved.
COULDN'T WAIT FOR ME, HUH?
JIM DAVIS 2-25

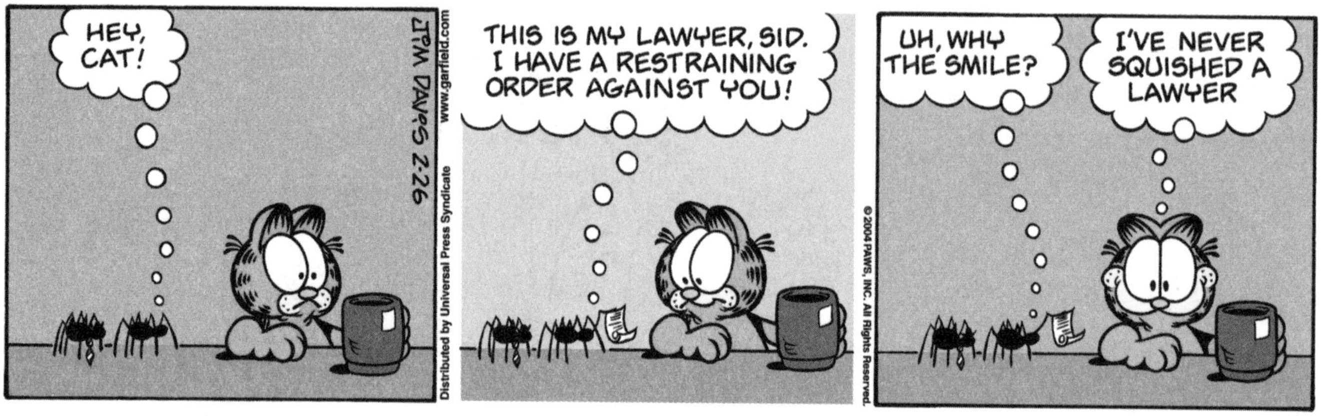
HEY, CAT!
JIM DAVIS 2·26
www.garfield.com
Distributed by Universal Press Syndicate
THIS IS MY LAWYER, SID. I HAVE A RESTRAINING ORDER AGAINST YOU!
© 2004 PAWS, INC. All Rights Reserved.
UH, WHY THE SMILE?
I'VE NEVER SQUISHED A LAWYER

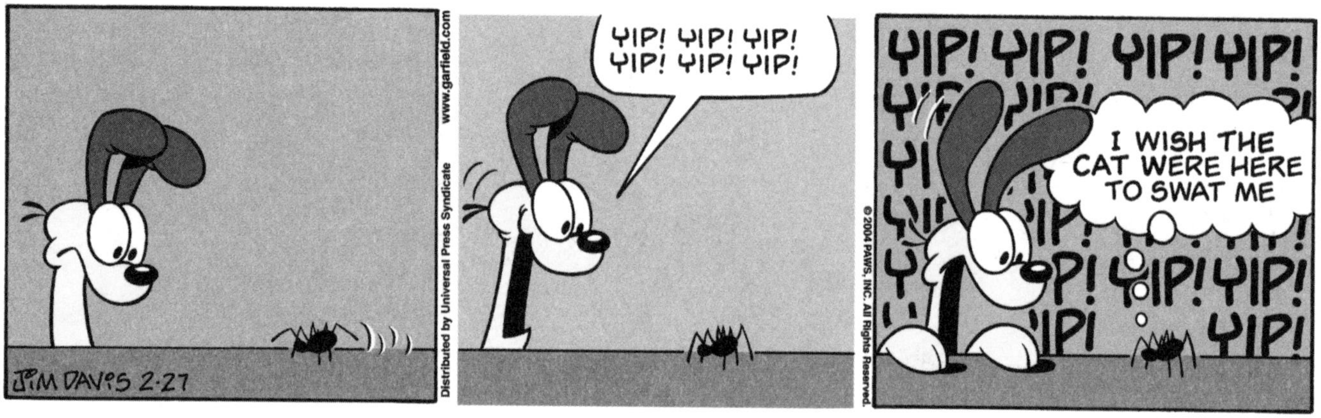
JIM DAVIS 2·27
www.garfield.com
Distributed by Universal Press Syndicate
YIP! YIP! YIP! YIP! YIP! YIP!
© 2004 PAWS, INC. All Rights Reserved.
YIP! YIP! YIP! YIP!
I WISH THE CAT WERE HERE TO SWAT ME

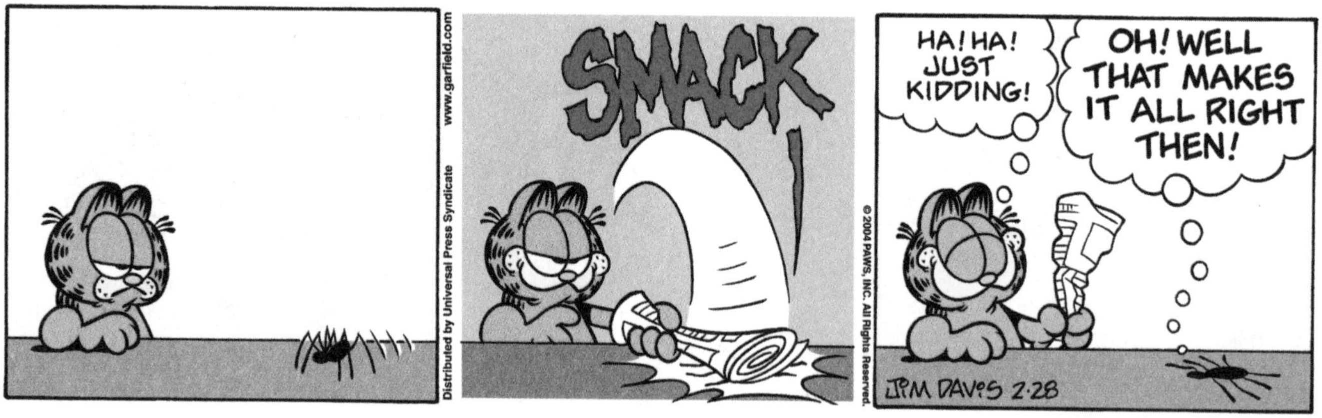
www.garfield.com
Distributed by Universal Press Syndicate
SMACK
© 2004 PAWS, INC. All Rights Reserved.
HA! HA! JUST KIDDING!
OH! WELL THAT MAKES IT ALL RIGHT THEN!
JIM DAVIS 2·28

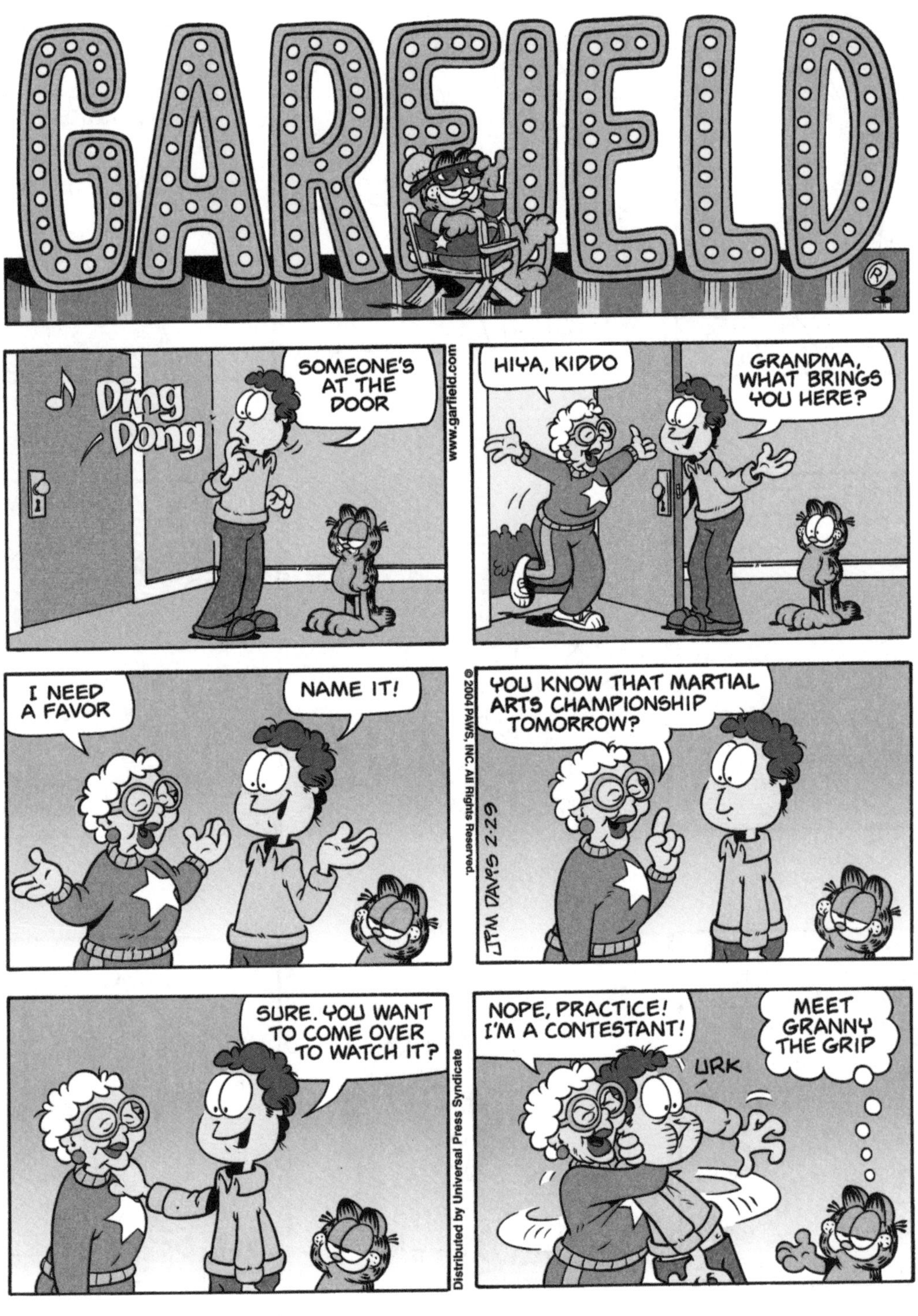
GARFIELD
Ding Dong
SOMEONE'S AT THE DOOR
HIYA, KIDDO
GRANDMA, WHAT BRINGS YOU HERE?
I NEED A FAVOR
NAME IT!
YOU KNOW THAT MARTIAL ARTS CHAMPIONSHIP TOMORROW?
SURE. YOU WANT TO COME OVER TO WATCH IT?
NOPE, PRACTICE! I'M A CONTESTANT!
URK
MEET GRANNY THE GRIP
www.garfield.com
© 2004 PAWS, INC. All Rights Reserved.
Distributed by Universal Press Syndicate
JPM DAVIS 2-29

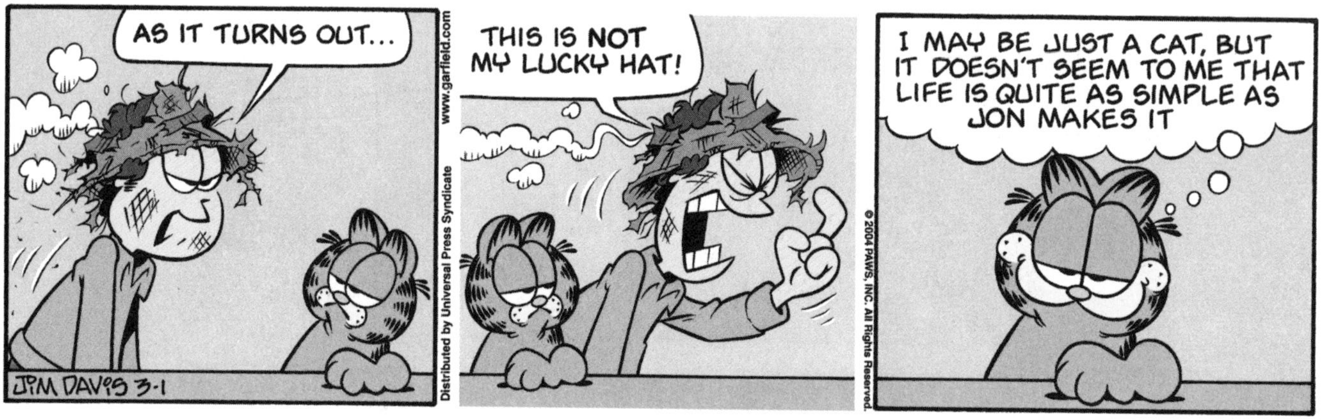
AS IT TURNS OUT...
JIM DAVIS 3-1
THIS IS NOT MY LUCKY HAT!
I MAY BE JUST A CAT, BUT IT DOESN'T SEEM TO ME THAT LIFE IS QUITE AS SIMPLE AS JON MAKES IT
www.garfield.com
Distributed by Universal Press Syndicate
© 2004 PAWS, INC. All Rights Reserved.

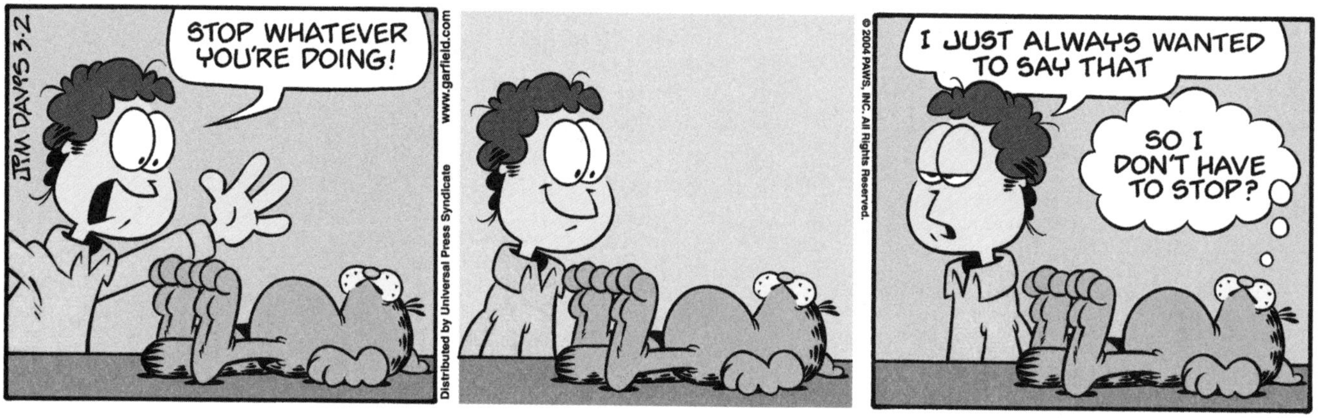
JIM DAVIS 3-2
STOP WHATEVER YOU'RE DOING!
I JUST ALWAYS WANTED TO SAY THAT
SO I DON'T HAVE TO STOP?
www.garfield.com
Distributed by Universal Press Syndicate
© 2004 PAWS, INC. All Rights Reserved.

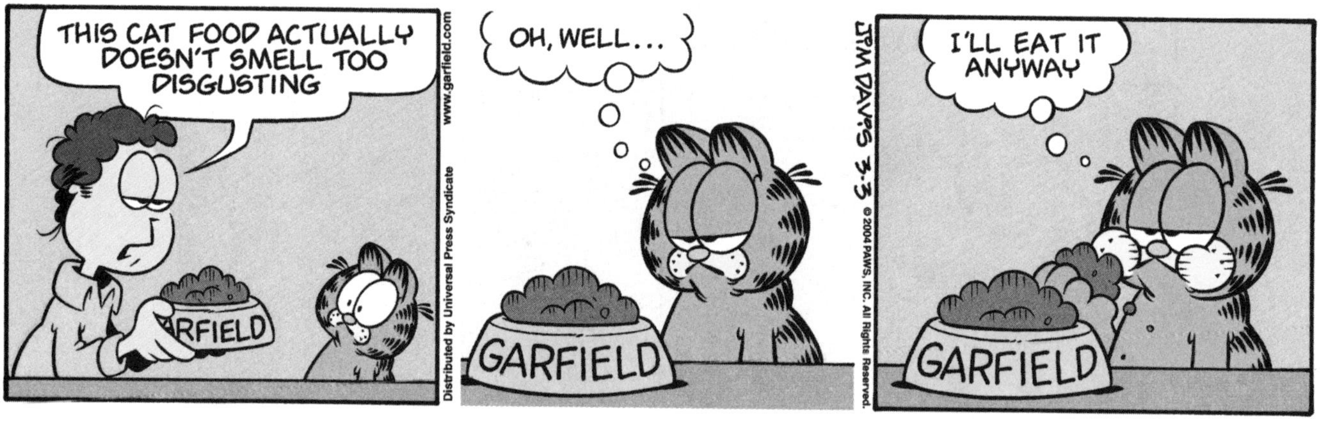
THIS CAT FOOD ACTUALLY DOESN'T SMELL TOO DISGUSTING
RFIELD
OH, WELL...
GARFIELD
JIM DAVIS 3-3
I'LL EAT IT ANYWAY
GARFIELD
www.garfield.com
Distributed by Universal Press Syndicate
© 2004 PAWS, INC. All Rights Reserved.

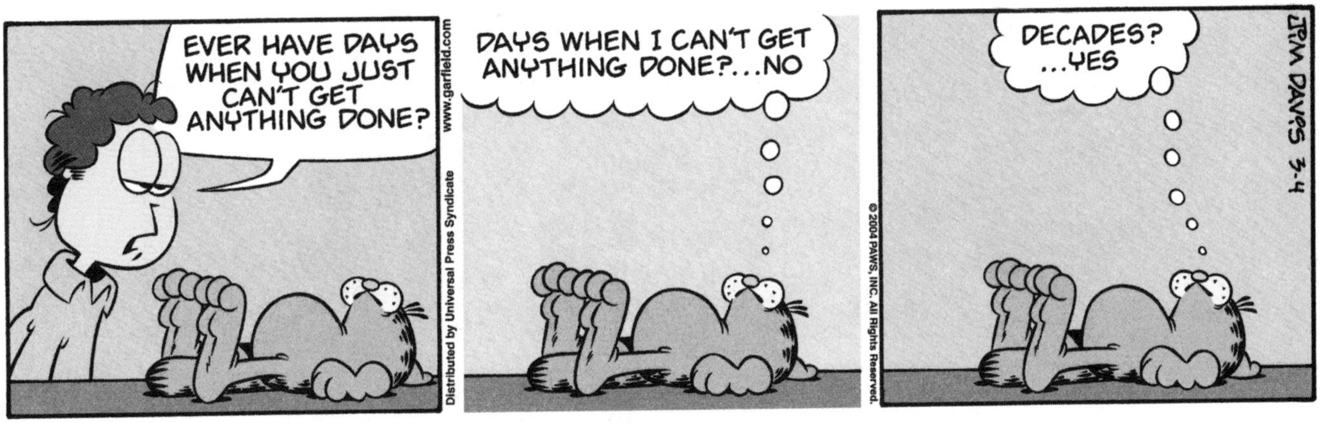
EVER HAVE DAYS WHEN YOU JUST CAN'T GET ANYTHING DONE?
Distributed by Universal Press Syndicate www.garfield.com
DAYS WHEN I CAN'T GET ANYTHING DONE?...NO
© 2004 PAWS, INC. All Rights Reserved.
DECADES? ...YES
JIM DAVIS 3-4

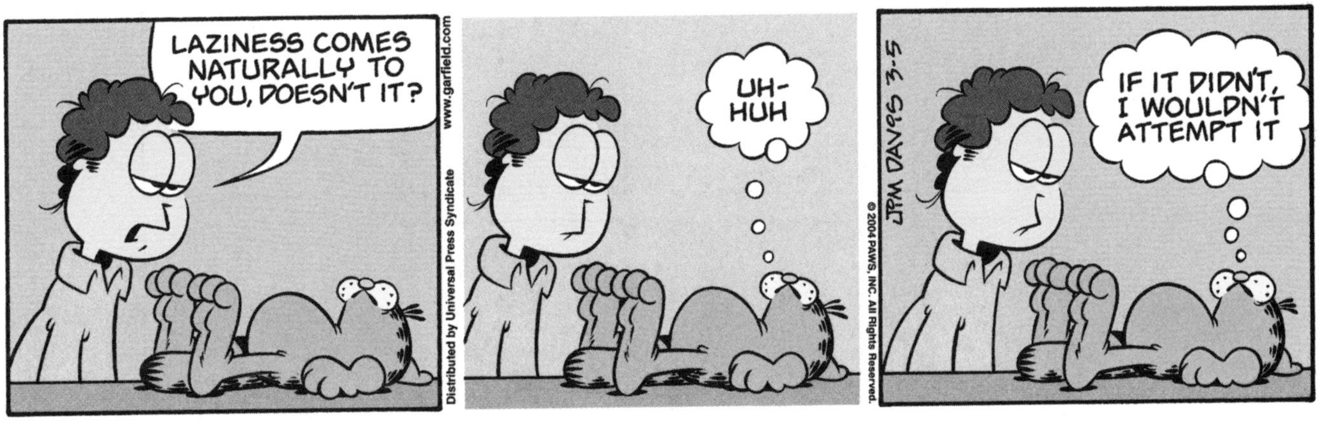
LAZINESS COMES NATURALLY TO YOU, DOESN'T IT?
Distributed by Universal Press Syndicate www.garfield.com
UH-HUH
© 2004 PAWS, INC. All Rights Reserved.
JIM DAVIS 3-5
IF IT DIDN'T, I WOULDN'T ATTEMPT IT

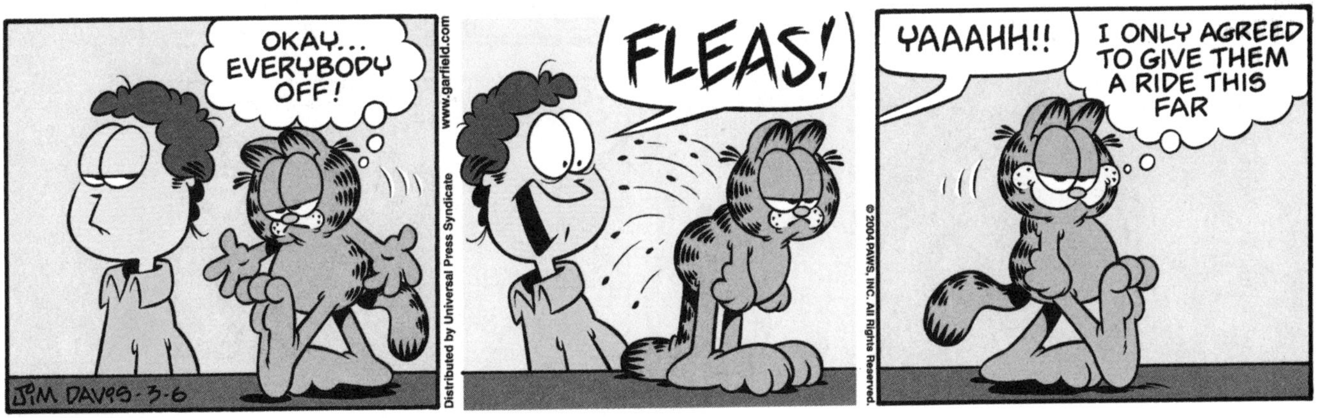
OKAY... EVERYBODY OFF!
JIM DAVIS 3-6
Distributed by Universal Press Syndicate www.garfield.com
FLEAS!
© 2004 PAWS, INC. All Rights Reserved.
YAAAHH!!
I ONLY AGREED TO GIVE THEM A RIDE THIS FAR

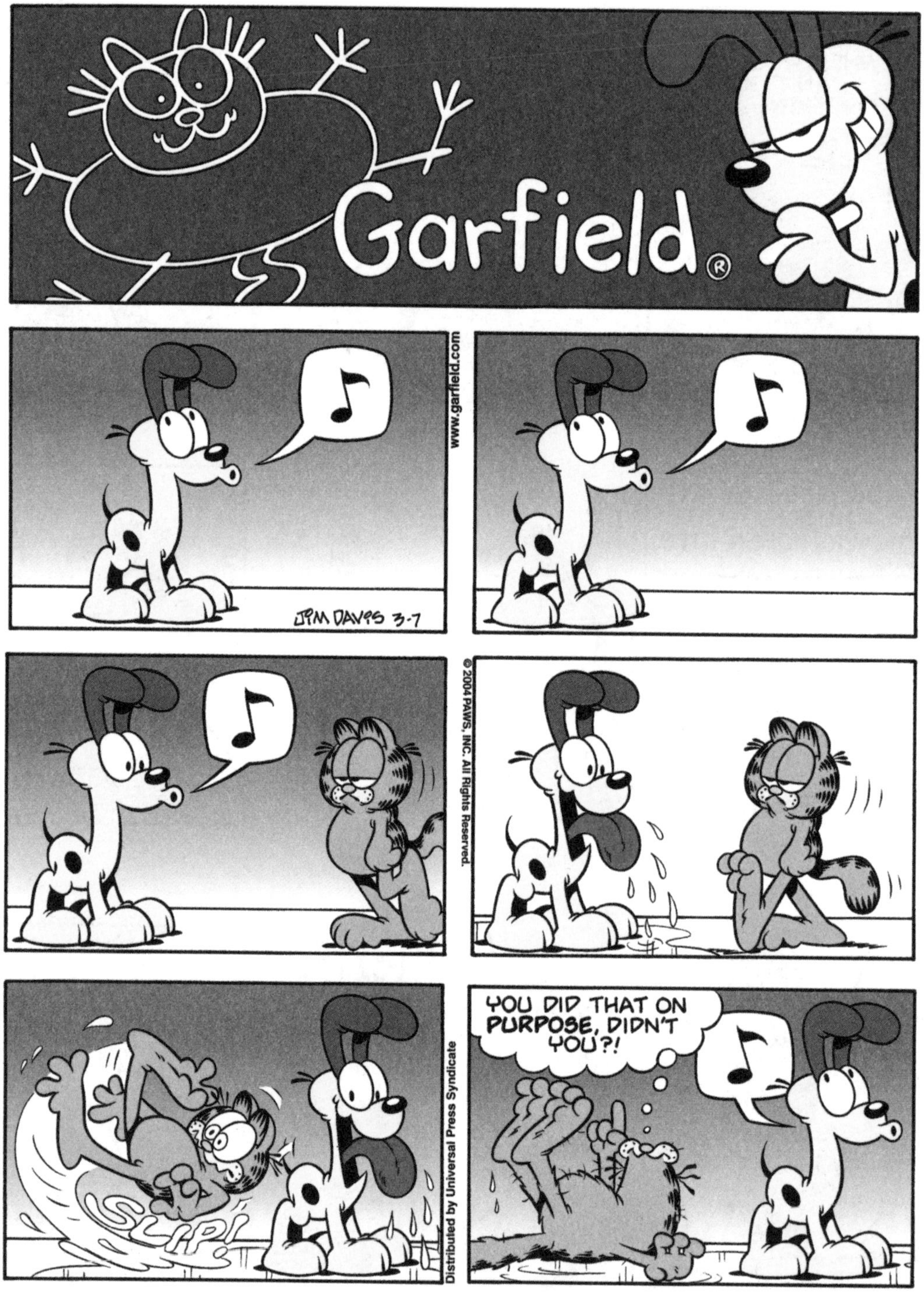
Garfield®
www.garfield.com
JIM DAVIS 3-7
© 2004 PAWS, INC. All Rights Reserved.
Distributed by Universal Press Syndicate
SLIP!
YOU DID THAT ON PURPOSE, DIDN'T YOU?!

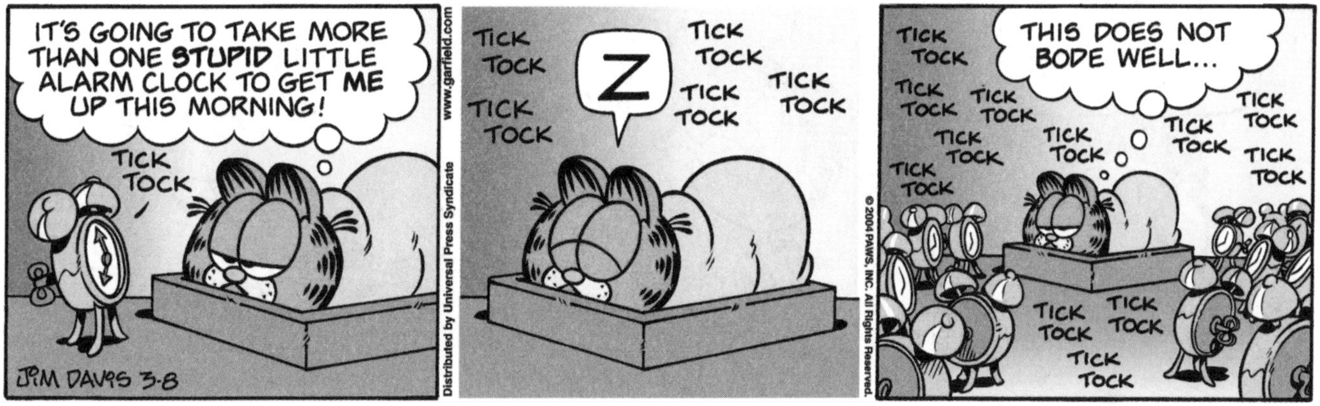
IT'S GOING TO TAKE MORE THAN ONE STUPID LITTLE ALARM CLOCK TO GET ME UP THIS MORNING!
TICK TOCK
JIM DAVIS 3-8
www.garfield.com
Distributed by Universal Press Syndicate
TICK TOCK
TICK TOCK
Z
TICK TOCK
TICK TOCK
TICK TOCK
© 2004 PAWS, INC. All Rights Reserved.
THIS DOES NOT BODE WELL...
TICK TOCK

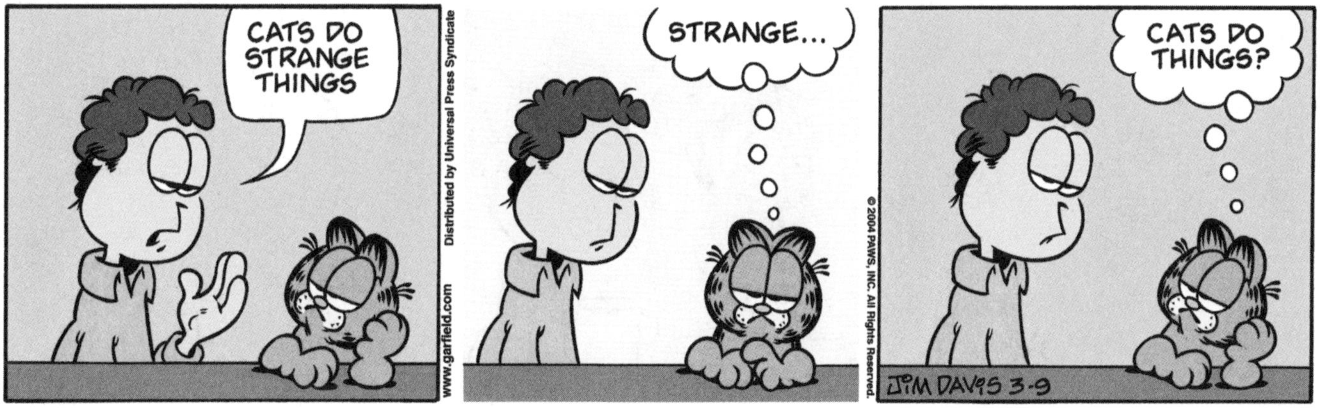
CATS DO STRANGE THINGS
Distributed by Universal Press Syndicate
www.garfield.com
STRANGE...
© 2004 PAWS, INC. All Rights Reserved.
CATS DO THINGS?
JIM DAVIS 3-9

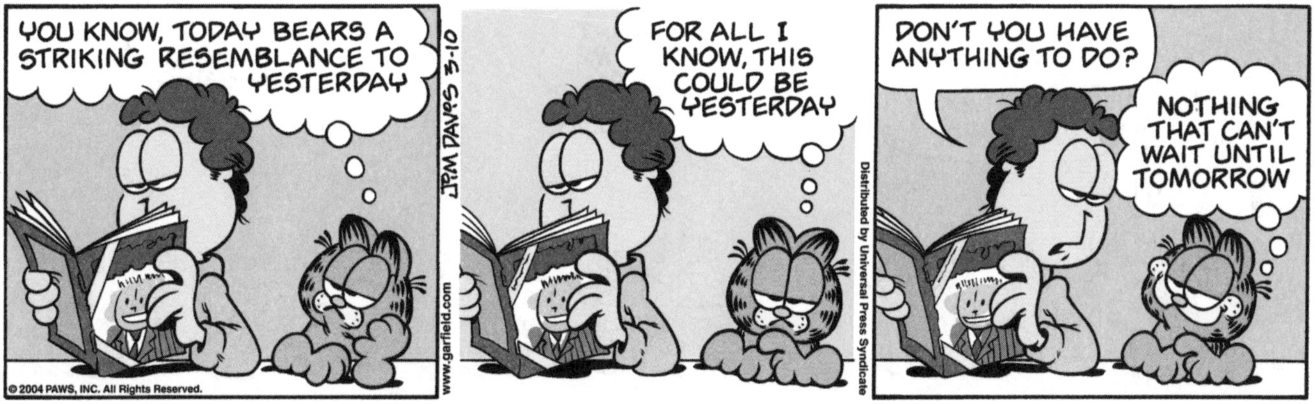
YOU KNOW, TODAY BEARS A STRIKING RESEMBLANCE TO YESTERDAY
© 2004 PAWS, INC. All Rights Reserved.
JIM DAVIS 3-10
www.garfield.com
FOR ALL I KNOW, THIS COULD BE YESTERDAY
Distributed by Universal Press Syndicate
DON'T YOU HAVE ANYTHING TO DO?
NOTHING THAT CAN'T WAIT UNTIL TOMORROW

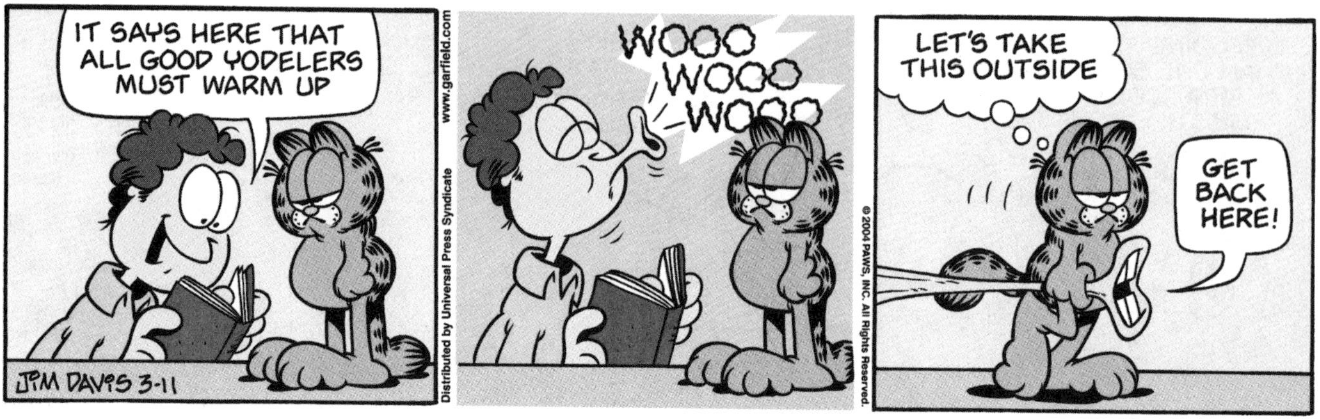
IT SAYS HERE THAT ALL GOOD YODELERS MUST WARM UP
JIM DAVIS 3-11
www.garfield.com
Distributed by Universal Press Syndicate
WOOO WOOO WOOO
© 2004 PAWS, INC. All Rights Reserved.
LET'S TAKE THIS OUTSIDE
GET BACK HERE!

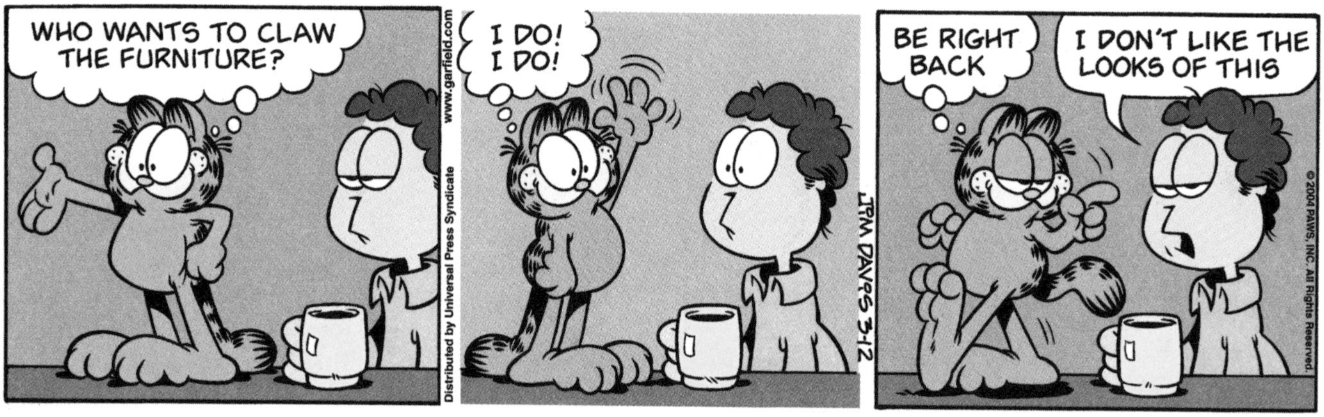
WHO WANTS TO CLAW THE FURNITURE?
www.garfield.com
Distributed by Universal Press Syndicate
I DO! I DO!
JIM DAVIS 3-12
BE RIGHT BACK
I DON'T LIKE THE LOOKS OF THIS
© 2004 PAWS, INC. All Rights Reserved.

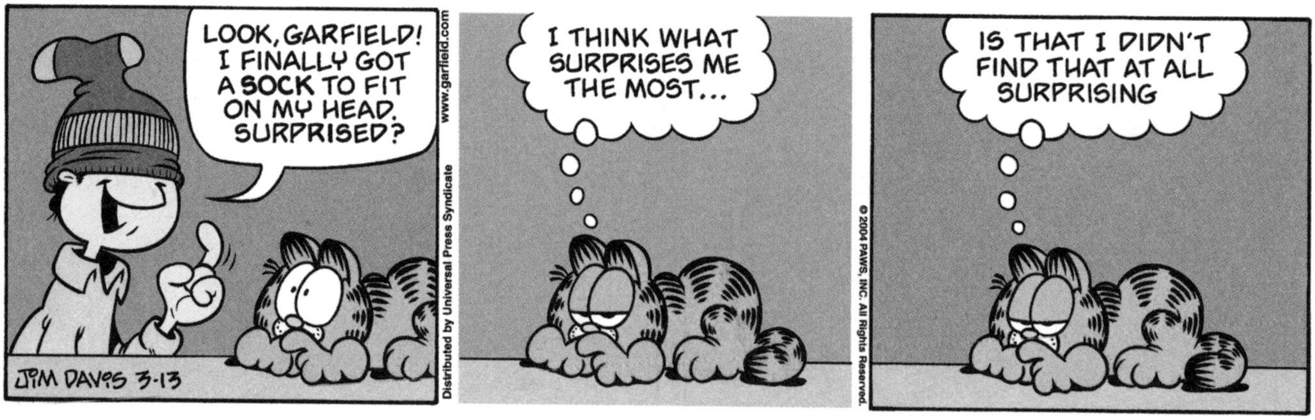
LOOK, GARFIELD! I FINALLY GOT A SOCK TO FIT ON MY HEAD. SURPRISED?
JIM DAVIS 3-13
www.garfield.com
Distributed by Universal Press Syndicate
I THINK WHAT SURPRISES ME THE MOST...
© 2004 PAWS, INC. All Rights Reserved.
IS THAT I DIDN'T FIND THAT AT ALL SURPRISING

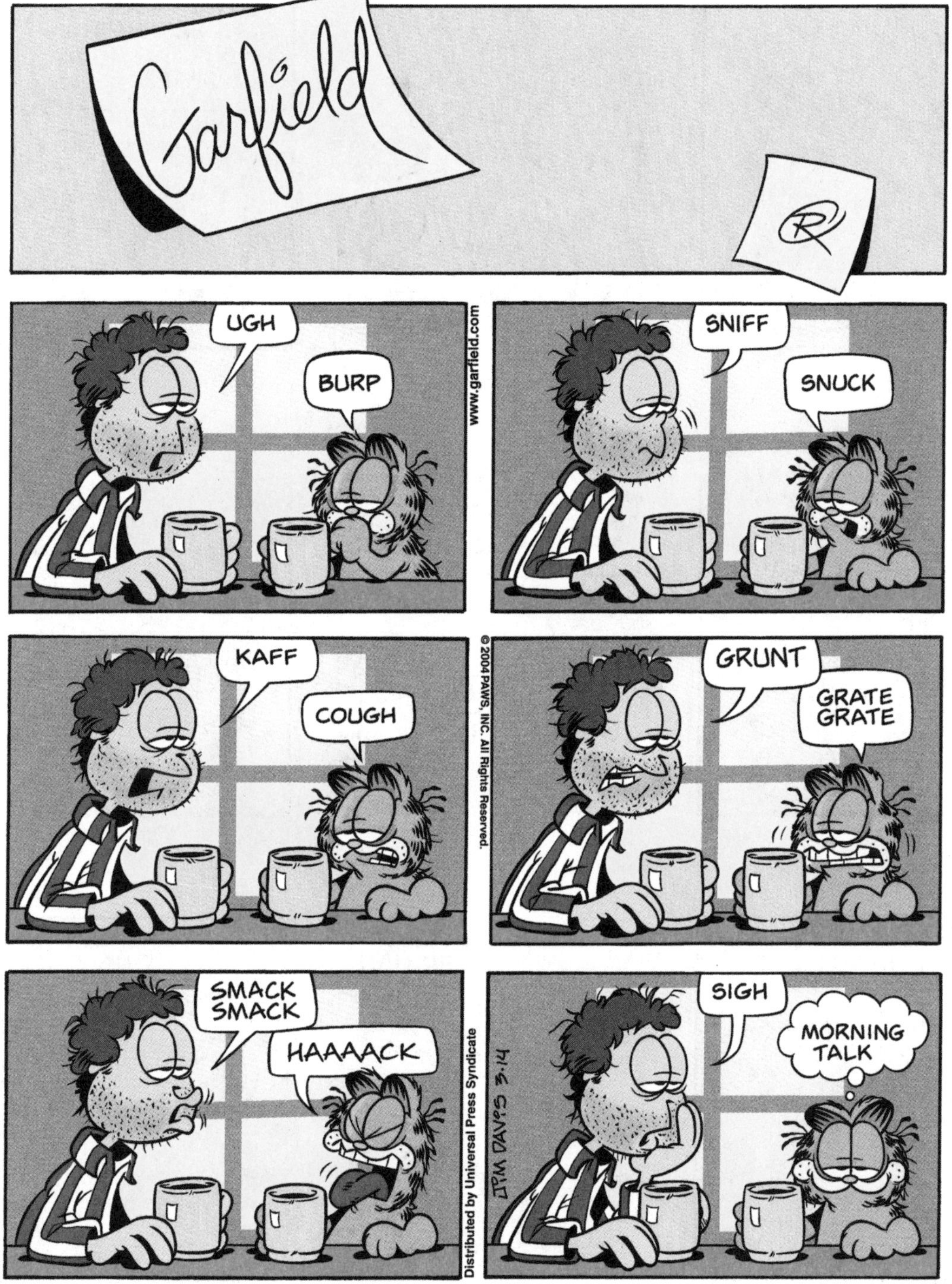
Garfield
UGH
BURP
SNIFF
SNUCK
KAFF
COUGH
GRUNT
GRATE GRATE
SMACK SMACK
HAAAACK
SIGH
MORNING TALK
JPM DAVPS 3.14

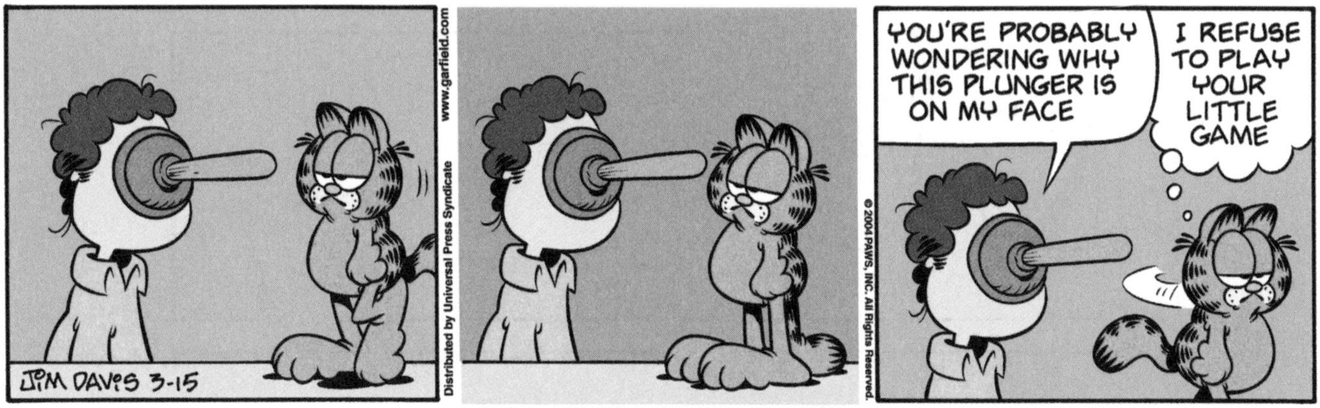
JIM DAVIS 3-15
www.garfield.com
Distributed by Universal Press Syndicate
YOU'RE PROBABLY WONDERING WHY THIS PLUNGER IS ON MY FACE
I REFUSE TO PLAY YOUR LITTLE GAME
© 2004 PAWS, INC. All Rights Reserved.

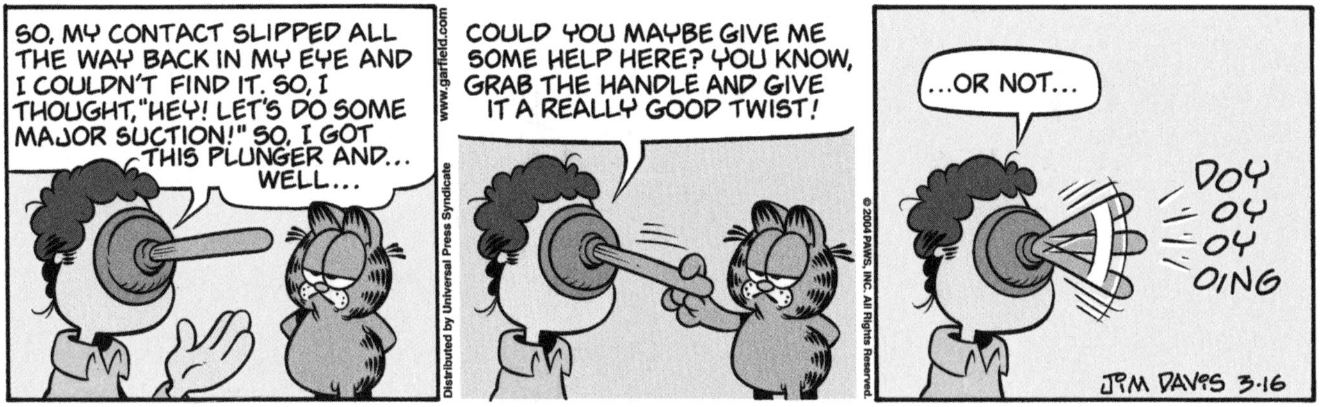
SO, MY CONTACT SLIPPED ALL THE WAY BACK IN MY EYE AND I COULDN'T FIND IT. SO, I THOUGHT, "HEY! LET'S DO SOME MAJOR SUCTION!" SO, I GOT THIS PLUNGER AND... WELL...
www.garfield.com
Distributed by Universal Press Syndicate
COULD YOU MAYBE GIVE ME SOME HELP HERE? YOU KNOW, GRAB THE HANDLE AND GIVE IT A REALLY GOOD TWIST!
© 2004 PAWS, INC. All Rights Reserved.
...OR NOT...
DOY
OY
OY
OING
JIM DAVIS 3-16

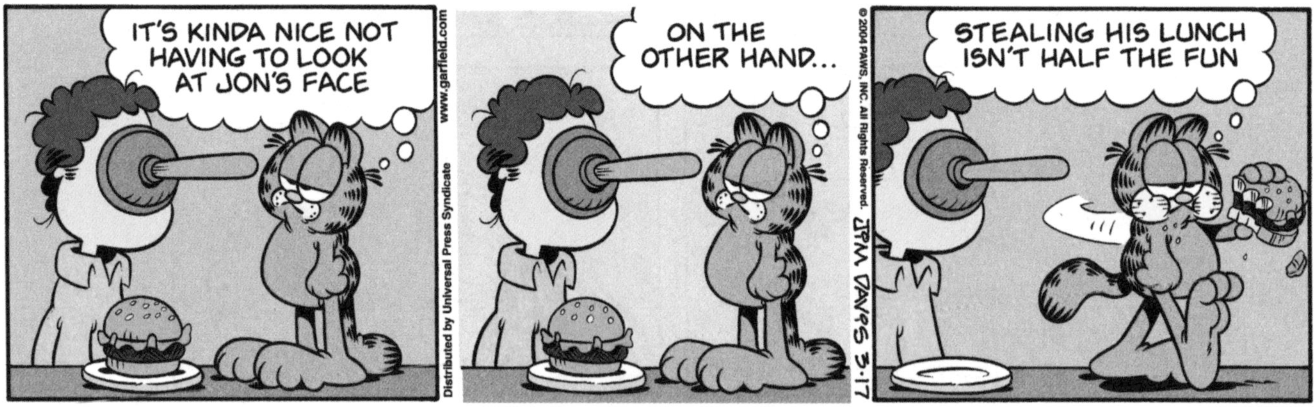
IT'S KINDA NICE NOT HAVING TO LOOK AT JON'S FACE
www.garfield.com
Distributed by Universal Press Syndicate
ON THE OTHER HAND...
© 2004 PAWS, INC. All Rights Reserved.
JIM DAVIS 3-17
STEALING HIS LUNCH ISN'T HALF THE FUN

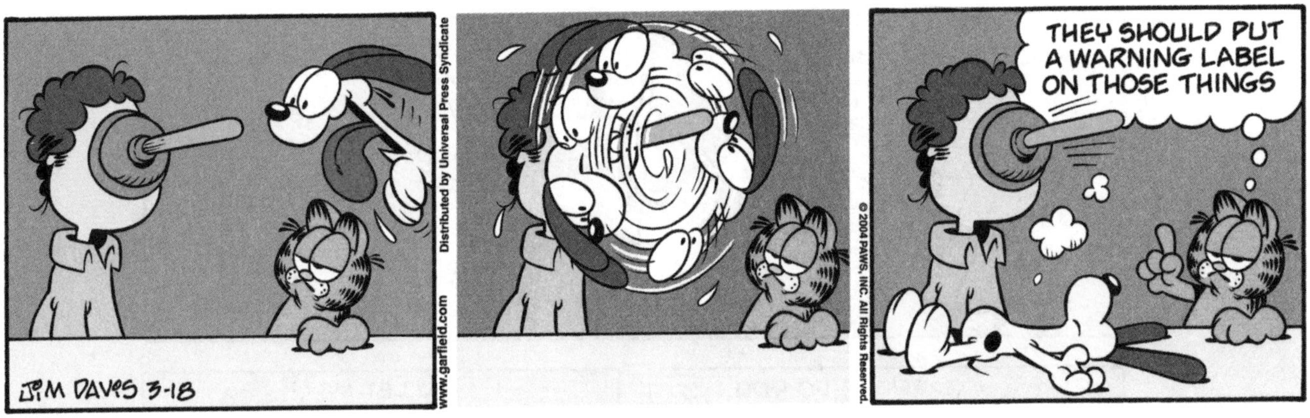
JIM DAVIS 3-18
www.garfield.com
Distributed by Universal Press Syndicate
© 2004 PAWS, INC. All Rights Reserved.
THEY SHOULD PUT A WARNING LABEL ON THOSE THINGS

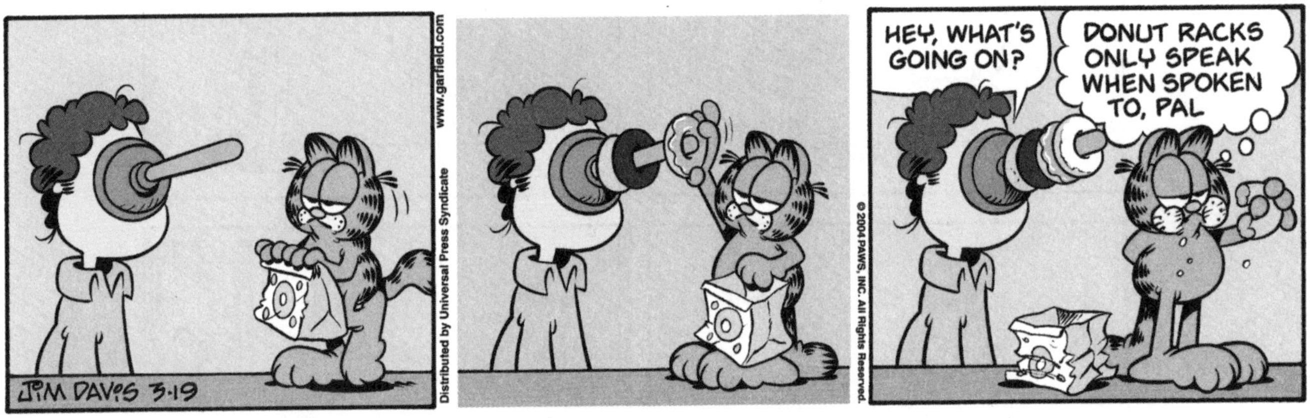
JIM DAVIS 3-19
www.garfield.com
Distributed by Universal Press Syndicate
© 2004 PAWS, INC. All Rights Reserved.
HEY, WHAT'S GOING ON?
DONUT RACKS ONLY SPEAK WHEN SPOKEN TO, PAL

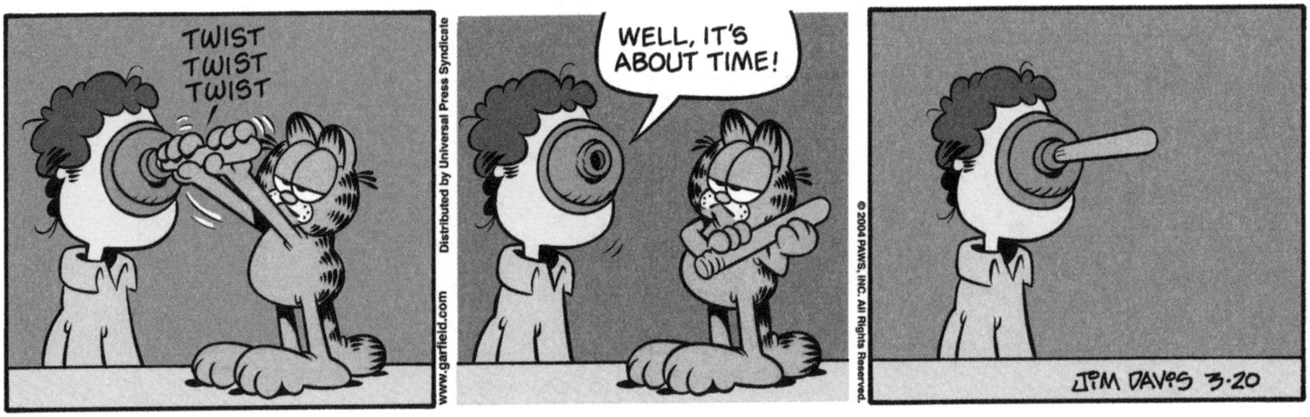
TWIST TWIST TWIST
www.garfield.com
Distributed by Universal Press Syndicate
WELL, IT'S ABOUT TIME!
© 2004 PAWS, INC. All Rights Reserved.
JIM DAVIS 3-20

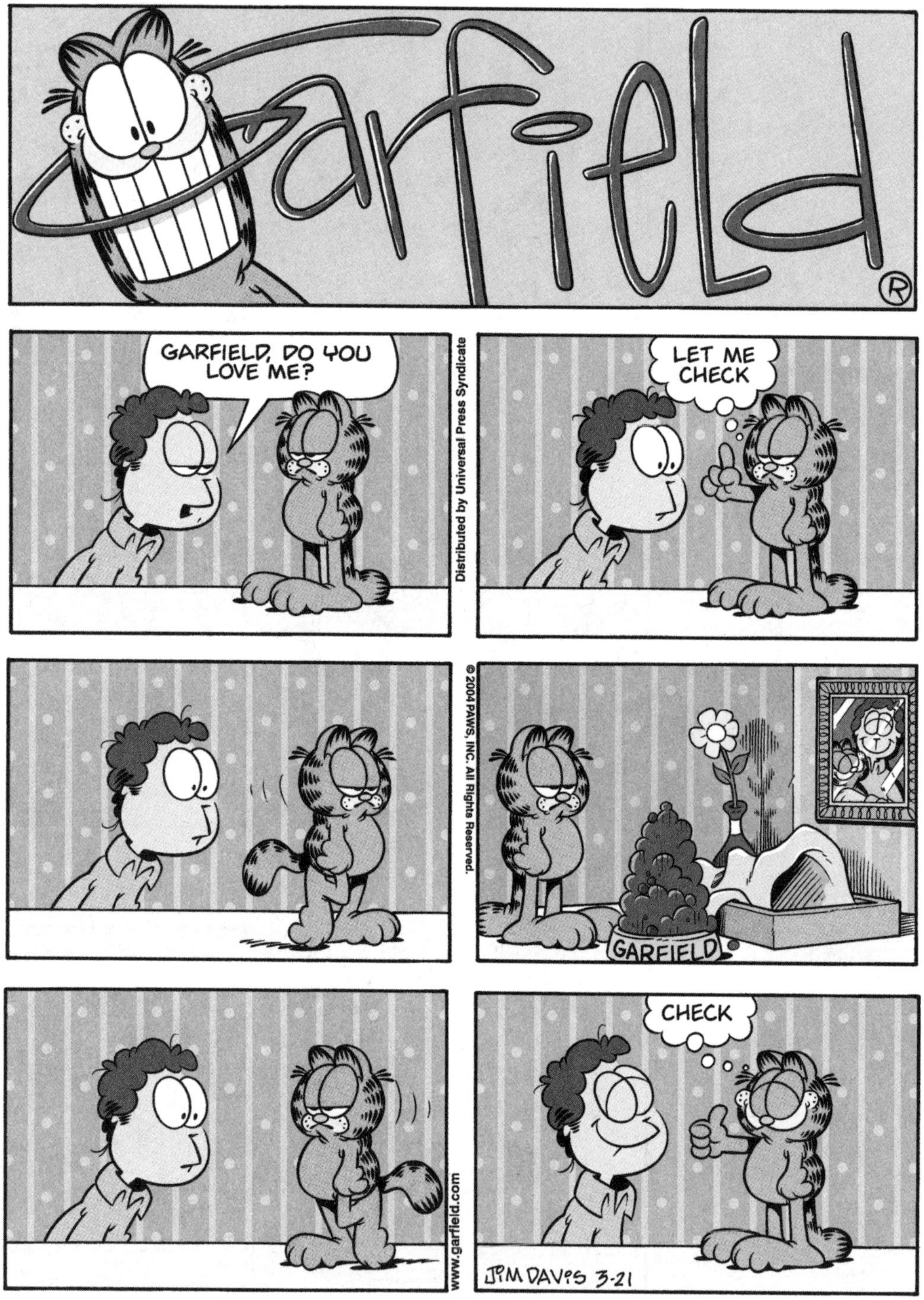
Garfield ®
GARFIELD, DO YOU LOVE ME?
LET ME CHECK
GARFIELD
CHECK
JIM DAVIS 3-21
Distributed by Universal Press Syndicate
© 2004 PAWS, INC. All Rights Reserved.
www.garfield.com

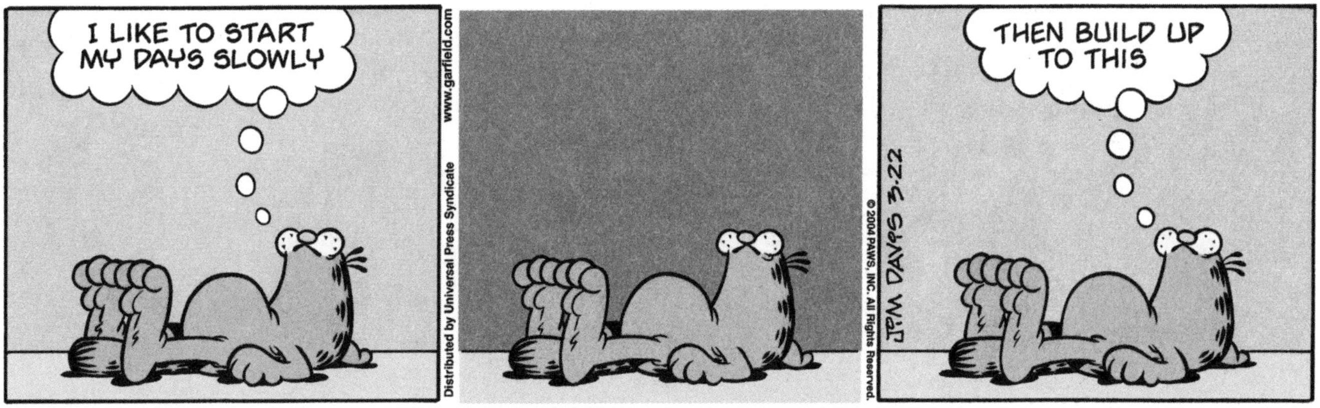
I LIKE TO START MY DAYS SLOWLY
THEN BUILD UP TO THIS
Distributed by Universal Press Syndicate www.garfield.com
© 2004 PAWS, INC. All Rights Reserved.
JPM DAVIS 3-22

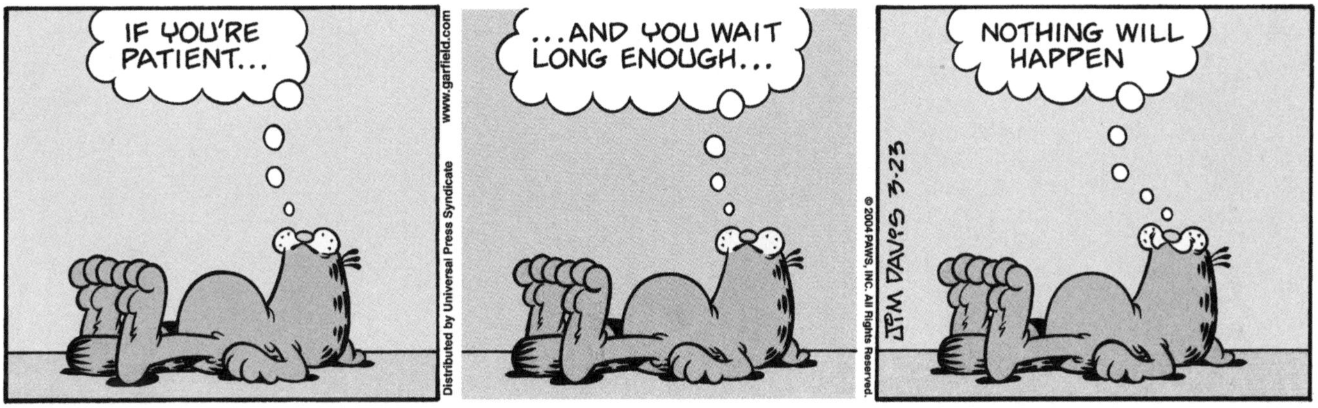
IF YOU'RE PATIENT...
...AND YOU WAIT LONG ENOUGH...
NOTHING WILL HAPPEN
Distributed by Universal Press Syndicate www.garfield.com
© 2004 PAWS, INC. All Rights Reserved.
JPM DAVIS 3-23

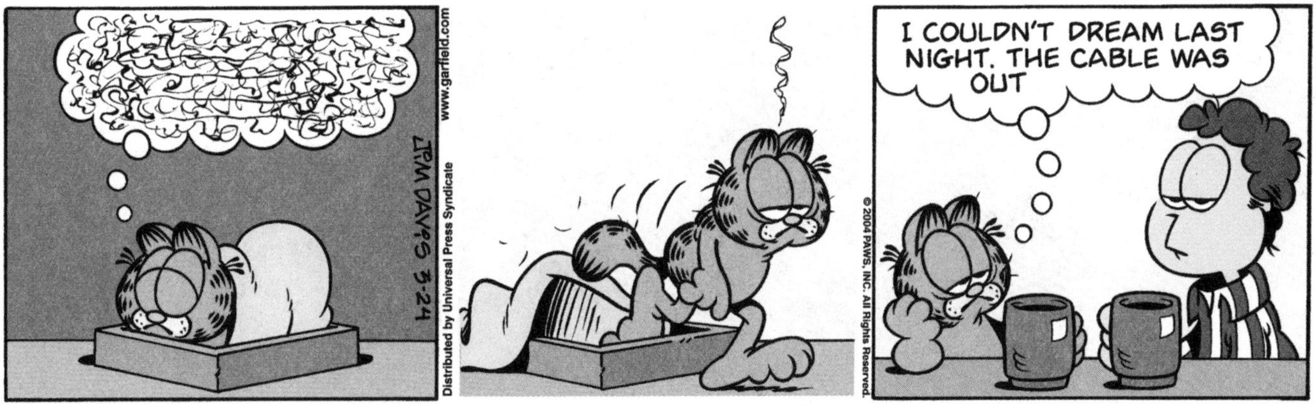
I COULDN'T DREAM LAST NIGHT. THE CABLE WAS OUT
Distributed by Universal Press Syndicate www.garfield.com
© 2004 PAWS, INC. All Rights Reserved.
JPM DAVIS 3-24

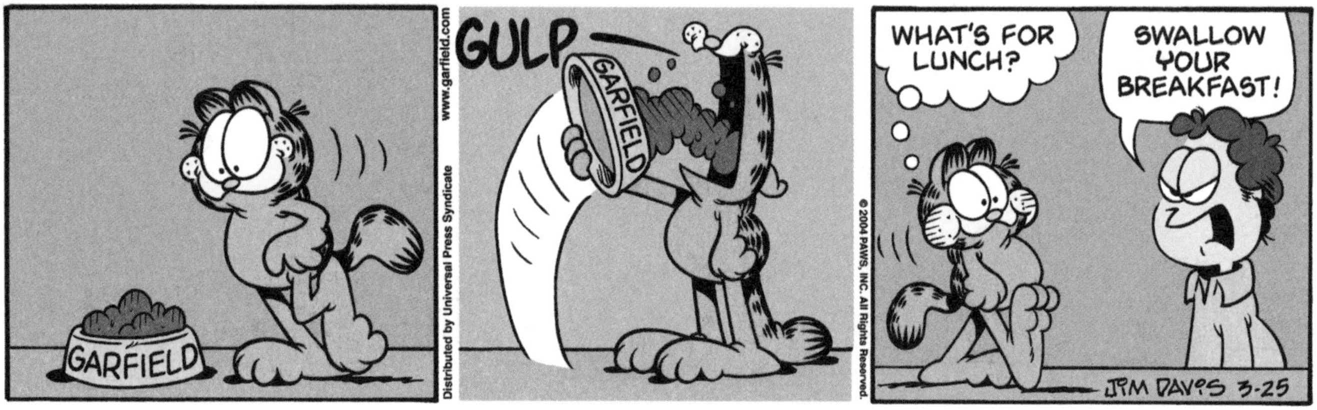
GARFIELD
GULP
GARFIELD
WHAT'S FOR LUNCH?
SWALLOW YOUR BREAKFAST!
Distributed by Universal Press Syndicate www.garfield.com
© 2004 PAWS, INC. All Rights Reserved.
JIM DAVIS 3-25

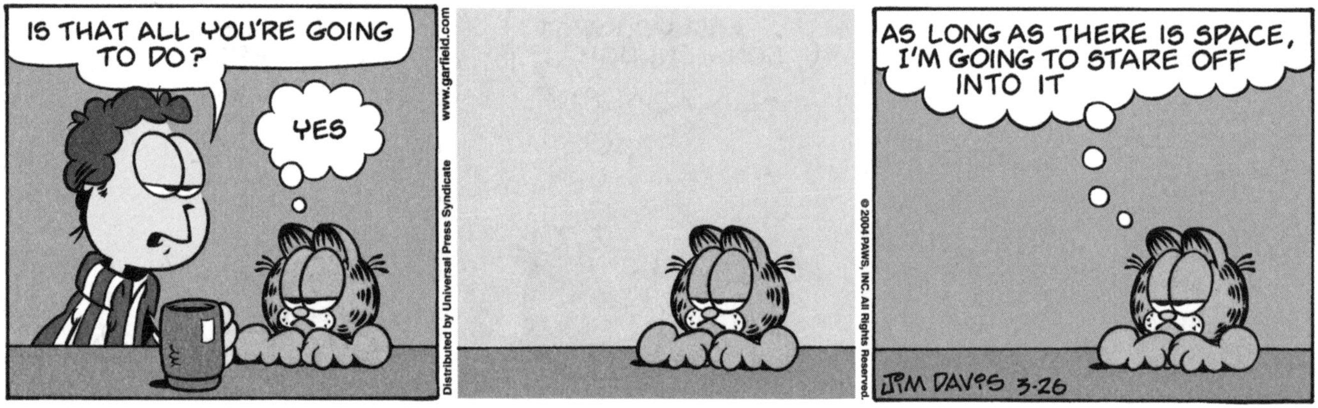
IS THAT ALL YOU'RE GOING TO DO?
YES
AS LONG AS THERE IS SPACE, I'M GOING TO STARE OFF INTO IT
Distributed by Universal Press Syndicate www.garfield.com
© 2004 PAWS, INC. All Rights Reserved.
JIM DAVIS 3-26

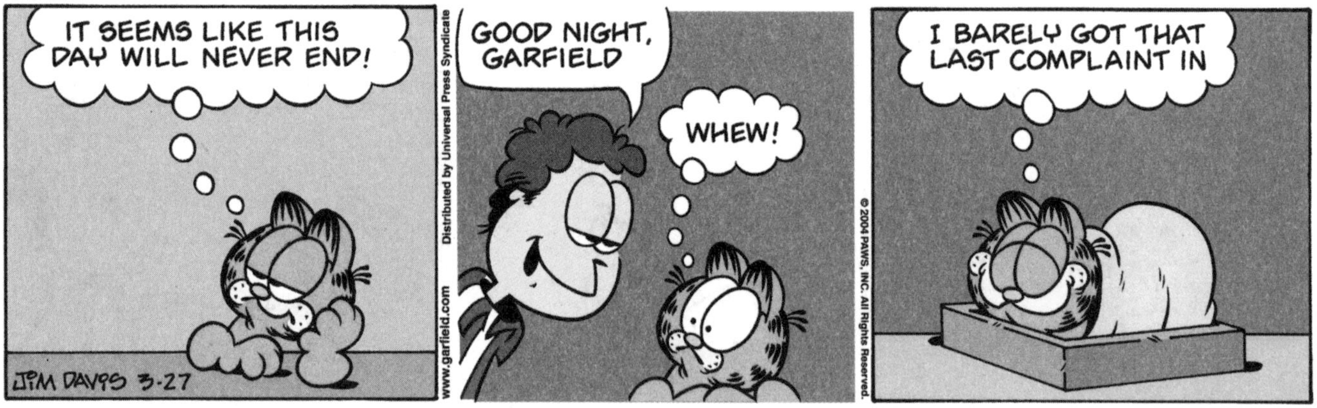
IT SEEMS LIKE THIS DAY WILL NEVER END!
GOOD NIGHT, GARFIELD
WHEW!
I BARELY GOT THAT LAST COMPLAINT IN
JIM DAVIS 3-27
Distributed by Universal Press Syndicate www.garfield.com
© 2004 PAWS, INC. All Rights Reserved.

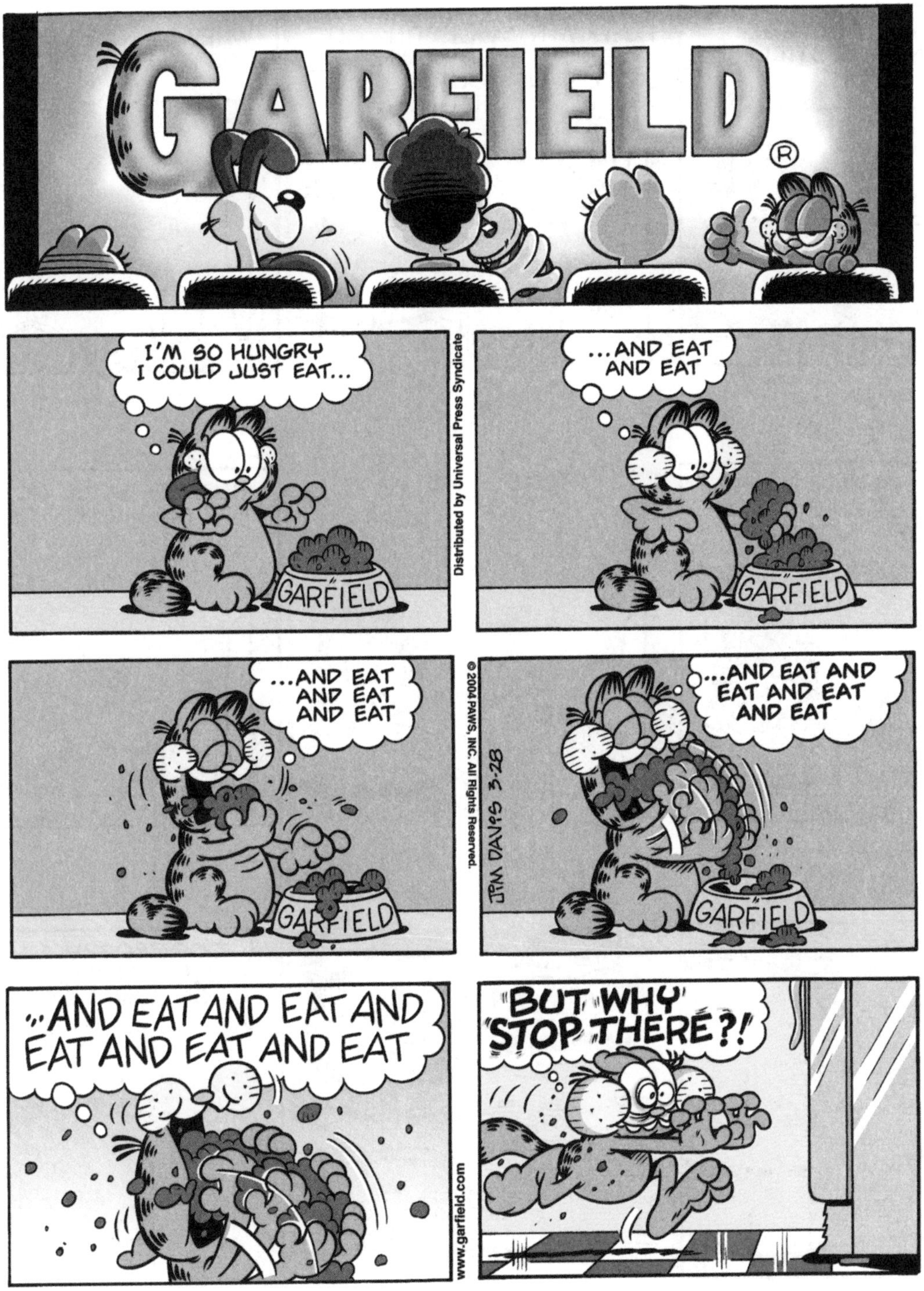
GARFIELD®
I'M SO HUNGRY I COULD JUST EAT...
...AND EAT AND EAT
...AND EAT AND EAT AND EAT
...AND EAT AND EAT AND EAT AND EAT
...AND EAT AND EAT AND EAT AND EAT AND EAT AND EAT AND EAT
BUT WHY STOP THERE?!
GARFIELD
JIM DAVIS 3-28
Distributed by Universal Press Syndicate
© 2004 PAWS, INC. All Rights Reserved.
www.garfield.com

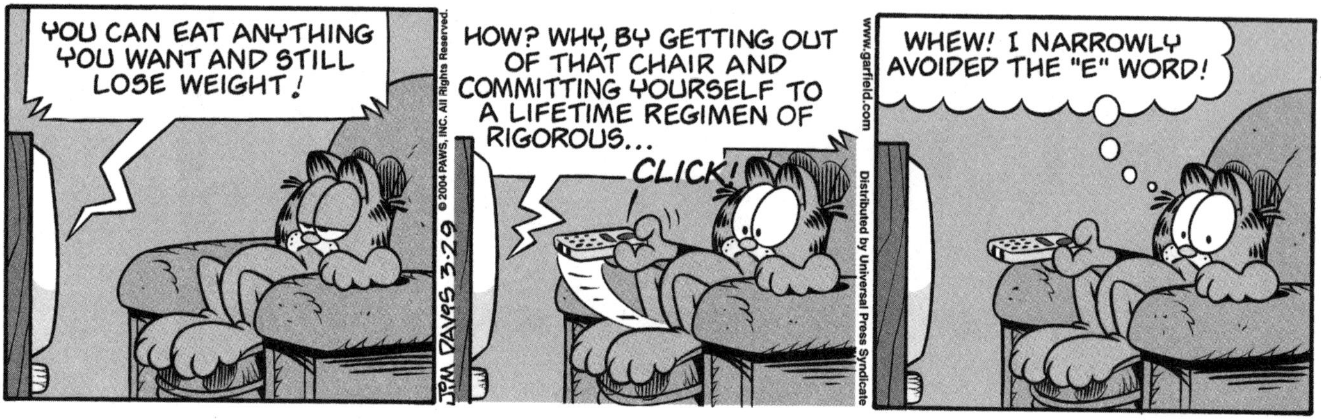
YOU CAN EAT ANYTHING YOU WANT AND STILL LOSE WEIGHT!
© 2004 PAWS, INC. All Rights Reserved.
JIM DAVIS 3-29
HOW? WHY, BY GETTING OUT OF THAT CHAIR AND COMMITTING YOURSELF TO A LIFETIME REGIMEN OF RIGOROUS...
CLICK!
www.garfield.com
Distributed by Universal Press Syndicate
WHEW! I NARROWLY AVOIDED THE "E" WORD!

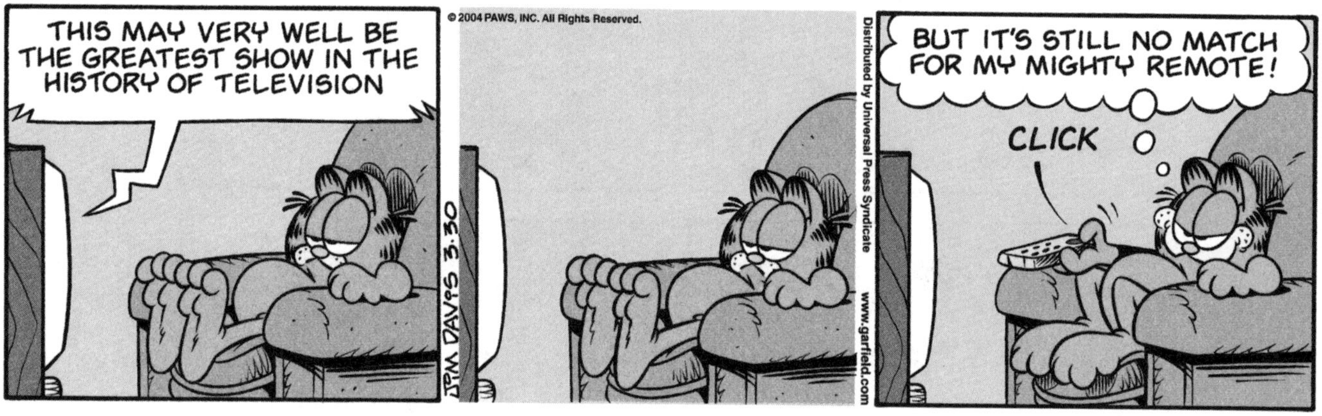
THIS MAY VERY WELL BE THE GREATEST SHOW IN THE HISTORY OF TELEVISION
JIM DAVIS 3-30
© 2004 PAWS, INC. All Rights Reserved.
Distributed by Universal Press Syndicate
www.garfield.com
BUT IT'S STILL NO MATCH FOR MY MIGHTY REMOTE!
CLICK

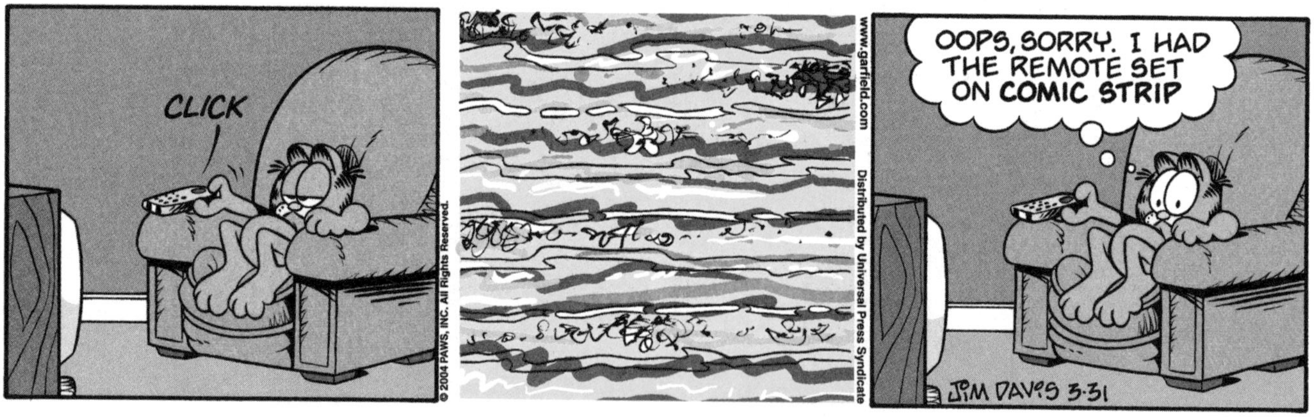
CLICK
© 2004 PAWS, INC. All Rights Reserved.
www.garfield.com
Distributed by Universal Press Syndicate
OOPS, SORRY. I HAD THE REMOTE SET ON COMIC STRIP
JIM DAVIS 3-31

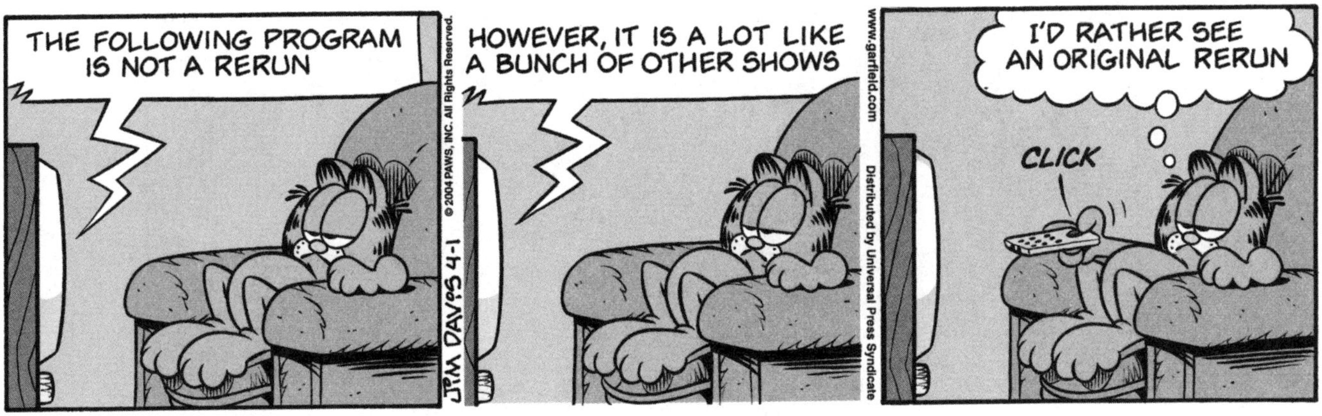
THE FOLLOWING PROGRAM IS NOT A RERUN
JIM DAVIS 4-1
© 2004 PAWS, INC. All Rights Reserved.
HOWEVER, IT IS A LOT LIKE A BUNCH OF OTHER SHOWS
www.garfield.com
Distributed by Universal Press Syndicate
I'D RATHER SEE AN ORIGINAL RERUN
CLICK

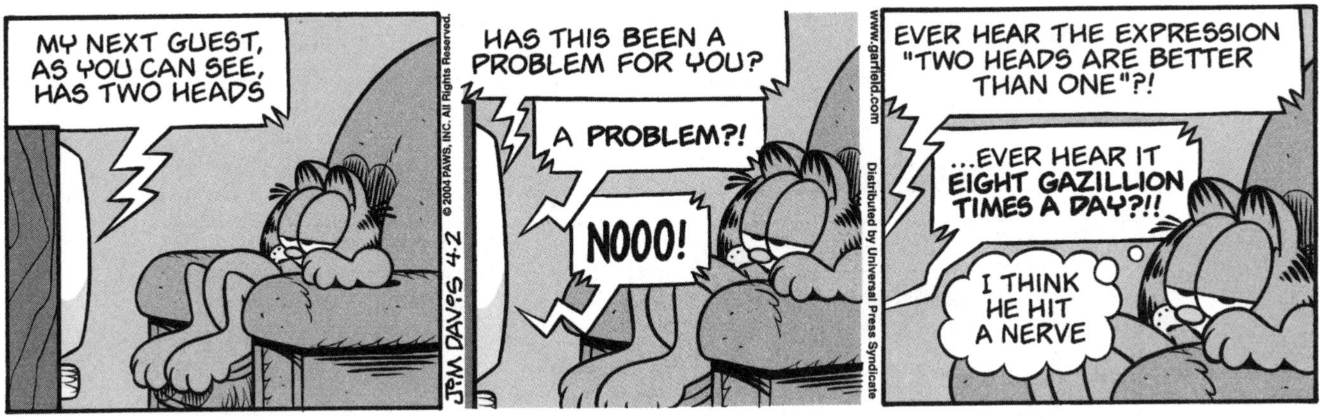
MY NEXT GUEST, AS YOU CAN SEE, HAS TWO HEADS
JIM DAVIS 4-2
© 2004 PAWS, INC. All Rights Reserved.
HAS THIS BEEN A PROBLEM FOR YOU?
A PROBLEM?!
NOOO!
www.garfield.com
Distributed by Universal Press Syndicate
EVER HEAR THE EXPRESSION "TWO HEADS ARE BETTER THAN ONE"?!
...EVER HEAR IT EIGHT GAZILLION TIMES A DAY?!!
I THINK HE HIT A NERVE

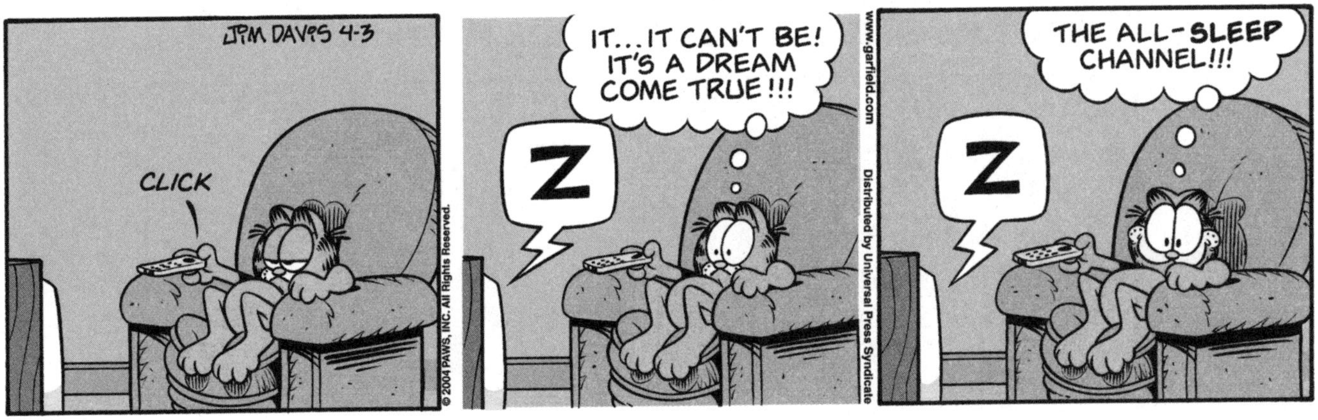
JIM DAVIS 4-3
CLICK
© 2004 PAWS, INC. All Rights Reserved.
IT... IT CAN'T BE! IT'S A DREAM COME TRUE!!!
Z
www.garfield.com
Distributed by Universal Press Syndicate
THE ALL-SLEEP CHANNEL!!!
Z

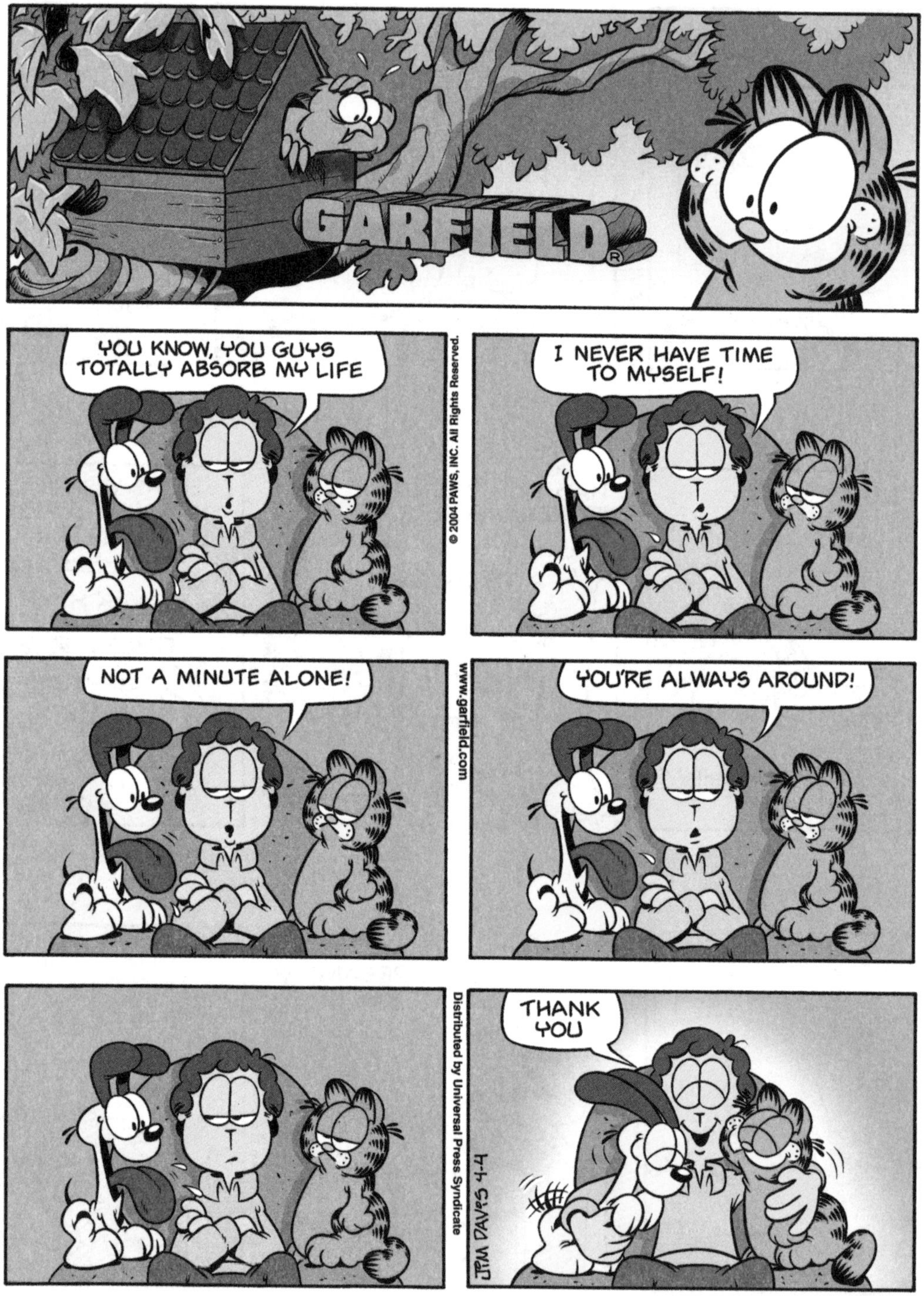
GARFIELD
YOU KNOW, YOU GUYS TOTALLY ABSORB MY LIFE
I NEVER HAVE TIME TO MYSELF!
NOT A MINUTE ALONE!
YOU'RE ALWAYS AROUND!
THANK YOU
JIM DAVIS 4-4

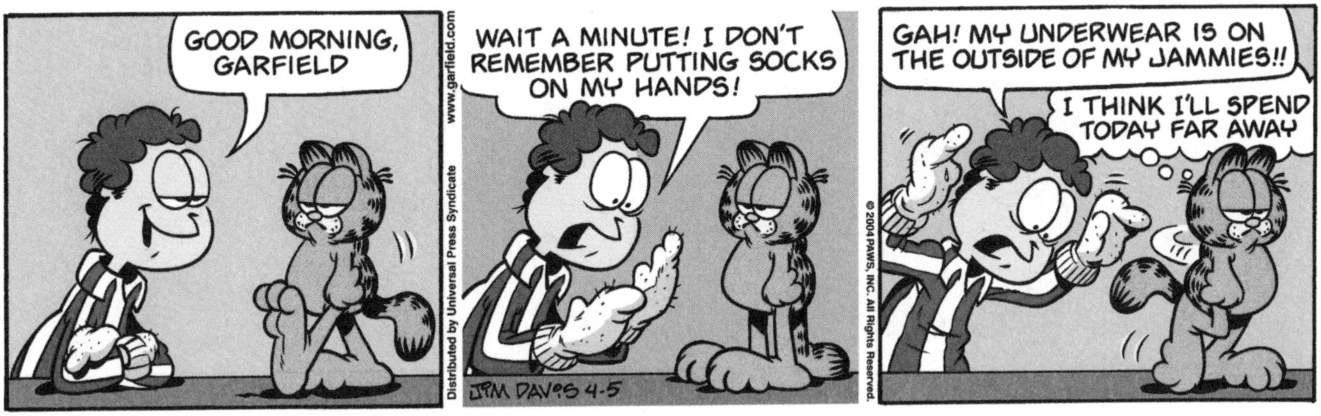
GOOD MORNING, GARFIELD
WAIT A MINUTE! I DON'T REMEMBER PUTTING SOCKS ON MY HANDS!
GAH! MY UNDERWEAR IS ON THE OUTSIDE OF MY JAMMIES!!
I THINK I'LL SPEND TODAY FAR AWAY
JIM DAVIS 4-5
www.garfield.com
Distributed by Universal Press Syndicate
© 2004 PAWS, INC. All Rights Reserved.

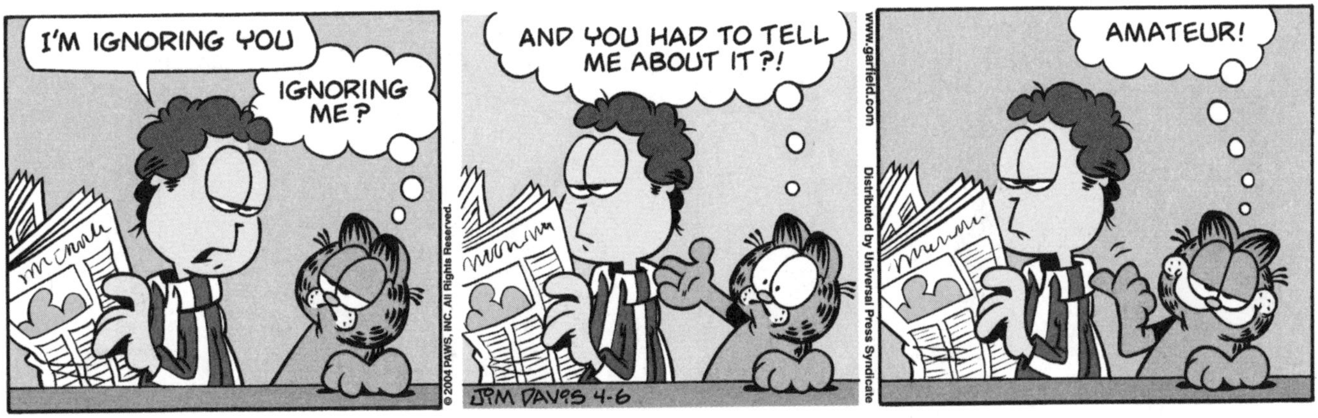
I'M IGNORING YOU
IGNORING ME?
AND YOU HAD TO TELL ME ABOUT IT?!
AMATEUR!
JIM DAVIS 4-6
© 2004 PAWS, INC. All Rights Reserved.
www.garfield.com
Distributed by Universal Press Syndicate

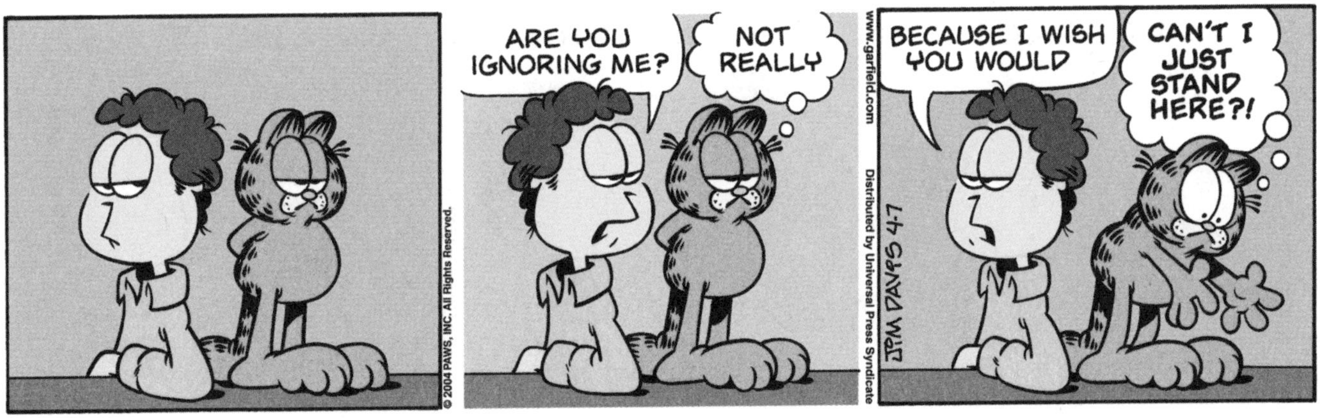
ARE YOU IGNORING ME?
NOT REALLY
BECAUSE I WISH YOU WOULD
CAN'T I JUST STAND HERE?!
JIM DAVIS 4-7
© 2004 PAWS, INC. All Rights Reserved.
www.garfield.com
Distributed by Universal Press Syndicate

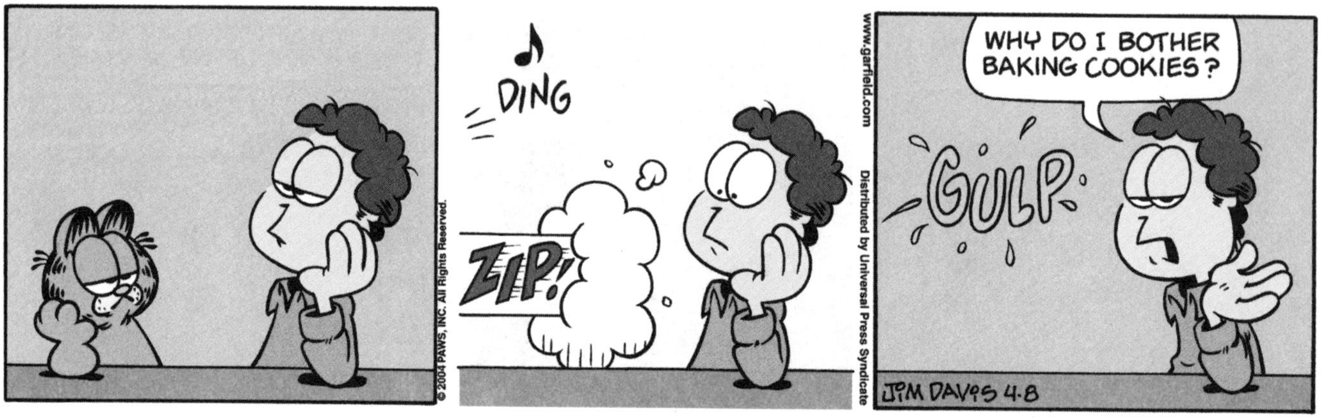
© 2004 PAWS, INC. All Rights Reserved.
DING
ZIP!
www.garfield.com
Distributed by Universal Press Syndicate
GULP
WHY DO I BOTHER BAKING COOKIES?
JIM DAVIS 4.8

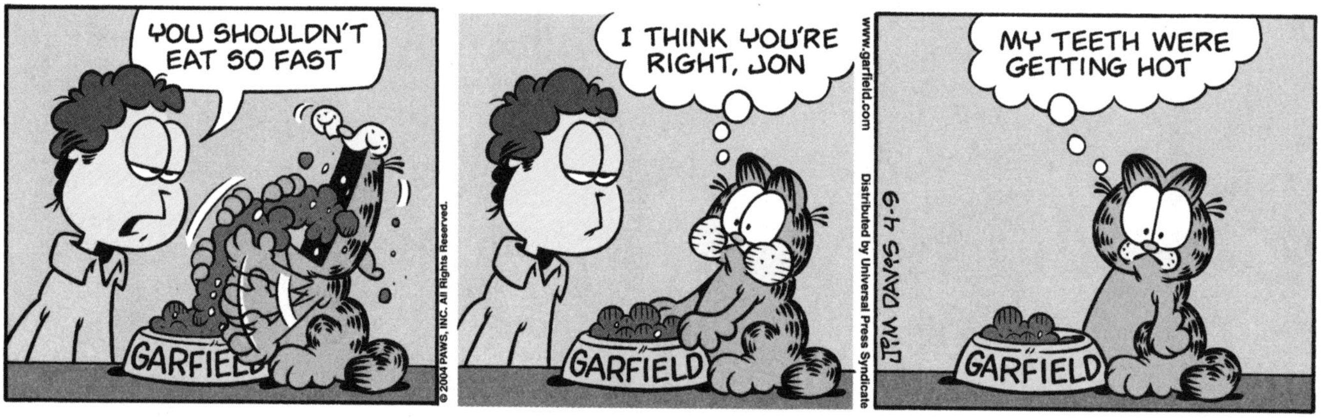
YOU SHOULDN'T EAT SO FAST
GARFIELD
© 2004 PAWS, INC. All Rights Reserved.
I THINK YOU'RE RIGHT, JON
GARFIELD
www.garfield.com
Distributed by Universal Press Syndicate
JIM DAVIS 4.9
MY TEETH WERE GETTING HOT
GARFIELD

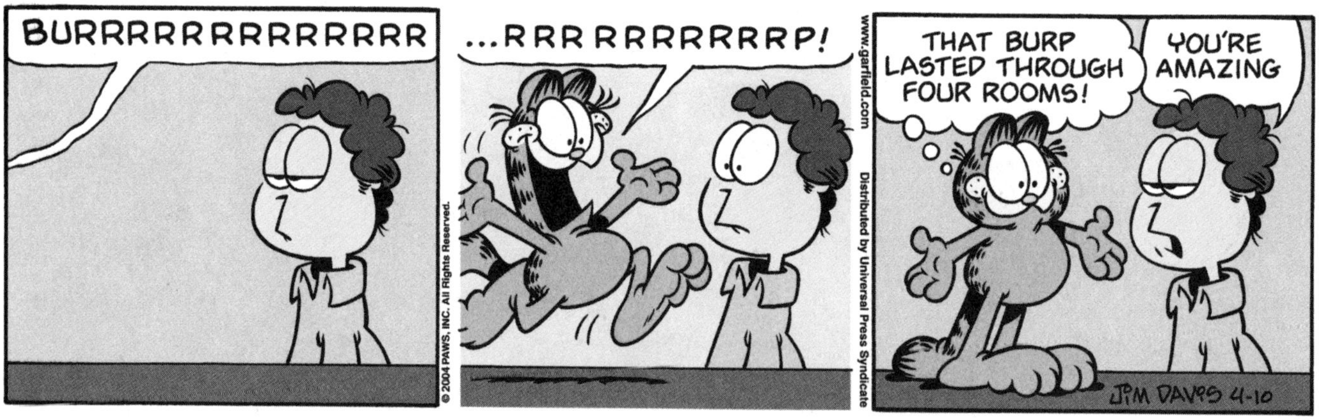
BURRRRRRRRRRRRRR
© 2004 PAWS, INC. All Rights Reserved.
...RRRRRRRRRRRP!
www.garfield.com
Distributed by Universal Press Syndicate
THAT BURP LASTED THROUGH FOUR ROOMS!
YOU'RE AMAZING
JIM DAVIS 4-10

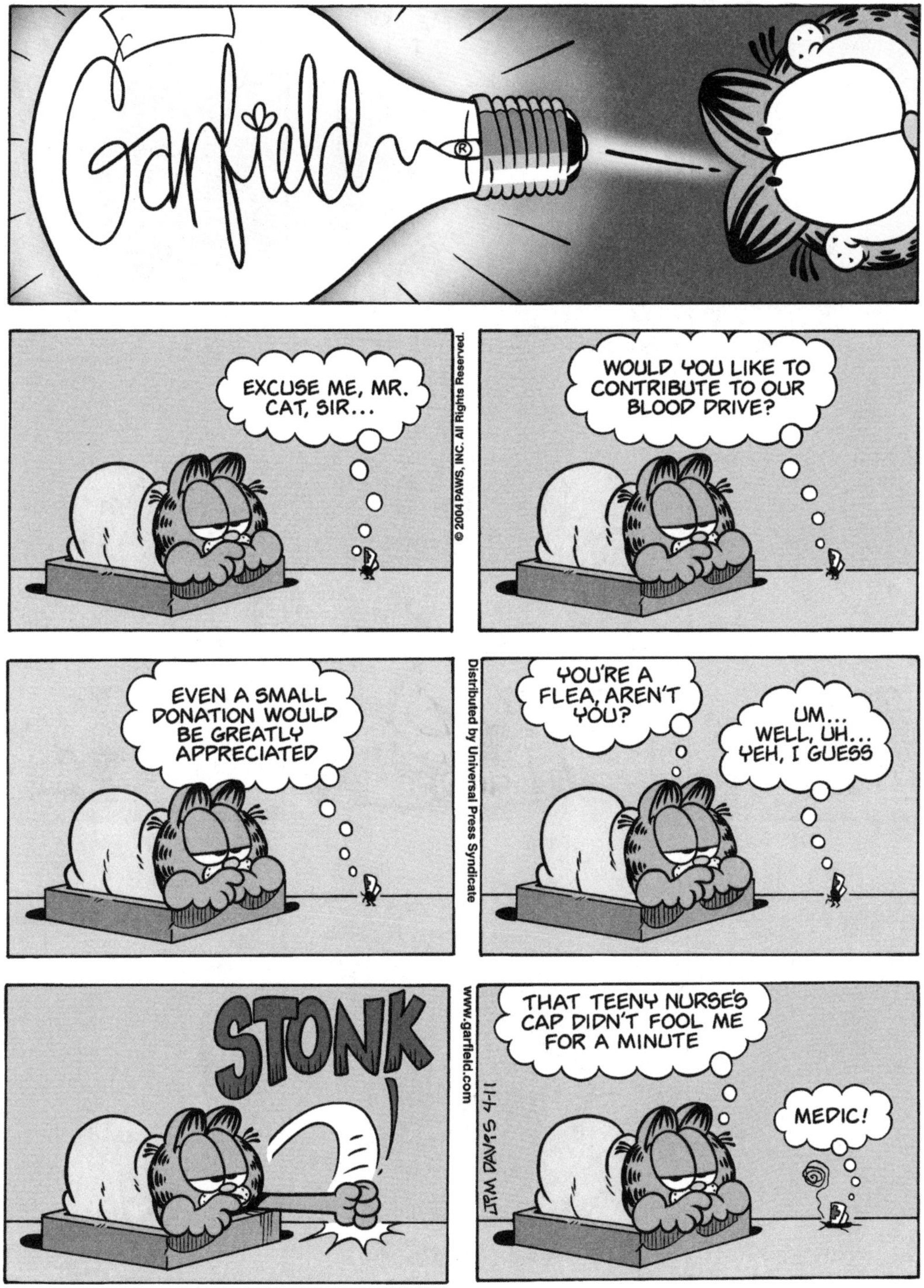
Garfield®
EXCUSE ME, MR. CAT, SIR...
WOULD YOU LIKE TO CONTRIBUTE TO OUR BLOOD DRIVE?
EVEN A SMALL DONATION WOULD BE GREATLY APPRECIATED
YOU'RE A FLEA, AREN'T YOU?
UM... WELL, UH... YEH, I GUESS
STONK
THAT TEENY NURSE'S CAP DIDN'T FOOL ME FOR A MINUTE
MEDIC!
© 2004 PAWS, INC. All Rights Reserved.
Distributed by Universal Press Syndicate
www.garfield.com
JIM DAVIS 4-11

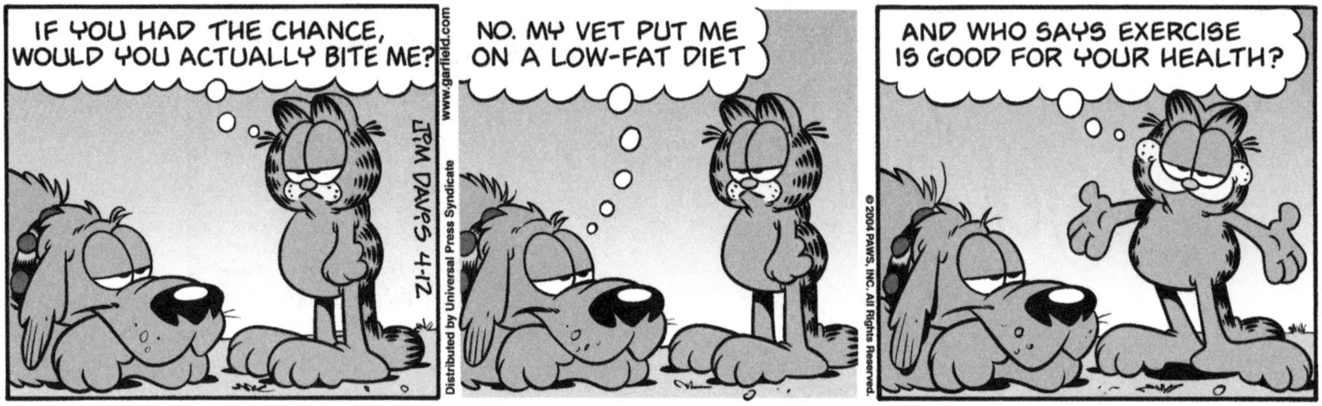
IF YOU HAD THE CHANCE, WOULD YOU ACTUALLY BITE ME?
NO. MY VET PUT ME ON A LOW-FAT DIET
AND WHO SAYS EXERCISE IS GOOD FOR YOUR HEALTH?
JIM DAVIS 4-12
www.garfield.com
Distributed by Universal Press Syndicate
© 2004 PAWS, INC. All Rights Reserved.

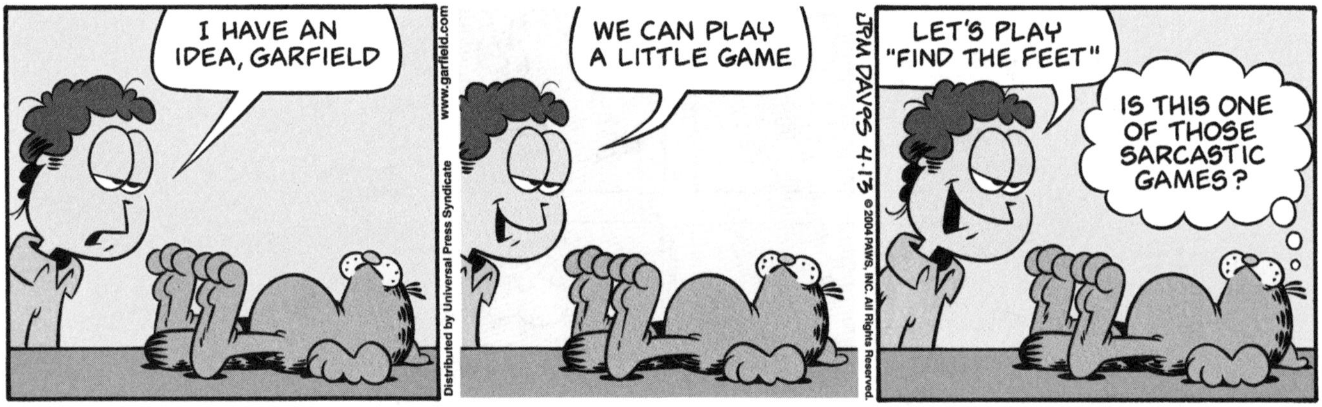
I HAVE AN IDEA, GARFIELD
WE CAN PLAY A LITTLE GAME
LET'S PLAY "FIND THE FEET"
IS THIS ONE OF THOSE SARCASTIC GAMES?
JIM DAVIS 4-13
www.garfield.com
Distributed by Universal Press Syndicate
© 2004 PAWS, INC. All Rights Reserved.

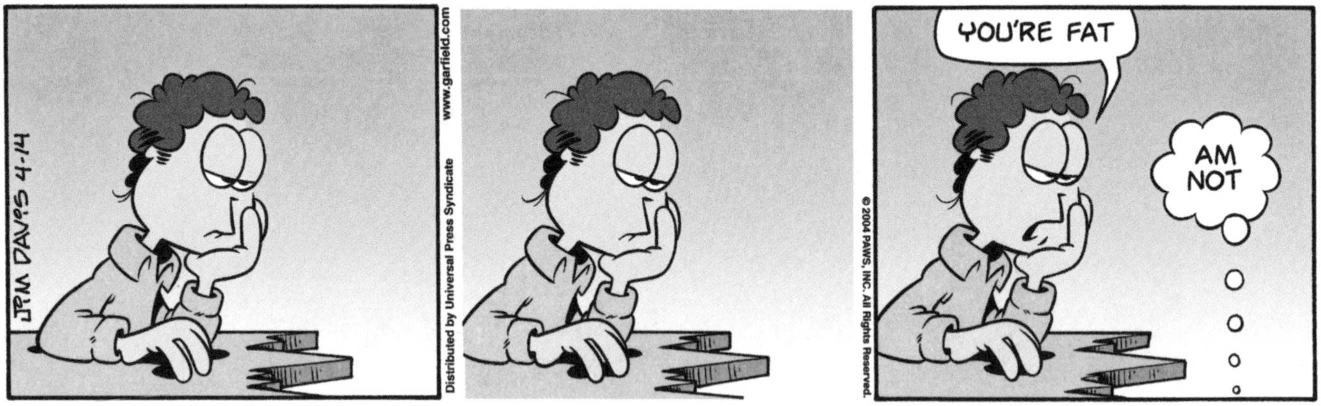
YOU'RE FAT
AM NOT
JIM DAVIS 4-14
www.garfield.com
Distributed by Universal Press Syndicate
© 2004 PAWS, INC. All Rights Reserved.

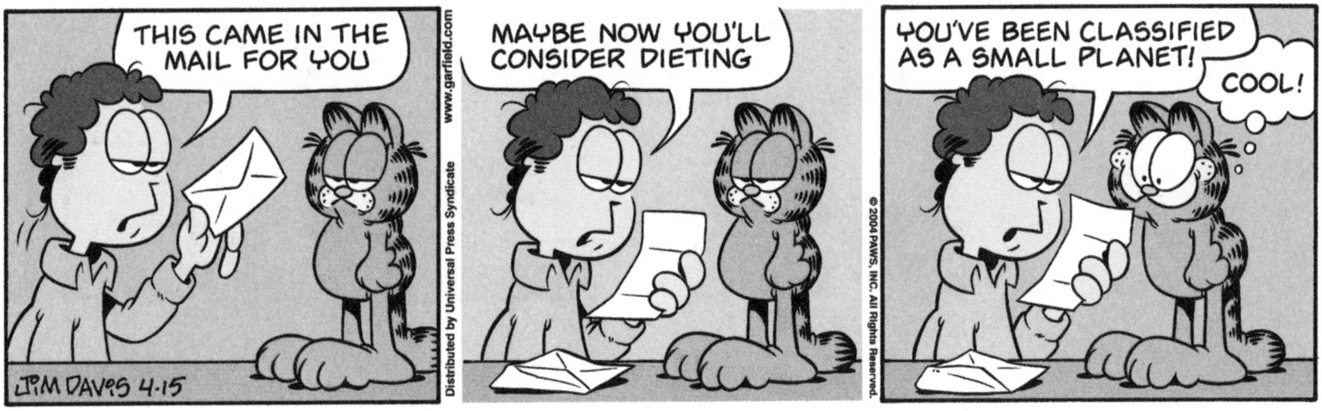
THIS CAME IN THE MAIL FOR YOU
JIM DAVIS 4-15
www.garfield.com
Distributed by Universal Press Syndicate
MAYBE NOW YOU'LL CONSIDER DIETING
© 2004 PAWS, INC. All Rights Reserved.
YOU'VE BEEN CLASSIFIED AS A SMALL PLANET!
COOL!

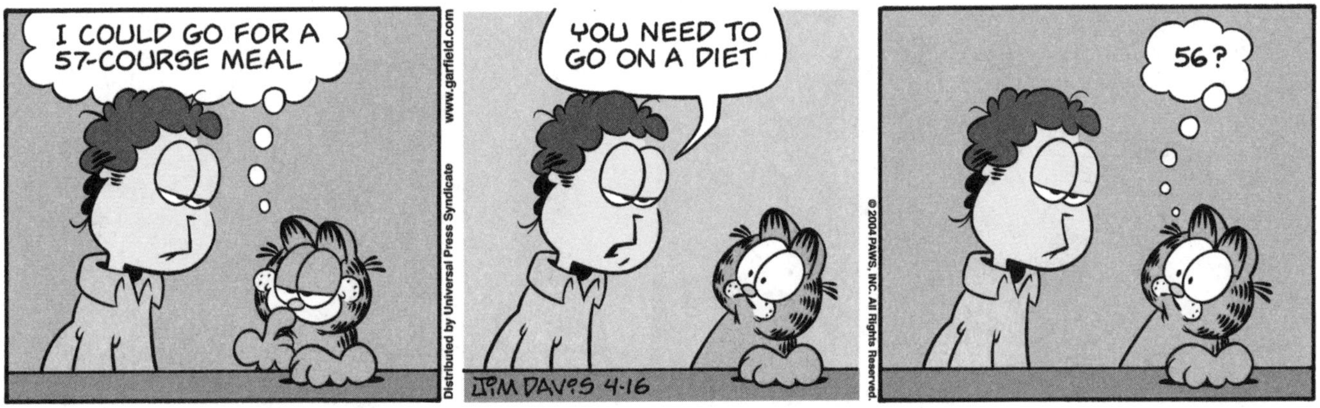
I COULD GO FOR A 57-COURSE MEAL
www.garfield.com
Distributed by Universal Press Syndicate
YOU NEED TO GO ON A DIET
JIM DAVIS 4-16
© 2004 PAWS, INC. All Rights Reserved.
56?

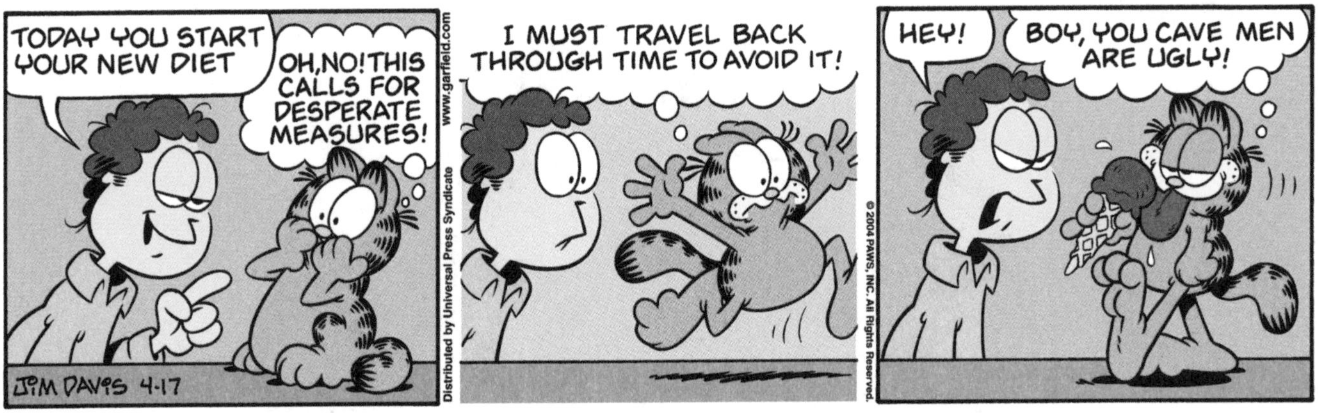
TODAY YOU START YOUR NEW DIET
OH, NO! THIS CALLS FOR DESPERATE MEASURES!
JIM DAVIS 4-17
www.garfield.com
Distributed by Universal Press Syndicate
I MUST TRAVEL BACK THROUGH TIME TO AVOID IT!
© 2004 PAWS, INC. All Rights Reserved.
HEY!
BOY, YOU CAVE MEN ARE UGLY!

Cats Rule Dogs Drool

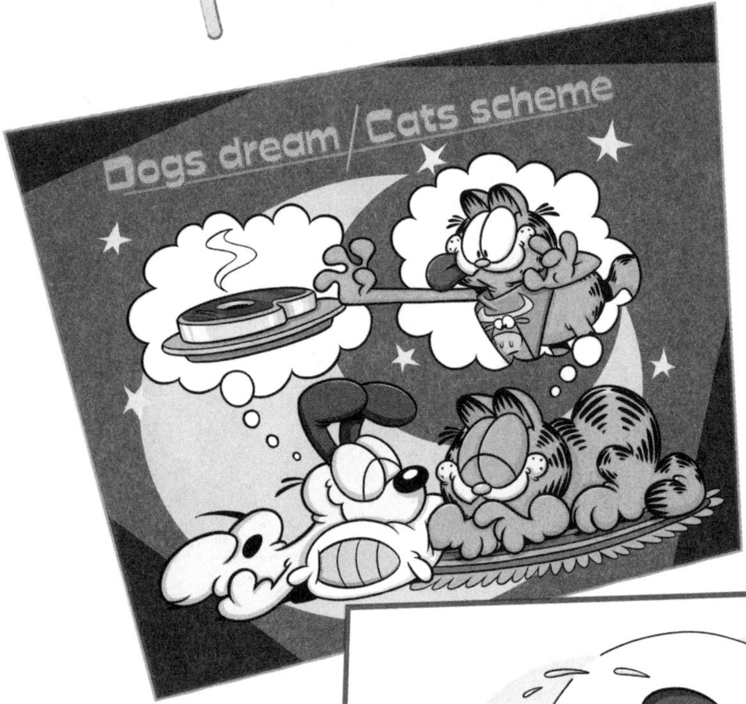
Dogs dream
Cats scheme

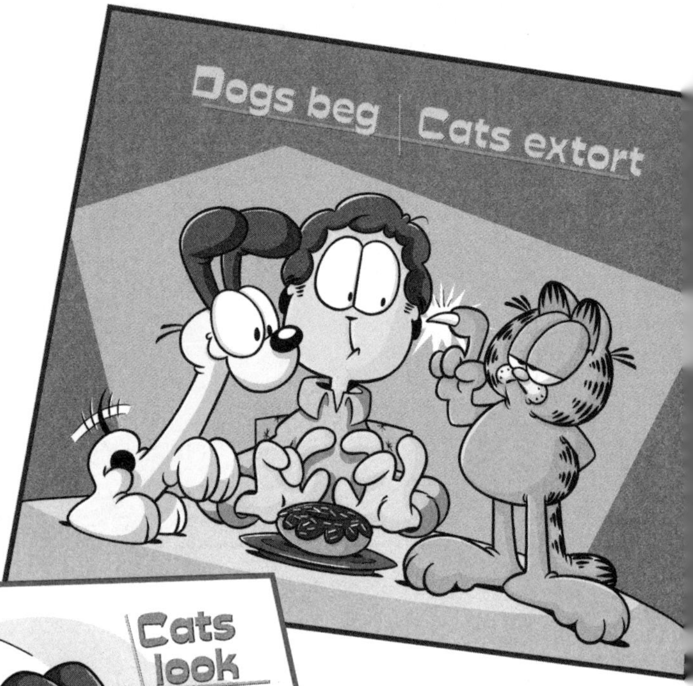
Dogs beg
Cats extort

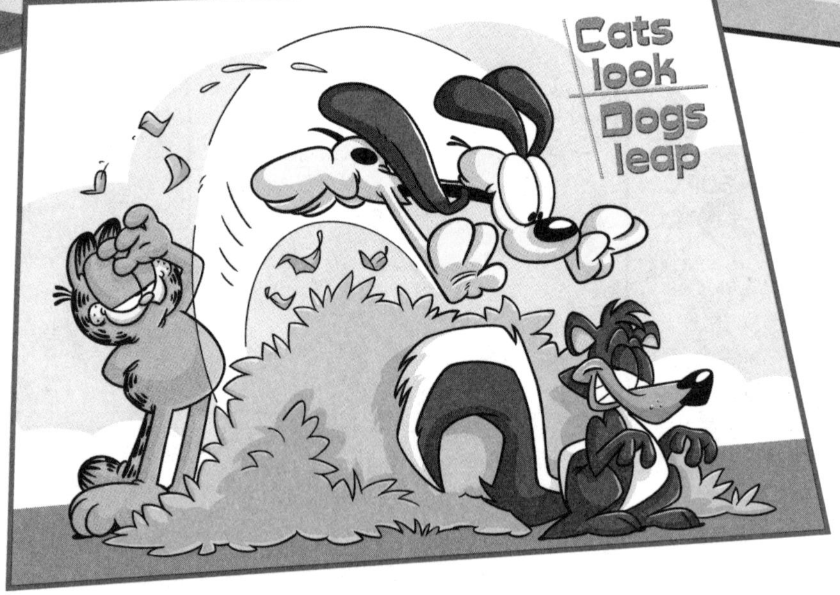
Cats look
Dogs leap

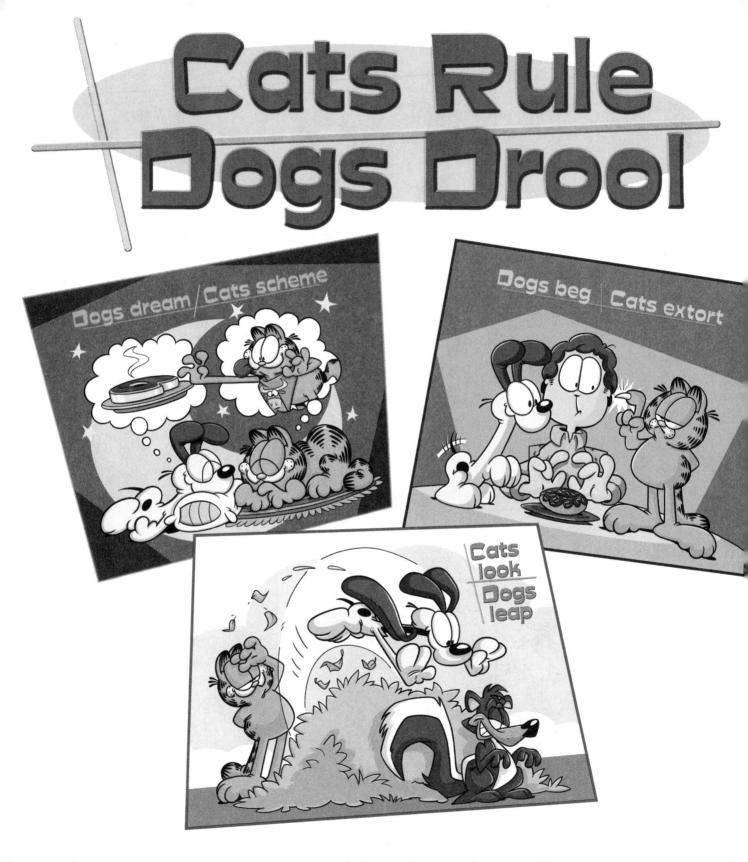

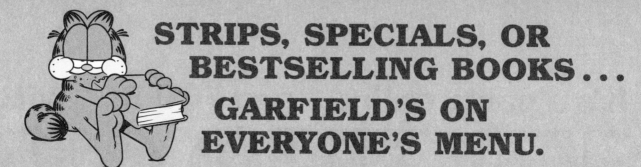

STRIPS, SPECIALS, OR BESTSELLING BOOKS . . . GARFIELD'S ON EVERYONE'S MENU.

Don't miss even one episode in the Tubby Tabby's hilarious series!

GARFIELD AT LARGE ....(#1) 978-0-345-44382-3
GARFIELD GAINS WEIGHT ....(#2) 978-0-345-44975-7
GARFIELD BIGGER THAN LIFE ....(#3) 978-0-345-45027-2
GARFIELD WEIGHS IN ....(#4) 978-0-345-45205-4
GARFIELD TAKES THE CAKE ....(#5) 978-0-345-44978-8
GARFIELD EATS HIS HEART OUT........(#6) 978-0-345-46459-0
GARFIELD SITS AROUND THE HOUSE..(#7) 978-0-345-46463-7
GARFIELD TIPS THE SCALES ....(#8) 978-0-345-46909-0
GARFIELD LOSES HIS FEET.................(#9) 978-0-345-46467-5
GARFIELD MAKES IT BIG....................(#10) 978-0-345-46468-2
GARFIELD ROLLS ON ....(#11) 978-0-345-47561-9
GARFIELD OUT TO LUNCH ....(#12) 978-0-345-47562-6
GARFIELD FOOD FOR THOUGHT......(#13) 978-0-345-47563-3
GARFIELD SWALLOWS HIS PRIDE....(#14) 978-0-345-91386-9
GARFIELD WORLDWIDE ....(#15) 978-0-345-91754-6
GARFIELD ROUNDS OUT....................(#16) 978-0-345-35388-7
GARFIELD CHEWS THE FAT...............(#17) 978-0-345-35956-8
GARFIELD GOES TO WAIST ....(#18) 978-0-345-36430-2
GARFIELD HANGS OUT.......................(#19) 978-0-345-36835-5
GARFIELD TAKES UP SPACE ....(#20) 978-0-345-37029-7
GARFIELD SAYS A MOUTHFUL ....(#21) 978-0-345-37368-7
GARFIELD BY THE POUND...................(#22) 978-0-345-37579-7
GARFIELD KEEPS HIS CHINS UP ......(#23) 978-0-345-37959-7
GARFIELD TAKES HIS LICKS..............(#24) 978-0-345-38170-5
GARFIELD HITS THE BIG TIME ....(#25) 978-0-345-38332-7
GARFIELD PULLS HIS WEIGHT..........(#26) 978-0-345-38666-3
GARFIELD DISHES IT OUT..................(#27) 978-0-345-39287-9
GARFIELD LIFE IN THE FAT LANE .....(#28) 978-0-345-39776-8
GARFIELD TONS OF FUN....................(#29) 978-0-345-40386-5
GARFIELD BIGGER AND BETTER......(#30) 978-0-345-40770-2
GARFIELD HAMS IT UP ....(#31) 978-0-345-41241-6

New larger, full-color format!

GARFIELD THINKS BIG........................(#32) 978-0-345-41671-1
GARFIELD THROWS HIS WEIGHT AROUND ....(#33) 978-0-345-42749-6
GARFIELD LIFE TO THE FULLEST.....(#34) 978-0-345-43239-1
GARFIELD FEEDS THE KITTY ....(#35) 978-0-345-43673-3
GARFIELD HOGS THE SPOTLIGHT ...(#36) 978-0-345-43922-2
GARFIELD BEEFS UP ....(#37) 978-0-345-44109-6
GARFIELD GETS COOKIN' ....(#38) 978-0-345-44582-7
GARFIELD EATS CROW ....(#39) 978-0-345-45201-6
GARFIELD SURVIVAL OF THE FATTEST ....(#40) 978-0-345-46458-3
GARFIELD OLDER AND WIDER..........(#41) 978-0-345-46462-0
GARFIELD PIGS OUT ....(#42) 978-0-345-46466-8
GARFIELD BLOTS OUT THE SUN ......(#43) 978-0-345-46615-0

DVD TIE-INS

GARFIELD AS HIMSELF................................978-0-345-47805-4
GARFIELD HOLIDAY CELEBRATIONS.........978-0-345-47930-3
GARFIELD TRAVEL ADVENTURES 978-0-345-48087-3

AND DON'T MISS...

GARFIELD AT 25: IN DOG YEARS I'D BE DEAD 978-0-345-45204-7
GARFIELD'S JOKE ZONE/INSULTS.............978-0-345-46263-3
GARFIELD FAT CAT 3-PACK/ VOL. 1 978-0-345-46455-2
GARFIELD FAT CAT 3-PACK/ VOL. 2 978-0-345-46465-1
GARFIELD FAT CAT 3-PACK/ VOL. 13 978-0-345-46460-6
SEASON'S EATINGS: A VERY MERRY GARFIELD CHRISTMAS 978-0-345-47560-2
GARFIELD'S GUIDE TO EVERYTHING 978-0-345-46461-3
ODIE UNLEASHED! 978-0-345-46464-4
GARFIELD'S BOOK OF CAT NAMES............978-0-345-48516-8
THE GARFIELD JOURNAL............................978-0-345-46469-9
LIGHTS, CAMERA, HAIRBALLS!: GARFIELD AT THE MOVIES........................978-0-345-49134-3